Praise for Mark Steel

Reasons to be Cheerful
'Polemic, passionate and consistently funny' *Independent on Sunday*

'Both intellectually rewarding and hilariously funny' *Time Out*

'Steel proves that radical leftism and an inspirational belief in collective action are not incompatible with jokes and self-criticism. Steel's humour is challenging rather than merely entertaining, riskily juxtaposing gravity and levity' *TLS*

Vive La Revolution
'An irreverent romp through the Gallic uprising . . . Illuminating and funny' *Daily Mail*

'An irreverent, engaging take on 1789 and all that, focusing on things you don't find in textbooks' *Time*

'Steel writes with zip and earnestness [with] an eagerness to impart knowledge. Terrific' *Time Out*

'Engagingly light-hearted whilst clearly thorough, the author has taken the events of the French Revolution and given them a human face, as well as neatly poking fun at the over-pomposity with which recent historians have dealt with the period' *Observer*

Also by Mark Steel

REASONS TO BE CHEERFUL
VIVE LA REVOLUTION
COLLECTED COLUMNS

WHAT'S GOING ON?

MARK STEEL

POCKET
BOOKS

LONDON • SYDNEY • NEW YORK • TORONTO

First published in Great Britain in 2008
by Simon & Schuster UK Ltd
This edition published by Pocket Books, 2009
An imprint of Simon & Schuster UK Ltd
A CBS COMPANY

1 3 5 7 9 10 8 6 4 2

Simon & Schuster UK Ltd
1st Floor
222 Gray's Inn Road
London
WC1X 8HB

www.simonsays.co.uk

Simon & Schuster Australia
Sydney

A CIP catalogue for this book is available
from the British Library.

ISBN: 978-1-84739-320-3

Typeset in Bembo by M Rules
Printed by CPI Cox & Wyman, Reading, Berkshire RG1 8EX

1

MAYDAY

I've always been suspicious of the lifestyle crisis. One of my first jokes when I began as a stand-up comic was about how a 'mid-life crisis' was only possible if you were comfortable enough to afford one, because you couldn't imagine a peasant in Vietnam traipsing through a paddy field with a wooden plough and telling his mate, 'Do you know, Li Wong, I just don't know WHERE my life is heading these days.'

It's clearly not a disaster, by itself, to turn forty. But that doesn't mean it's altogether healthy. For a start, once you're forty everything's finite. If you average one foreign holiday a year you've probably got about thirty-five left. It's the same with books. You've got to be selective now as there's time for only about another thousand or two. Even bananas – at, say, two a week, you're down to roughly your last 3,600, so a disappointing banana now carries a poignancy that didn't apply at nineteen.

Also, and I don't think this is being paranoid, the older you get the nearer you are to dying. I noticed that whenever I saw the obituary page in a newspaper, I'd automatically look at the deceased's date of birth first. If it was some old geologist born in 1919, that would be quite comforting. But anything later than 1950 would be disconcerting, so then I'd check what they'd died of, and maybe gasp, 'Oh thank Christ for that, he was a junkie. That doesn't apply to me then.'

And then you have to put up with other 40-year-olds proclaiming they LOVE being this age. The worst are those who pretend they're still as youthful as ever by saying, 'Martin and I certainly aren't over the hill. You should have seen us last month, jigging in the aisles to Fleetwood Mac at the Birmingham Exhibition Centre.'

It's harder if you are still in touch with current youth culture, because then you realise how old you seem. For example, I love much of the British hip-hop known as 'grime', but was wary of going to a live gig. Then I went to see Lady Sovereign and realised why. I was surrounded by tongue-studded 17-year-olds taking pictures of each other with their mobiles, and felt they were all thinking, 'That bloke must be a) from the record company, b) the drug squad, c) about to run through the crowd and grab his daughter shouting "So THIS is where you come when you say you're round Sarah's studying," or d) on a register having recently been exposed in the *Sun*.'

On top of these problems I had an extra one specially designed for someone in my time and place. I grew up confident that I would be part of the generation that would change the world so that people would matter more than profits. Such was my success that, around the time I reached forty, it seemed to be universally accepted as a fact – as undeniable as gravity or Napoleon's defeat at Waterloo – that nothing can be built or made or done properly without someone making a huge profit. And in Britain as much as anywhere the government appears to believe there's a scientific law, perhaps first stated by Isaac Newton, that states: 'If a substance shall not have Balfour Beatty involved in it, then that substance will surely melt.'

Libraries, prisons, schools, sports projects, transport, everything depends on attracting business. Now, if you suggest to most people in authority that something could be made without businessmen making money from it, you feel like an eccentric

Victorian telling his friends over a brandy that you've invented a flying machine. They look at you as if to say, 'My God, sir, I contend your scheme is PREPOSTEROUS.'

Any route through a school, even a primary school, takes you past adverts for Sainsbury's and posters proclaiming that the computers were generously provided by Tesco. Maybe next the lessons will be pay-per-learn, so the first five minutes are free but after that you have to pay a pound or the teacher goes all fuzzy. Or they'll be sponsored, so science teachers will announce flatly, 'In this experiment, we're, um, going to try to see, ahem, how much of this green, er, green liquid, is displaced by this object here. And the liquid we're using is, er, Lilt, with the totally tropical taste that puts the fizz back into physics. It's tangy, it's cheery, it proves quantum theory.'

Then there's the unfathomable railway companies, that most people consistently state have become worse since the unreliable days of British Rail. Maybe the chaos of the transport system could be utilised for the Olympics with the introduction of a special 'London triathlon' in which you have to get a bus to Brixton, an underground to London Bridge and a Connex South Central back to East Croydon – do that in less than five hours and you *deserve* a gold fucking medal.

The fear with the Olympics is that as of now we already seem to be four years behind, although it's only three years since we were told we were holding them. I have a dread that when the time comes, the athletics track will still be rubble and the swimming pool will be half-built with no water in it, so the swimmers will be told to run backwards and forwards along the bottom.

Whenever a leading politician makes a comment about anything cultural, it's along the lines of Tony Blair's assessment of British music: 'a valuable and integral part of our trade across the world.' Or the minister of culture extolling an award-winning British film by saying, 'This shows the importance of the film industry as a source of foreign earnings.' The idea that anyone might paint or write or sing for a purpose other than boosting their share price seems beyond their comprehension. If Blair was asked what he thought of the *Mona Lisa*, he'd probably say, 'It should be applauded as one of the leading exporters of smiles throughout Europe.'

Even the traditionally rebellious environment of the rock festival fizzes with sponsorship, from Orange tents and Nokia fields. At the Reading festival, noted for its love of thrash heavy metal, they have the Carling stage, so bands such as Slayer scream and roar about kicking arse and cocksuckers, under a 50-yard-wide banner for the most famously weedy lager in existence.

I watched the black music awards on television one night, aghast at the way each winner was presented with their trophy while carefully positioned in front of one of those huge boards bearing the name of the sponsors. So we saw a series of strident singers and rappers, wearing clothes and expressions carefully designed to say 'Fuck you and all you stand for', wiggling slightly to the left to ensure they didn't obscure the logo for AXA Equity & Law. The hip-hop scene seems especially proud to embrace big business, as if no dirty urban street musician can keep it real unless he's appeared on adverts and set up a clothing chain.★

I sometimes fear I'll see a protest against this blanket sponsorship, but THAT will be sponsored, and demonstrators will be asked to turn up at 1.00 p.m. for the HSBC march against big business.

A few weeks after I was forty I played the minor part of father in the birth of my second child, Eloise. Compared to the drama that leads to the birth of a first child, the second-time-round parents can be shamefully nonchalant. In the months before our son was born, there was a frantic assembly of romper suits, bibs, sterilizing stuff and essential ointments. For the second baby I popped into

★If 50 Cent is interested, I've thought of an advertising campaign he might like to consider. It's for Bisto gravy, and he'd stand in front of a gleaming BMW rapping 'It goes like a shot, but I know it's not, as hot as BISTO – it's got a flow as hot as a ho's G-spot.'

Safeway on the way home from the maternity ward for a packet of nappies. For the first child, the birth itself is a procession of bewildering dramas that defy planning. You're aware there's a bit where 'the waters break' but even so, the morning of the birth began with us dipping our finger into this puddle on the sheet grimacing 'What the fuck's THAT?' Then the covers were yanked back, we took a moment to study the alien substance, then shrieked so that anyone passing outside would have thought we were auditioning for a part in *The Godfather*. Then came a day of thrashing and screaming in a hospital ward, while every few minutes a new person would enter wearing a green pinny, shove past me and plug in a big square machine covered in dials, a contraption that resembled what people in the 1930s believed a time machine would look like. And in the confusion I'd want to say, 'Who are YOU?', but you feel such an unwanted nuisance when you're a father in a maternity ward that you don't say anything, and probably wouldn't if they picked up the bed, along with the mother, lifted it on to a truck and drove off in the direction of France.

But the second time, even the baby seemed casual. I was woken at around half past six in the morning with the words, 'The contractions have started and they're every five minutes.'

'Doesn't that mean you're about to have the baby?' I asked.

The answer was the most definitive possible. It was, 'Er, oh yes, I suppose, AWAAAAGHEEUGHYYYIWEEEEEEOOOOO. UGH UGH UGH AWAAAYYY FUCK FUCK.'

So I rang the midwife and she said she was sure her shift patterns had been rearranged and that it wasn't her covering this birth. I asked, 'Well, who IS covering it?' and she said something that I couldn't hear because behind me it sounded as if a live wrestling match was in progress. There was a 'YAAAAAY' and then a deep breath followed by 'HNNNNNNNYEEEAGH', and it would have seemed perfectly natural if this had ended with 'NO NO NO NO' and 'a ONE, a TWO, a THREE – ding ding ding – and the WINNER by a fall and a submission . . .'

The midwife phoned back and assured me she definitely wasn't supposed to be on duty and she couldn't understand WHY I'd been asked to ring her, and added that I'd probably have to deliver the baby myself. So I called the hospital again and was put through to some other department. Then an ambulance arrived from somewhere with two paramedics, and there was a knock at the door and there were TWO midwives, who stood in the doorway arguing furiously about who was supposed to be covering this one as the baby started to emerge. A friend arrived to take our son for the day, then as my partner was being lifted through the January snow past the increasingly animated midwives, with the blue light reflecting off her white plastic gown, and the neighbours peering through their frosty windows at this scene of eight people equally bewildered and loud for different reasons, a man in his sixties who'd recently taken over the local paper round arrived. 'Where d'you want your paper today, mate, 'cos I can't seem to get to your letterbox,' he asked.

I think I said, 'What? I don't know, anywhere, she's having a baby, look.'

'Yeah all right, mate,' he said. 'But if I leave it here on the step with all this snow it'll get wet and ruined.'

As if at the end of a day like that, I was likely to say, 'Oh, that's two things gone wrong today; first the birth was a shambles, now my crossword's gone soggy.'

My partner was instructed to try to hold the baby in until we got to the hospital. Within a few minutes of our arrival Eloise slid out, and on top of the joy that accompanies these occasions I felt fantastically smug as it was still only eight o'clock. 'We've got up and had a baby,' I thought, 'and some lazy fuckers aren't even out of bed yet.'

An hour later, the three of us were installed in a room at the Mayday Hospital in Croydon. As my partner and I perused the new infant in this most glorious human moment, the door opened. In came a woman wearing a perfectly pressed white blouse and pleated skirt. The two parents and possibly the baby gazed at her. What could she want? 'Good morning,' she said, in the voice of a travel rep advising you where to board the bus for the excursion to the ruins of Knossos. And she began a prepared spiel: 'Now – many new parents find that with all the hectic goings-on that follow a birth, they simply don't have time to take that precious photo of their new-born angel in the special first hours. So for a very reasonable charge I can remove that worry from your shoulders and take the precious pictures that mean you'll have a memento of your baby's precious first moments to treasure in the years to come.' And she revealed a camera and a display of lenses. I wonder if, on a slow day, she's tempted to branch out into other sections of the hospital and burst into the cardiac unit to say, 'Good morning. Many people find that in the precious hours following a triple bypass operation they simply don't have the strength to take that precious photo as their life hangs in the balance. Well now there's no need to worry . . .'

She'd probably trained as a photographer, maybe owned a plethora of certificates, and now the only job available was a franchise offered by the hospital, in which they let her sell her skills and intrude on new-born babies in exchange for taking a cut themselves. It's probably a scheme that won high praise from the finance department of the health authority as an innovative means of securing extra revenue.

Maybe one day they'll allow advertising during the birth. A couple of actors will stand at the end of the bed and, as the cord is being cut, one will exclaim, 'Blood, meconium, afterbirth – that will NEVER come out. I might as well throw these sheets away.' Then her mate replies, 'Hold on a moment – you haven't tried New Maternity Daz.'

There's a nagging thought that probes at the margins of the mind whenever you stumble across one of these brazen displays of profiteering. Because it would be churlish to complain if the Health Service was delivering babies and transplanting kidneys and mending spines to everyone's satisfaction, that this is all very well but then they ruin it all by offering to take your picture. But the mentality that leads to excitable executives searching hospitals for any overlooked money-making potential doesn't stop at franchising florists, phone lines and photographers. It's part of a belief that the system can't function without incentives for business. So the cleaning and catering is run by businessmen as eager as the lady with her camera.

Compared to the wondrous way in which modern hospitals routinely ensure most births are conducted with utter safety, it may seem a minor point to grumble about the photography lady. But it's not the imposition that's upsetting, it's the feeling that every area of life is now run for profit, even when you're one hour old.

The sense that your value, the 'success' you've attained, is determined by the wealth and status you've accrued through your business ventures drove the 'morals' of New Labour.

In his book *The Point of Departure*, Robin Cook recalled a conversation he and Roy Hattersley had with Blair, in which they questioned why the Prime Minister had sent his son to a selective school. 'After all,' said Hattersley, 'with all the advantages of being the son of a prime minister he'd do well wherever he went.' Blair replied that he didn't want his children to end up like the kids of Harold Wilson. So Hattersley pointed out that one of Wilson's sons was a headmaster and the other was a professor at the Open University, and Blair said, 'Well, I would hope my sons do better than THAT.'

And you know that by 'better' he doesn't mean more valuable to society, or more inspiring or even more content, he means possessing more wealth and status. But if that is the modern definition of success, it can't be just through the influence of New Labour. From every corner we're bombarded with the message that success means profit, even on an individual level. Your house is no longer somewhere in which to live, it's an investment, a foot on the ladder, a fiscal gilt-edged unit of equity. All through the day enthusiastic estate agents on television programmes with titles like *Hot Property* advise couples how to buy a cottage in the 'up and coming area of Northampton' and double its value by converting the loft into a skating rink. Sometimes you can feel them itching to say, 'And there's no panic for a quick sale as you can rent the place out to three families of Somali asylum-seekers, who are GUARANTEED to make the payments as they'll be terrified you'll grass them up and get them deported and tortured, creating a fluid return on your investment all round.'

A friend in Greenwich, which has been designated 'up and coming', told me a woman who'd recently moved into her road came running up to her in the street, arms waving in panic, bellowing, 'Oh my God, I've just come past your house and had such a shock.' My friend braced herself for the dreadful news. A fire? A dead body in the garden? The woman said, 'Do you realise that with your property, you're not fulfilling your true potential?'

TV shows such as *Dragons' Den* and *The Apprentice* can make sense only if we accept 'success' is another word for 'profit'. If someone appeared before Alan Sugar and said their plan was to become the most caring generous nurse in Britain, creating a trail of patients overwhelmed at such selfless kindness, the programme makers would splutter and garble, unable to know how to respond – like a car when it's been filled with diesel instead of petrol by mistake.

There's nothing especially novel about large companies eagerly making vast profits with little regard for the consequences; what *is* new, is that it appears to be universally accepted by all major parties that it can't be any different. The world *must* be run by big business. We can't confront them, we must involve them. For example, if Tesco are able to buy computers for schools in return for their mass advertising campaign inside classrooms, why wouldn't it be possible to compel the company to do the same without giving them the right to plaster their logo at the eyeline of the nation's children? It wouldn't be that unfair, would it, if the tax system were such that the major supermarkets had to cough up a portion of their profits (made from the parents of those children) towards education. If you propose this now, you're treated as a quaint novelty, like one of those people who stand at by-elections on an education platform proposing to abolish maths and teach kids how to levitate instead.

Similarly, throughout the debates on global warming, every initiative seems to include 'bringing business onside', with complex formulas to try to persuade big corporations not to continue destroying the planet. No one suggests this with less serious crimes. Imagine if someone announced, 'The important point in dealing with street crime is coming up with a plan that can bring the muggers on board.'

Yet the multinationals certainly haven't vanquished all opposition. If anything, the numbers opposed to their onslaughts are greater than ever.

There seems to be a demand for anti-globalisation literature, that is, suitably enough, unprecedentedly global. One British Conservative, an ex-editor of *The Spectator*, complained he had a shock when he visited New York because 'The shop window of every bookshop looks as if it's been filled by members of the Socialist Workers Party.' Naomi Klein's *No Logo* was an international bestseller, Noam Chomsky could sell out vast theatres in a few hours;* there must have been some bemused clerks at Ticketmaster who assumed he was an offshoot from Radiohead. And this was all before the prospect of war in Iraq brought millions into the streets to try to stop it happening. Since then, while the numbers demonstrating has decreased, there's no sense that opinion, in Britain or around the world, has swung in favour of big business or of war. For example, when Michael Moore toured Britain following the release of his anti-war film *Farenheit 9-11*, huge theatres sold out within hours.

---

*When I was in Iceland, an excited student informed me that his student group had booked Chomsky for the largest theatre in Reykjavik in six months' time, and it was already sold out. I'd been speaking in the student union bar the previous evening and felt delighted at getting about ninety. How do you think that made ME feel, eh Chomsky?

The overwhelming majority in every poll supported the idea that the railways should be taken back into public ownership. The arguments against the exploitation of farmers and factory workers around the world became so widespread that major stores erected huge signs proclaiming their goods were 'Fairtrade'. This revulsion against the ethics of big business reached so far beyond 'the Left' that I would find myself enthusiastically agreeing with an angry voice decrying the effects of globalisation on the radio and discover I'd boomed 'bloody right, mate' at an ex-field marshal or chairman of the British Mustard Marketing Board or something. It was now mainstream to hold a rebellious attitude towards war and big business – properly mainstream, like Des Lynam or *The Lion King*. And yet there was something else at the heart of this resentful attitude, which was confusion.

If the number of people who wished for a more humanitarian order was enormous, hardly anyone could articulate what they thought ought to be done about it. Even the millions who'd marched against the war – maybe especially them – felt no one was listening, so what could they do. Indeed the confusion extends so far that hardly anyone among this disgruntled number is even sure who they should vote for in a general election.

This is in contrast to most of the last 100 years, when there was a much smaller number of outraged people but an established set of organisations competing with each other to attract their support. The Labour Party had been a natural home for most of those who opposed the bullying ways of the rich and powerful. Now, if you try to explain that to anyone under the age of thirty, they look at you as if you've said something truly surreal, as peculiar as if you had suggested the Church of England started out as an aquarium.

So, as Labour has enjoyed the greatest period of electoral success in its history, its membership has halved and its youth movement has vanished entirely. Now if someone in their twenties joined the Labour Party, it would almost certainly be as a career move. It's almost reached the point where choosing which party to join is like deciding on a public school. Prospective members will sit with their parents studying the prospectus and league tables, making comments such as 'Labour offer a wider variety of opportunities in the law and media but the Conservatives are still ahead if you want to go into landowning.'

The environmental movement has grown slightly, and the Green Party vote has gone up a little, but not much when you consider how prominent that issue has become.

Even the trade unions, whose reason to exist is as the first line of resistance against the bullying and cost-cutting, have declined in numbers, from 8.8 million in 1993 to 7.8 million in 2003. Thirty years ago the union leaders were celebrities. Now, even the name of the TUC general secretary would be known only by those with a close interest, on a par with the president of the Acupuncturist Association or Leyton Orient's goalkeeper.

The Liberal Democrats attracted hundreds of thousands of votes from Labour at the 2005 election as a result of the war in Iraq, but like a nun who mistakenly gets drunk and has a roll in a barley field with a nearby farmer, they seemed to react to this by pledging to become more duller than ever, to make sure no such fun could ever happen again.

So where was it all going to, this vat of discontent? If it were possible to set up a party with a manifesto that stated: 'We're sick of big business running everything for its shareholders and wish we'd never had anything to do with George Bush and his wars but we're buggered if we know what to do about it,' it would stand a good chance of winning millions of votes.

In this situation, you might imagine, the far left should be doubling its membership every week. But it hasn't. There have been two instances in which it has crept on to the edge of the mainstream, with the election of Respect's George Galloway in Bethnal Green in 2005 and the achievements of the Scottish Socialist Party, before running into magnificently exotic disasters.

In fact, left-wing groups have shrunk, and seem more distant than ever from those they ought to attract; including the Socialist Workers

Party, of which I'd been a member since I was 18. And so, for the first time in my adult life, if someone asks me what I reckon we should do to stop the grubby people wrecking the world, I find myself saying, 'I'm not really sure.'

But for all the fear and anxiety that accompanies this age, at least there ought to be the compensation of certainty in my personal life. The one thing the person in their forties doesn't envy about teenage life is the instability. There can be trauma, but not usually the same agonising confusion of being nineteen; you shouldn't fall in love with three different people in a day, one of whom is the mother of one of the others. Not if you're forty. Nor should you refuse the last possible lift home from a party on the grounds that someone you fancy smiled when they passed you the cork-screw so you reckon you're in with a chance – the result being you have to walk home on your own five miles through the snow.

At forty, your relationships with siblings and surviving parents may be tiresome, or even nonexistent, but they're likely to be stable one way or the other. Once you're forty you're probably aware whether you're gay, or love being in France or like burning down public buildings, and by now are living your life accord-ingly. I had a house, a partner of the opposite sex, a son and a daughter and a garden. If I'd done a quiz in a Sunday magazine called 'Are you a conformist?' I would have scored more points than Cliff Richard.

If something appears stable, however, when it collapses the impact is much greater. I realised this when my domestic life fell apart and I found myself sleeping in the living room on a settee. Obviously this entails a great deal of emotional upheaval, but one of the most uncomfortable aspects is that you find yourself thinking, 'I shouldn't be sleeping on a settee in the living room – I'm FORTY.'

Lying awake pondering, I'd take advantage of the modern world and watch the variety of all-night digital channels. One night there was a documentary on Bravo about a man who was convinced he was a zebra. He even had stripes tatooed across him. And with the birds beginning to tweet, the main thought in my head was, 'Not that serious about it are you, mate, or you'd fuck off and take your chance in the Serengeti with the pumas.' Quiz channels, oodles of soft-ish porn, reruns of *The Sweeney*, and a programme called *Britain's Roughest Pubs* which included an interview with a landlord of a decrepit lap-dancing bar saying earnestly, 'One bloke got a bit overexcited, whipped it out and splodged on my upholstery. Well, I banned him for a MONTH.' And on the shopping channel, a programme called *Curtain of the Day*. And this camp bloke going for it – 'Now we've seen some curtains today but this IS the one – oh my goodness, just look at the drapes.' The drive of business to make a profit had reached so far it had found a way to exploit the discomfort of my marital breakdown at three in the morning. I was in my forties and more confused than at any time since I was nine – and than I'd expected to be again until I was eighty-six.

2

NEW PROJECTS

It takes a lot of effort to make people cynical. We start by merrily trusting every word of our parents, teachers and presenters of *Blue Peter*, never imagining they could be hungover/winging it/buzzing from coke. We accept charming explanations for how things work long after we've witnessed forensic evidence that suggests they can't be true. Presumably even when Richard Dawkins was six, he didn't say to his mum, 'If the money was left by a tooth fairy, how does it know the rate for every country? Does it have a celestial calculator constantly keeping tabs on every exchange rate? Either you're in on it or you're an irrational fantasist, Mother.'

We believe the brightly coloured children's stories that inform us the world is made of smiling butchers, jolly policemen and friendly animals who play together and would no more eat each other than Daddy might eat Mrs Whittaker next door. At school we accept the Bible is a multiplex full of feelgood tales, such as cuddly Mr and Mrs Noah who build a lovely bouncy ark for all the cheerful creatures, and even the most precocious child doesn't say, 'Hang on, this is a story about God murdering virtually every creature on his Earth because they aren't worshipping him enough.'

When we first fall in love we believe it will last for ever, despite the mounting historical evidence that this isn't always how it turns out. And we want to believe there are great figures out there, dripping with integrity, who will descend like Robin Hood and slay the baddies with their greed and corruption and injustice. Such is our endearing capacity for self-deception that millions of people believed in Tony Blair.

Because of all that's happened since, it's hard to remember accurately the joy of the day he became Prime Minister, in the same way you can't recall the elation and passion of the early days of a relationship once you're sitting with a solicitor constructing a demand for half the house and access to the kids. But that shouldn't rob us of that night of joy. Mellor, Hamilton, Portillo – it appeared every creep in Britain was being humiliated in public, and I started wondering if Dimbleby was about to say, 'Now we're going over to Telford, where Noel Edmonds is being dangled naked so children can spray him with cat sick.'

The thrill of that time was real enough, strangers smiling at each other on trains, in the hope that the days of being ruled by hypocrites, liars and arms dealers had come to an end. A video of the election-night TV coverage went into the best-selling charts, as did a book called *Were You Up for Portillo?* For a while the election of Tony Blair was presented as one of those events that should unite all humanity in joy, like when Torvill and Dean won their gold medal, and any Tory spokesman who objected looked as churlish as if they'd been at the Winter Olympics and said they wished Torvill had slipped and broken her ankle.

It was especially remarkable because the change promised was extremely limited. Blair and his colleagues had spent three years reassuring big business that they would work in its interests and had promised to stick to the Tories' spending plans. (At the time we didn't realise this included sticking to how much you have to spend to get a peerage.) In his first week in the job Blair invited Thatcher to Downing Street for tea. But so many wanted to believe . . . For a while everything the new government did appeared bold and exciting. They announced the independence of the Bank of England, and millions of people marvelled:

'WOW – that's AMAZING. Wasn't it independent already then? So what does that mean then? Anyway – that's BRILLIANT.'

The declaration that the government would pursue an 'ethical foreign policy' illustrated the triumph; it seemed to usher in a new era of humanity. Because the regime it replaced was so tainted, all New Labour had to do to look fresh and overflowing with goodness was to declare it would be ethical. As if any government would announce it had met long into the night and decided that on balance it should be UNethical. But no matter how little they promised, there was a different ATMOSPHERE. And even if New Labour said, 'No, there isn't,' many people would have given them a squeeze and said, 'Oh you daft things, you're too modest.' Because we wanted to believe.

It's a mistake to assume this only affected the naive. Even those most cynical about New Labour thought there would be SOME change.*

It's often assumed the goodwill evaporated because of Iraq. But it was already disappearing before then, so that by the general election of 2001 there was the lowest turnout of voters since the First World War. And although Labour won easily, there was none of the enthusiasm of four years earlier. The argument that was common before his first election, that Blair was waiting until he was Prime Minister to turn radical, was revived by a few people who suggested he was waiting for his second term, when he'd really have the opportunity to be radical. By the time he resigned, I expected some would suggest it was a shame, because if only we had waited until 2035, in the crucial eleventh term he'd have been really quite radical.

It wasn't the specific policies that created the sense of betrayal – the student fees, the fiasco of the dome, etc. – as much as the realisation that the values of this government were so similar to those of the last one. They didn't just help giant corporations, they

---

*Six years later the comedian Linda Smith put it succinctly, 'I had no illusions of Blair whatsoever; absolutely no expectations at all – none. And even I'M disappointed.'

begged to be their best friend, to enjoy their holiday homes and sit by their swimming pools. They oozed big business. When Peter Mandelson was on TV you felt he might call security and have you thrown out of your living room for being too common to watch him. Blair himself was SO impressed by wealth and celebrity he even became friends with Cliff Richard.

Labour's membership, which blossomed in the years before they were elected, began to crumble – from 400,000 in 1997 to 198,000 at the end of 2005. In the traditional Labour areas, the support suffered most of all, not necessarily because the government had become too right wing, but because Labour had become so distant and removed from the people on which the party had been built.

Becoming a parent doesn't necessarily make you more conservative, but it does make you reassess certain questions. For example, once my daughter was about three, I amended my liberal views on sexuality slightly and became adamant that my son would grow up straight and my daughter gay, so that no boys would be coming round for either of them.

On the other hand, when my son was six we watched the final of *Big Brother* together, and when Davina addressed the housemates with her customary 'This is Davina speaking – you're LIVE on Channel 4 so NO SWEARING' my boy said, 'I'd love to be in that house now, Dad, so I could say "Hello, Davina. Bloody hell, arse, shit."' And I was so proud.

The campaigning socialist does face an awkward moral problem with the arrival of children: how to get them to be wary of all authority except yours. One morning, when I was merrily tapping my feet to Rage Against the Machine howling 'Fuck you, I won't do what you tell me', my son turned it off to watch cartoons instead. And as I bellowed, 'OY – YOU'RE NOT ALLOWED TO DO THAT,' I realised I'd created a philosophical dilemma that would have kept Descartes busy for a year.

Luckily you have the opportunity to watch other parents make mistakes and learn practical lessons as you watch them plead, 'PLEASE put the lighter fuel down, darling, what did we say about explosions?' The phrase that makes me squirm the most is 'I'm WARNING you.' Warning them WHAT? When the kid calls their bluff, the beleaguered parent has to resort to 'RIGHT. I'm going to count to THREE.' At this point *I'm* hoping the kid carries on, because I'm dying to see what happens at three. Otherwise I'd feel as if I'd watched a play but missed the ending. But of course they haven't written the ending, so it goes 'One', then an agonising dramatic gap – 'Two . . .' Now a ridiculous pause, like the moments before the announcement of who's been knocked out that night on a reality TV show, and eventually a floundering 'RIGHT, that's IT', but WHAT? You feel so cheated. I find it hard not to shout, 'OY – you promised something would happen at three – so go on, burn his teddy or SOMETHING.'

One thing you learn from being involved in trade union campaigns is that, if you make a demand to management, you've got to be able to back it with the threat of some form of action if they don't agree to it. The great battles in the history of the labour movement wouldn't have got far if the leaders had said, 'Stop those wage cuts at once or I'll count to three.'

The finest case I saw of issuing a meaningless threat was from a mother struggling to get her boy out of the car outside the school. He wasn't getting out for some reason, so she yelled, 'Get out NOW – otherwise you'll NEVER watch television again for the REST OF YOUR LIFE.' Imagine trying to enforce that one! Every trip to any house would begin with an instruction to turn off all tellies, even when he was thirty. As an old woman, she'd be ringing his mates to make sure he wasn't trying to sneak a look at the 2038 World Cup Final, and leave instructions on her deathbed that guardians must be appointed to ensure he didn't catch so much as the first landing on Mars.

The next test for a parent is a bunch of questions: 'How much does the moon weigh? Why can't cats talk? Who invented cheese?' There are also the social dilemmas: 'Mr Parkin said today that the first person to help you whenever you're worried is a policeman.' What do you say? You can't reel off a forty-five-minute precis of the miners' strike. Just as you can't send your daughter in with a note that says, 'It is my view that public services, especially education, should be funded by public money and not be dependent on charity. Therefore I am NOT signing up to my daughter's sponsored bounce on the bouncy castle at the summer fair.'

But in 2001 came a particularly tricky moment. Everyone has their own version of how they heard the news, and no matter how mundane it's always interesting. A classmate of my son's was staying at our house while his parents went to New York for their wedding anniversary. They flew back overnight and came to the school in the morning, where they met their son and asked if I could pick him up in the afternoon so they could catch up on some sleep. 'What a trip,' they enthused. 'Yesterday afternoon we were up the World Trade Center.'

That afternoon I was in a local second-hand bookshop when the phone rang. The shopkeeper exclaimed 'bloody hell' and put the phone down. As I paid for the book, an academic tome on the peasants in the French Revolution, he said, 'Apparently there's two planes just flown into the World Trade Center.'

I drove home, half expecting this to be a meaningless story, a product of confusion and exaggeration, but what I found when I arrived was the grotesque confirmation beaming live from New York. I stood duly aghast, unable to sit down, just as I can't when I'm watching the dramatic finish to a Test match or game of football. And I think I flicked through the channels, fascinated to see which ones were carrying on as normal. I seem to remember the shopping channels were unmoved; I suppose when there's diamanté ear-rings to be shifted it helps keeps things in perspective.

As the first tower collapsed, a dual horror was unfolding. There was the obvious devastation, slaughter and unimaginable suffering at the heart of the extraordinary images, but also the sickening certainty that this wouldn't go away, like an earthquake or tsunami. The aftermath would spit and explode for decades. You don't do this to empires and get away with it. It was the equivalent of a bunch of barbarians marching into Ancient Rome and blowing up the Colosseum. I went out to pick up the boys from school, still less than an hour since the first plane struck, and in place of the normal scene of jovial parents receiving drawings of flowers and arranging sleepovers, there was a chaotic shuffling, anxious questions being exchanged between mothers as if a calamity from which their kids had to be firmly protected was taking place at the end of the road.

My lad and his friend skipped home, oblivious, and played with a train set while I stared at the images on the screen and listened to the bemused reporters. 'Can we watch cartoons, Dad?' asked my son after a while. 'Not today,' I said, and they carried on with their trains. 'Thankfully they haven't noticed any of this,' I thought, 'as I've no idea how I'd explain it, morally, politically or even architecturally.' Then a minute later my son said to his friend, 'It's a good job your parents aren't up the World Trade Center today or they'd be dead,' and pushed Percy the Engine along the wooden rails.

The next morning the inevitable reactions were fully activated. One of the dads said, 'Did you see them bastards celebrating on the news? Jumping up and down and laughing? In fucking Palestine or whatever. How can they be so heartless about innocent civilians getting killed like that? Fucking bastards.' This was at ten past nine on the way back from the school. I started to offer a reply, but he wouldn't have heard if I'd said I'd organised the whole thing myself as a protest against Dido reaching number one in the charts. 'What we've got to do now is fucking bomb them, really fucking bomb them, kill a million of the bastards. I'd fucking laugh, I would, I'd fucking laugh,' he said. And he'd completed that circle in about sixty words, taking him no more than twenty yards from the school gate.*

*On the other hand, a journalist I know was making a documentary in San Francisco about the porn industry. The actors were all ready to go when the news came through. After a discussion they took the collective decision that, in the circumstances, they didn't feel quite as erotic as they'd intended, and as a mark of respect abandoned filming for the day.

For a day or so after the Twin Towers collapsed, it seemed inde-
cent to consider anything beside the immediacy of the calamity;
the individual anguish, the desperate tales you imagined belonged
to the photocopied faces pasted on to walls under a forlorn
'Missing'. Then the choreographed wailing started. Almost every
newspaper columnist was obliged to tell us that 'These days I give
my children that extra hug before they go to bed' – as poignant as
a vicar saying at a funeral 'She was a fine woman' about someone
he's never met. I wondered whether the gardening columnist
would eventually inform us that 'Since that fateful afternoon I
watch my houseplants with a more focused intensity, unable to
sleep without giving them an extra capful of Baby Bio.'

They all felt lucky as they had been so close to being there
themselves, although the winning comment was Peter Hain's,
who said,'My wife and I were at the World Trade Center twelve
years ago, which made us think – "It could have been us."'

There was the lavishly cynical, such as the full-page easyJet
advert appealing to the government not to compensate major air-
lines for lost revenue. It began: 'Firstly our thoughts are with the
people of New York, and the dreadful suffering they have
endured.' Then it went on to argue that, nonetheless, it would be
unfair if all this was to thwart easyJet's business strategy for the
forthcoming year. It must have crossed the minds of advertising
agencies to tell us 'A Milky Way is the bar you CAN eat between
lighting candles for the suffering but spirited and courageous
people of New York.'

It all contributed to produce an outlandish atmosphere of fear.
When some powder was spotted leaking from a bag in a
Liverpool postal sorting office the whole area was evacuated, and
for a day we feared we were under threat from anthrax. Except
the powder turned out to be spilt Horlicks. Thankfully we didn't
behave like that in the Second World War, because back then
everything was powdered. Hitler wouldn't have needed the
Luftwaffe, just half a dozen badly packed sacks and he'd be rolling
into London.

A comedian I know went to a gig on the Isle of Skye, where he was told hardly anyone had bought tickets as they were afraid to go out, with all that had happened. Because in the hills of Pakistan there might have been an Al Q'aeda cell declaring 'After the Twin Towers, now for an even *greater* blow against the infidel – destruction of the function room in the Rose and Crown on the Isle of Skye.' The only event that went ahead regardless, without even a nod towards the unfolding carnage, was the arms fair, put on in London's Docklands by Reed-Elsevier for the world's arms dealers.

The 24-hour news channels carried a permanent strap across the screen saying 'War on Terror', and the number of days this had been going on, September 11th being day one. Yet in the first two weeks of this War on Terror the American response was applauded by virtually all politicians and commentators as 'restrained' and 'thoughtful'. Typical was Simon Jenkins in *The Times*, who told us, 'The leash of common sense has restrained the dog of war.'

George Bush hadn't 'lashed out' as people expected, but 'carefully and diplomatically built a coalition' so opposition to US action seemed churlish. Typical of the confusion caused by this state of affairs was the statement by Paul McCartney that, although he was a pacifist, he couldn't be at this time of war. Which is as daft as being a vegetarian between meals.

For a while anything critical of the American establishment would be leapt on as insulting to the victims of the Twin Towers. The American writer P.J. O'Rourke, described as a 'satirist' and hailed for his irreverence, said he wouldn't be attempting to write anything funny for a while as 'Now is not the time for jokes.' And yet, if you peeked behind this façade of stoic heroism, Bush was virtually writing his own jokes against himself. He announced one day that 'The noose is tightening around Bin Laden' because 'we have frozen his bank account'. Did that mean that up until that day Bin Laden had merrily been strolling down to the cashpoint, but now he'd ring up to book cinema tickets and be told, 'I'm afraid your account's been frozen Mr Bin Laden'? I wondered if George Bush would announce next that the noose had been tightened even further because they'd cancelled his Blockbuster video card. On another occasion Bush said, 'We could do a deal with the *moderate* Taliban.' Who were they then? Presumably they thought, 'Well, one tower yes, but not *two*.'

The bombing of Afghanistan made it easier to voice opposition, for the obvious reason that the bombs were killing civilians.

The fleeting images of wailing, rage and confusion were familiar, like those from New York. The women waving their arms and gesturing to the rubble behind them may have been wearing black headscarves and crying in a different language, but the anguish, the bewilderment, the need to find someone to scream at were a perfect echo of the scenes by the remains of the Twin Towers. But beyond the immediate carnage, there was another reason for not backing the US bombing campaign. A clique existed at the top of American society who believed that, following the end of the Cold War, the US should be able to assert its role as the only world superpower, to reap the rewards for having seen off communism. In 1997 these people devised the 'Project for a New American Century'. Shortly afterwards their friends in the US Department of Defense issued a statement declaring that America must attain 'full spectrum dominance', meaning any opposition to US interests anywhere on the planet could be immediately dealt with.

One of the first aims of the Project creators was an invasion of Iraq, followed by the installation of a regime friendly to the US. When Bush became President he appointed to his cabinet sixteen signatories to the Project, including Paul Wolfowitz, Richard Perle and Donald Rumsfeld at Defense. Any troop movements, bombing campaigns and invasions launched by these men were part of this strategy. The Twin Towers carnage may have altered the timing and detail of their plan but not the overall Project.

So next stop after Afghanistan was always going to be Iraq. The Twin Towers was a convenient excuse, but no more the real reason for the war than the sudden concern for women's rights in Arab countries. That was why when Bush and Blair and their supporters bowed their heads on all those occasions to remember the slaughtered of New York, I couldn't join in. Because anyone who is deeply moved by one set of tragedies while ignoring, and even justifying, those on the other side, in reality is not genuinely touched by either. It's just an arm of their propaganda.

Blair went to New York a couple of months later to stand with Bush for the three-minute silence to commemorate the Twin Towers victims. Cherie spent £2,000 getting her hair done for the occasion. I waited for the exact moment the silence started, then played 'I'm So Bored With The USA' by The Clash at top volume with all the doors and windows open. And I've rarely felt so stupid as when it ended, because the track is only two minutes and twenty seconds long, and for forty seconds I fiddled about trying to think of some other symbolic thing to do in the silence.

According to one biography of Che Guevara, when Che met his future wife, Hilda, 'They spent the evenings reading Marx and Mao together, and fell in love.' Which must have made for an unusual romance – Che whispering into her ear, 'My sweet, when I gaze into your deep succulent eyes I, like Mao, am reminded that power comes through the barrel of a gun,' as he gently unbuttoned her dress.

For me, the origins of socialist love blossomed within an even more unlikely environment, performing at a comedy event for the Broad Left section of a trade union conference, held in the function room of a decaying hotel in Bournemouth. I doubt whether Mills & Boon have ever published a story, even one aimed at their trade unionist market, that reads: 'She felt his arm brush hers, sending a tingle racing up to her neck and down her spine like an electric shock. "You seem deep in thought," he said. Her heart began to gallop, her cheeks flushed and she gasped, "I'm wondering whether to reword our motion on Health and Safety legislation to include Scotland and the North-East, which traditionally act as separate regions not governed by the National Executive."'

In that creaking hotel, a maze of swing doors and short narrow staircases with a hundred places where you had suddenly to duck or face an evening in Accident and Emergency with concussion, was someone who sparkled through the smoke and lager, laughing, persuading and enjoying the in-jokes and drunken circular arguments about resolutions and nominations for positions with very long titles. She drank, danced and explained the following day's conference debates all at the same time. She introduced me comprehensively to twenty people in ten minutes, flipping between them to deliver foot-stamping retorts, never for a moment stumbling for a syllable, like a trade unionist version of one of those chess players who plays dozens of opponents at once. And while her repartee ricocheted between the personal, the comical and the political, it was always affectionate and always very, very loud.

Everything and everyone seemed to matter to her, so that as she gesticulated to the delegate from Bristol who was slumped over an ashtray, or grabbed a friend to gyrate to Abba in the days when to do so was *genuinely* ironic, I wondered, and worried, that she'd forgotten about me altogether. But she kept returning, maybe to explain why my jokes about vegetarians had caused uproar among the contingent from Stoke, or the need to elect the man slumped over the ashtray to the Finance Committee, or to enthuse about a collection she'd helped organise for people in jail in some dictatorship or other, or to hand me a bottle of beer with a smile comprised of suggestiveness and danger.

And all this energy and anticipation was so urgent, as if the anger and joy and youthful vital rows she orchestrated throughout the room would determine the course of world events – from the basement of a crumbling hotel that served tinned tomatoes still cold in the middle and unfeasibly small eggs for breakfast.

I've no idea why men are initially attracted to certain women. I suspect most of the surveys, reports and studies in psychoanalysis make matters too complex. Most single blokes, if they're being truthful, when asked whether they're attracted to women who are confident or vulnerable, organised or flaky, ambitious or carefree, would say, 'I don't know – I'll have ANYONE. I haven't had sex for six months, do you think if I had an offer I'd say, "No thank you, you're twenty per cent too sentimental and not interested enough in current affairs?"' On the other hand, surveys that conclude that huge breasts and compact bottoms are the main criteria probably make us out to be more stupid than we really are. Which is why someone like Anthea Turner, who possesses all the physical attributes that ought to make her the ideal beacon of attraction for straight men, due to that chilling vacant demeanour, remains strangely sexless.

For whatever reason the attraction that began in Bournemouth seemed almost immediately long-term. Within days of meeting her, the doubts and hesitancy that infest with caution the male 30-year-old mind were swiftly dispatched, as if they were a mild virus. Even through the early gooey phase of long phone calls in the afternoon, when every journey had to be marked with a present (I did a gig in Darlington and brought back a saucer with 'Darlington' written on it, the only Darlington-specific object I could find), there was a certainty that once the initial rush of passion receded, we'd remain entwined for many years in a settled chaotic stability.

Every time I met her off a train she was with someone, gesticulating, laughing and debating with the relaxed buoyancy and candour you share with old friends or your favourite relative. 'Hi,' she'd call out across the platform, then approach and introduce her companion.

'Where do you know each other from?' I'd ask, and her companion would say, 'Oh I just met your girlfriend when I got on at Watford Junction. Now remember, the party's on the nineteenth so see you there.'

This engaging exuberance revolved around an intelligence that became apparent on our first date, when I showed her an episode of *The Simpsons*, back in the days when people still said, 'You don't watch that, do you? I thought it was a kids' show.' And not only was she instantly hooked, but she spotted a subplot involving Krusty the Klown I'd never even noticed.

That pulsating fizz, which could attract friends at an instant, could also send them into a scurrying retreat as words flew in all directions, accompanied by a jagged wave of one hand or both, or all four limbs at once. Sometimes we'd be talking in a bar when a friend would come across and whisper, 'Are you all right?'

'Yes,' I'd answer, surprised.

'Oh, it's just that from over there it looks as if your girlfriend's about to have a fight with the people sitting opposite.'

'No, she's just a bit animated,' I'd assure them, and she'd carry on thrusting out an elbow as she described to the people opposite why she preferred Devon to Cornwall.

The combination of astute, extrovert and loud was a guarantee of incidents. We went to Paris in the spring, and instead of discovering a romantic café where we could stroke each other's fingers in tranquil contrast to the hectic bustle of the waiters, we found a bar in which every single person had a scar they'd earned in a fight.

'You are from London?' asked a man with one eye.

'Yes, South London,' I replied.

'Ah, South London,' he said. 'Ha ha. I had a brother who was murdered there.'

When we took a ride on the ghost train at Brighton pier it caught fire, and a man in a boiler suit came through the skeletons to usher us to safety. And when she left her squalid flat because the landlord refused to fix the electricity when it packed up, we turned on the taps and wrecked his threadbare carpets, which resulted in the police being called and giving those carpets more attention than they'd ever received before. She was late arriving at a recording of my radio show because she'd been caught up in a demonstration which ended in a pitch battle with the British National Party. And we once saw a Norwegian ska band, because we fancied going away at Christmas and suddenly she said, 'Hang on, I met some Norwegians at a party and they gave me their number.' She rang them, and we ended up staying with them in Oslo and going to the gig in an illegal drinking club, and on the way back the tram crashed.

Maybe the volatile spark was the core of my attraction, because it would guarantee I could never descend into a suburban quagmire of middle-aged comfort involving charity golf events and barbecues where everyone discusses property prices and recipes for mulled wine – not when even a dinner party with the neighbours has the potential to erupt into a plate-throwing fight over the social implications of the *X Files*.

But even the most frenetic of people are tranquil for long periods. George Best must have had nights when he dozed off in front of *Columbo*, and Henry VIII probably had evenings when he stayed in listening to someone gently playing the harpsichord. Between our memorable explosive moments were the more memorable peaceful ones, the days of ringing in sick and cancelling appointments to stay in bed, and the tenderness that can render buying a fridge or spending an hour in a grimy pub romantic.

So we moved in together and bought a house and planned a family and charted the rest of our lives together, and on the rare occasion another woman smiled at me with a hint of interest I quickly mentioned my girlfriend, and that gave me a smug satisfaction greater than any pursuit from my single days.

Sometimes, though – just sometimes, around once every four months – her enthusiasm and tension would go beyond thrilling and become unsettling. Apparently out of nowhere the volume would rise up and up, and I'd find myself pathetically flailing, standing in a corner unable to do anything useful – like when your car's broken down and your mate who's a mechanic is under the bonnet fixing things while you stand gormlessly behind him. 'What's the matter?' I'd ask, uselessly, and maybe try to answer the words being shouted, with feeble comments such as 'We don't have to go to Canterbury if you don't want.' And after a while it would all be calm, until the next time. During those incidents it was as if she became someone else. It was like living with a lovely, effervescent, wonderfully bright and fun person who suddenly became a Tory and started yelling in the middle of the night about immigrants and business being crippled by tax, but by the next morning was fine again.

We put some thought into the cause of these moments, but as each one receded into the past it didn't seem to matter. Maybe we'd exaggerated it. But it was like the bit near the beginning of a science fiction film, when the main character shrinks just a little or discovers one fingernail has turned into a small claw. We'd try to forget about it, but in the back of our minds we knew this would be a major part of the plot later on.

3

I WAS SO MUCH OLDER THEN

The generation born in the 1960s finds it hard to understand that, to the genuinely young, we're old. Especially if you smoke dope at dinner parties and still play Blondie and Ian Dury, you can be certain you'll never turn into your parents, without seeing that you're turning into an *updated* version of your parents. It strikes you when you spend time with a 23-year-old. How can they have never seen *Porridge*, or not know who Norman Lamont is, or not find it rude when you're talking to someone and in mid-anecdote the bastard answers his mobile and starts an entirely new conversation while still looking straight at you, so for a moment you're left puzzling why, during your story about being stuck in a lift, he's said, 'Yeah yeah man, I've spoken to TJ and he's cool for Tuesday.'

Around the time of the new millennium, I'd noticed a new response from many people in their twenties to any mention of socialism. Instead of the regulation retorts such as 'What's wrong with wanting to be rich?' or 'It will never work', I'd hear, 'Socialism? What's that then?' It wasn't a request for an explanation, the way you might ask, 'So what IS the theory of relativity?' It was merely evidence that they'd barely heard of the subject. The first time this happened I answered, 'You know – socialism' in the tone you'd use if someone said, 'France – what's that then?' But why should anyone that age have heard even a fleeting explanation of socialism, or communism?

Socialism, to me, meant that society should be organised according to what benefits humans, rather than what makes a profit, whereas at the moment a handful of people own and control the world's resources, so that the richest 400 own the same amount of wealth as the poorest 2 billion – and that's not right. Hope, though, lies in the fact that the vast majority, who have no choice but to sell their labour, can resist all that's imposed on them if they stick together. The majority could even collectively run society, in the interests of that majority rather than the profit-obsessed interest of the handful.

But then, to complicate matters, a series of tyrannies such as the Soviet Union and Mao's China went by the name of socialism, and thoroughly ruined the brand name.*

When most of these regimes collapsed between 1989 and 1991 and the full scale of the horrors they'd inflicted became indisputable, most socialists reacted with a mixture of devastation and bemusement. The SWP had never considered these regimes to be socialist, so I naively thought people like me would be protected from the humiliation that socialism would inevitably suffer. We were like the innocent kid that just happened to be hanging about with the bad kids in the gang when they were all arrested. We could simply say, 'It wasn't us – we opposed these tyrants more than anyone.' But that was never going to be the case. Socialism was understood to be finished. To most people, still campaigning for it years later seemed as futile as shouting, 'Come on, we can still win this' to a boxer after the crowd's gone home and he's being driven off in an ambulance.

On top of that, many parties around the world associated with socialism distanced themselves from it, or reinterpreted it to be

---

*Linda Smith told me of a friend who had the archetypal English communist parents. She remembers them sitting in the kitchen distraught at the news on the radio that Russian troops had invaded Czechoslovakia. Eventually her mum sighed and said, 'Oh well, let's have a nice cup of tea and see what it says in the *Morning Star.*'

meaningless with statements like, 'We still believe in socialist values, which are to be fair, and to look to the future.' And no one did that more thoroughly than New Labour under Tony Blair. On the few occasions he mentioned socialism, it not only diluted the ideology but made it utterly surreal. For example, at the 2003 Labour conference he told us, 'I want the middle class fighting to get into the state education system. That's what the founders of socialism dreamed of.' So Karl Marx's dream must have been for the workers to lose their chains so they could build a new world in which advertising executives sent their sons to St Joseph's, as it did *very* well in the league tables and won't be much further for the nanny to go in the mornings.

Eventually we reached a point beyond socialism being discredited, to one where it wasn't known at all, except in connection to the most banal statements. Explaining what you meant by socialism to a 23-year-old would provoke the same sort of half-fascinated response that you'd get if you said you were a member of the Ancient Order of Illuminati. 'And this is still going on, this socialist thing, is it?' they'd ask, as if you'd told them you belonged to a church that still worshipped Zeus.

With the Soviet Union dismantled and the socialist movement vastly weakened, Western leaders seemed to believe they had secured everlasting victory, as if everything had been leading to this final battle between good and evil, like at the end of a science fiction film.

This assumed that with socialism apparently out of the way, when a corporation or a government, in order to boost profits, ripped up someone's land, herded people into slums, or – to be more British about it – shut down a library, no resistance would follow. But in reality no one ever fought injustice because they were a socialist, they fought injustice because it annoyed them. So a new generation responded to the inequalities of the new century by getting drawn to radical ideas. It's just that few of them were attracted by socialism.

Individual old socialists could still be immensely popular, most

notably Tony Benn. At Glastonbury in 2005 I saw the moving
spectacle of 4,000 people squeezing into a giant marquee to hear
him. Most of them looked between fifteen and twenty years old,
although maybe that calculation was distorted by the fact they all
displayed nose studs and an array of other piercings. In itself this
made me realise the prejudice of age, because a bit of me wanted
to say, 'You lot are hardly a threat to authority. All they'd have to
do is fly a plane over the place with a huge magnet and you'd all
be off.'

I was talking to Tony Benn behind the marquee a few
moments before he went on, as he sipped tea from his Thermos,
joked with my son and worried about where to put his canvas
haversack while he was speaking. Out of everyone in the whole
festival he seemed the most unlikely person to draw a vast young
crowd, as he struggled to keep his pipe alight in the breeze. Then
he shuffled on to the stage and a roar went up that made me
wonder whether I had one of those peculiar neurological diseases,
and that what I thought was Tony Benn was actually the White
Stripes. How does an 80-year-old socialist live up to expectations
like that? Perhaps he'd have to whip out a guitar and launch into
a thrash-metal version of his speech on the suffragettes. 'Well,' he
eventually said with a mixture of bemusement and humility, 'you
might be surprised to know I've decided we should give up
protesting. We should give up protesting and start DEMAND-
ING.' (In truth he speaks with such affection and so little
aggression, even the word 'demanding' was said in a font halfway
between normal and capitals).

And the place went wild. Screams, whoops and if you listened
carefully enough, probably the click of teeth on tongue studs. It
was as if he'd started with his biggest hit. Maybe if he'd opened
with a line about the Iraq war the crowd would have called out
'DEMANDING – do DEMANDING, we want DEMAND-
ING' until he did it. And they stood enraptured, as the speaker
put the case for a world that sought priorities other than war and
profits. So many politicians devise elaborate schemes to make

them palatable to the 'youth', posing with rappers and being filmed talking to schoolkids about the Scissor Sisters, when you can tell what they're really thinking is, 'Look – if you're going to rob me, please don't take my glasses or my Visa card.' If only they realised the way to a hoodie's heart is socialism.

I can in all honesty declare the scene made me shed a tear. The generation derided by so many from left and right as thoughtless, insolent and obsessed only with celebrity saw as a hero someone with nothing to offer but conviction and principles. But did any of them follow their icon's precedent and commit themselves to the Labour Party? Did they bollocks. Young campaigners may appreciate old radicals, read their books and check out their websites, but they won't join their organisations. Somehow all these groups have failed to connect, and the link between the Left and youth now seems almost completely broken.

When I first became an activist, at eighteen, I would generally reckon that at most events I was about five years younger than the average age. Now, twenty-nine years later, I found that statistic roughly the same. I've spoken at several events and rallies where I had planned to make a reference to someone like Missy Elliot, but looked at the audience and realised that unless I could make the same point using Neil Young I might as well drop that section altogether. It's wonderful that so many people have defied the stereotype and retained their youthful activism, but my gaze sweeps the room and I think, 'Before long, when we're all on a demonstration, instead of chanting "What do we want?", we'll be yelling "What did we come out here for?"'

The most distressing part of this trend is when the older people don't seem to notice. They can be like a group of friends growing older together, not realising they've got older at all because they still go to parties together and play Madness and the Damned and everyone laughs when someone makes a joke about Jeremy Thorpe.

I've been at rallies where the chair has announced how MAR-VELLOUS it is to see so many young people in the room, when the only people under thirty were the kids of someone who's been coming to these events since the miners' strike and couldn't get a babysitter.

One sign that, despite being forty or over, you're still in touch with today's youth to a certain extent, is to realise you're not in touch with them at all. For example, because I have some flimsy knowledge of contemporary rap, I conducted this conversation with the teenager who works in my local grocery shop. 'Ah, you listen to hip-hop, don't you? Have you heard the latest Lowkey album? And the first Plan B?'

'Man, I never knew you play that shit, right. Yeah Lowkey bruv, he's *sick*. He was wiv Doc Brown's crew init, but you feel Lowkey man, you must know Cuba Ranks you get me, you know who had beef wiv Fat Joe?'

'No. No, I don't know Cuba Ranks.'

'You know bruv, he produced for Kalashnikov, used to MC at the Brix Club init.'

'Eh, oh I think I know, no I don't.'

'You don't know him? Bruv you must know, he left Asher D's label saying he didn't check for him when he mixed wiv Skinnyman's crew.'

'I'll have a box of Weetabix and some hummus please.'

It's futile to try to escape being forty. Because no matter how you act, you'll still have friends who drag you into the world of forty-ness. I've stared in catatonic bemusement as someone's explained that 'Michael and I had a row all Thursday night about which light fittings to get for the hallway,' and all I can think is, 'I remember when you set fire to a litter bin in the High Street for no reason.' I have a fear that soon I'll meet someone I once broke into a derelict building with as a squatter, and he'll say, 'The wife and I are hoping to go to the Lake District in the summer.'

Perhaps the most depressing phrase from 40-year-olds who've become too comfortable is, 'We've had the builders in – it was sheer HELL.' Right. So if the medieval painters and poets who depicted several layers of hell with the bottom one portraying eternally tormented souls writhing in perpetual agony as they boiled in molten lead knew about YOUR plight, they'd have added an even more horrible layer, in which people had to walk round some bags of plaster to get to the kitchen, would they?

There's also those who move to the fucking countryside. Rural areas are evidently not as uniformly conservative, incestuous and unaware of post-1950s technology as they're portrayed in Londoners' jokes.* The population will usually include poets and bands and maybe an MC and a CND group, but the ones who've moved from a big city 'to bring up the children' are infuriating. And smug. 'Oo, while you're stuck on the underground we're in the marshes identifying species of herons,' or 'The produce is SO fresh – if we fancy some beef we just ring Farmer Newman and he comes straight round and strangles a cow in the living room.'

Even avoiding these traps doesn't make you a soulmate of the strident, nervous, belligerent, unsure volcano that is the 19-year-old rebel. Most obviously, you can't hope to maintain similar hours. The problem isn't just physical, it's that at nineteen I had nothing much to do the next day, and even if I had it was usually something that it would be fun to cancel, like work. Right up to forty there was a thrill attached to the spontaneous one-off binge, whereby at pub closing time someone would shout, 'I know where there's an all-night bar – at the back of a pet shop in Lewisham.' And soon I'd be past the slurring stage of drunkenness into the comfortable tired haze, philosophising and enjoying the silences, until the birds were tweeting, which somehow I'd see as my achievement: 'It's getting light and I'm STILL here – you couldn't beat me, darkness.'

*However, I was once visiting a friend, who now lives in London but came from a village in Suffolk, when his mum rang. Very excited, she asked him if he'd seen that their village had been in the newspapers. He said 'No' so she insisted, 'You didn't see it? Our village, this week, was in ALL the newspapers.' He said, 'No, what was it about?' And she explained, 'Well, they done this survey, right 'cross country, and it turns out OUR village is the most inbred village in all Britain. 'Ow 'bout that?'

But as I progressed through my forties I had a recurring moment of misery. Somewhere in the middle of London, with drinks flowing and jokes requiring less and less quality to earn big laughs, I'd notice it was twenty to twelve. I'd log that thought, but then have a couple more drinks until thinking, 'I really must go, it's twenty to twelve.' Then take a while to say goodbye, perhaps while swigging half the pint I'd been bought despite saying I was definitely going, and wander round to the doorway in Leicester Square where a perpetually smiling Arab man in a white robe with a clipboard organised unlicensed minicabs. Then I'd wander off as directed, find the dented Toyota Carina, struggle with the broken seatbelt before giving up, and suddenly notice the green figures on the digital display.

'That can't be the time, mate, is it, mate?'

'Yes, yes, time.'

'No, it can't be. It can't be three forty-six.'

'Yes, yes, three forty-six time.'

And then would come one of those moments, like when you stub your toe or drop the keys down a drain, when you try desperately to think of a way of turning the clock back a bit. For a while you really are thinking, 'There must be SOME way of doing it.' And all the way home, as Magic FM oozed out Phil Collins and 'Fernando' and that one by Luther Vandross about his dead father, I'd be coming to terms with the fact that in about three hours I'd be woken by a five-year-old jumping on my neck, shouting, 'Daddy be a horse.'

Eventually, not only did I stop but was delighted to stop. In such ways, stage by stage, the responsibilities of parenthood defeat the excesses of youth. To those who remain unburdened by the demands of family life, this can seem an unbearable restraint, as they say things like 'Are you SURE you can't get away for the absinthe festival this weekend?' And they give you a look that says, 'Aah it's SUCH a shame' as if you've got an incurable allergy that's been featured on Comic Relief.

Despite the occasional yearning for lost revelry, most parents embrace their role, rarely regretting the exchange of unlimited mobility for the joys of domesticity. This is in spite of the way parenthood is ordered. Ideally it should be organised so the new parent is eased into their role, with a gentle transition from carefree to frighteningly responsible for offspring. Instead the hardest bit comes right at the start, having to tend to an utterly helpless baby that can do fuck-all. Then it gets progressively easier, as with each task they learn to do themselves – such as going to the toilet or getting dressed – your own workload decreases.

Eventually, by the time they're about four, they're not so demanding physically and taking them out is like enjoying the company of a little mate. You're just left with trying to answer awkward questions like 'Did they hang Saddam Hussein because he was very naughty?' or 'Why did the man at the bus stop say he'd like to give Gabby Logan one up the gary?'

But as if by divine intervention, to nip in the bud any notion that decreasing domestic pressures might lead to a life of predictable cosiness, my partner and I began to subside beneath an avalanche of hostility that seemed specially designed to prevent any prospect of middle-aged complacency.

One morning there was an episode of terrorism that left me quite disturbed. As I awoke there was a story on the radio news that a suicide bomber had blown himself up, along with a number of other people, in a bar in Casablanca. Later that morning I arrived at Broadcasting House where I was working on a radio programme, and said to a group of people in the Light Entertainment department, 'I'm sure you all had exactly the same thought as me when you heard about the bomb this morning.'

They looked puzzled. 'When you heard about that bomb in Casablanca, you must have had the same thought as me,' I repeated.

'What?' they all said.

'That as the suicide bomber went into the place, the barman must have said, "Oh of all the bars in all the towns in all the world you have to blow up mine."'

They looked horrified. It wasn't until that moment that it occurred to me that other people don't necessarily think like that. I felt how I imagine people with Asperger's syndrome feel, if they ever twig that not everyone counts objects in a room and works out that number's cube root.

It must be a trial to live with a comic and their disconcerting habits. Only comics, for example, feel such inconsolable anguish in a curry house, because they're halfway through telling a hilarious joke and it's trodden on by the waiter interrupting with 'Your starters, please' and delivering your onion bhajis. Only comics come away from a funeral feeling numb and hollow because another comic's story about the dead person got a bigger laugh than their own. So my partner would probably have been able to make a case that if you're going through a period of manic volatile anxiety, it may not be advisable to be living with a comic.

For around ten years our awkward moments remained an unwelcome nuisance that we could learn to live with, like diabetes. But then they grew, like the engine noise you know you shouldn't ignore, but do anyway until it suddenly clatters with doom. In some ways the more dramatic episodes were the most manageable. But when there was a low level of rumbling discontent, it was tempting to deal with it as a genuine argument, for example by exhaling a puff of exasperation and saying, 'But you *asked* for custard.' And that way we could descend into the world of the classic bickering couple, boiling with a sense of injustice while enunciating one word at a time with tensely bent fingers and a galloping heart, 'You – said – turn – left – so – I – turned – left.'

There'd be the gruelling moments following a chilling exchange when neither of us would speak as we brushed past each other, each of us leaving a trail of unsettling frostiness, the sort that people who reckon their house is haunted tell you about, and it felt as if we'd sprayed every room with icy tension from an aerosol. Then a neighbour would call out 'Hi, yoo-hoo, anyone there?' and my partner would suddenly abandon her scowl and cheerily discuss the latest episode of *Buffy the Vampire Slayer*. Which makes you even more livid, unable to de-clench a single muscle while wanting to shout, 'OY. We're supposed to be GRUMPY here. You might have been faking it for effect so you can switch it off as soon as an outsider arrives but I *really fucking* MEANT it – er, sorry, Barbara.'

Or we'd play out that dreadful scene in which you've snapped at each other with particularly malicious venom but you're not really in a position to leave the room to allow the acrimony to cool down. For example, having just been described as 'a selfish shitty lump of shit', you've still got to sit next to each other for the foreseeable future because you've just turned on to the M6 at Lancaster.

From time to time we'd hold a series of informal summits, after the children went to bed, involving discussions that went on until about one in the morning, so that each session was probably longer than the United Nations take to discuss the crisis in Kashmir. And because I fidget, I'd make things worse by getting up to change the CD, which must be exasperating if you're midway through a heartfelt soliloquy about feeling unappreciated. Or the television would be left on, with the sound off, and even when your partner's describing feelings of sickening helplessness it's hard not to react to something that comes into the corner of your vision, and say, 'Bloody hell, Ronnie O'Sullivan could get a maximum 147 break here.'

We'd stumble through each crisis, then there would be a month when the irritation cleared up as if it was a rash and be replaced with the thrills of calm, the comfortable excitement of family tranquillity. Like someone whose just vanquished a raging blaze, maybe you ought to conduct an immediate search for the cause of the uproar, but your instinct is to think you've been through enough turmoil for one day, so you have a cup of tea and assume it will never happen again.

In an organisation such as the SWP a sense of camaraderie develops, different from that in a sports club or social group, because it's

based on ideas that last all week, not just on the night of the meeting. Being a member influences the conversations and debates you
have, and has a huge bearing on the books you read. And the link
between members seems even stronger because on a regular basis
you're collectively denounced for trying to ruin the country.
These workplace courses that take the staff on bonding sessions
involving paint-ball fights should see how strongly you bond once
you're jointly accused by the *Daily Mail* of inciting a nationwide
epidemic of violence with your friends in Haringey Council and
Al Q'aeda. Or worse, of being a bunch of middle-class students.

But mostly the sense of belonging was driven by a set of ideas.
Throughout this time the SWP was almost unique in assessing
that the cause of socialism was best pursued outside the Labour
Party, and that countries such as Soviet Russia represented the
opposite of what we hoped for. Crucially, the party was sane
enough to be aware that the project on which it had embarked
could easily look utterly insane. But almost imperceptibly, through
the early years of the new century, the SWP went into decline
until, like at the end of a party, you suddenly look round and
realise loads of people have gone. Where we'd once held regular
public meetings attracting a youthful energetic crowd, the local
branches shrivelled until they barely existed. One reason for not
noticing this is that hardly anyone resigns, they're just no longer
motivated to come. And they honestly do mean they would come
but they really really can't make it this week. That, you assure
yourself, explains the small turnout. The real problem is they
don't think it will make any difference whether they attend or
not. Whereas I don't suppose in the middle of the French
Revolution anyone ever said, 'Jean-Paul can't make the people's
militia tonight, he's waiting in for a settee to be delivered.'

The SWP branch of which I'd been a member met at the local
Labour club, but the numbers dwindled from a weekly average of
twenty a few years earlier, and we were relegated to the basement, where we met around a disused pool table. On a good
week there were five, but one of these was convinced he was a

secret detective and another used to wear shorts all winter, bark like a dog and be afraid of crossing the road. Still, if we'd acted as we should and asked them to stop coming and instead attend the relevant department of social services, we'd have been down to three, and the Labour club would have asked if we needed the whole pool table or could make do with sitting round one of the pockets.

For a while I assured myself this was a quirk of my area but I'd hear similar stories from everywhere, and the shrinkage was most apparent to me from the social scene. Ten years earlier, if I was doing a show in a club or theatre, the local SWP branch would arrive as a lively contingent of the audience, appearing youthful whether they were or not, and would usually make an endearing if awkward request such as 'During the show, could you mention the public meeting we're having about the crisis in the Lebanon?'

Afterwards they'd ask if I wanted to go round to Barry's house for some drinks and if I liked I could crash out there, and I'd expect them to say, 'You can move in if you like, it'll be a laugh and you'll enjoy living in Bristol.' But now, although the total audience was far bigger than before, the SWP contingent would comprise the odd old friend, or maybe a couple who would say hello, have a debate about whether they could have one quick drink without being late for the babysitter and tell me they hadn't really seen anyone else in the SWP much lately.

At one regional meeting for the whole of South London there were around fifty people, of which none was under thirty. These meetings used to attract four times as many, so I hoped there'd be an attempt to explain how this could be rectified. Instead four people began their speeches by saying, 'This is the most exciting political time of my life.' To which the only sane response was, 'What – THIS?' Were they really thinking, 'Nelson Mandela being released was so-so, but I never thought I'd experience the thrill of seeing fifty middle-aged people slouched in a church hall.' Then someone opened with a different angle: 'My branch decided to have a joint meeting with two other branches. On the

night I was a bit disappointed at first because only three of us
turned up. But then we had an excellent discussion . . .' at which
point someone behind me restored some sanity by muttering, 'Oh
for fuck's sake, don't try and make this good.'

Once upon a time the local SWP branches were chaotic caul-
drons of activity that often connected with all that was vibrant and
energetic in a city. In most towns you were never far from a line
of hastily slapped-up *Socialist Worker* posters; they were almost an
accepted part of any city centre, and there must be people who
supposed the government ensured every area had them, just as
everywhere has to have a library and a fire station. But no more.
Shopping centres on Saturday mornings were meant to have
someone selling balloons, teenagers in bright red uniforms giving
out leaflets for Pizza Hut and a circle of people shouting, '*Socialist
Worker.*' They were *meant* to. If a local branch couldn't sustain this
they should have applied to the council for a grant to keep it
going on grounds of maintaining local heritage. But now those
hubs of high-volume agitation are extremely rare.

The local branch held weekly meetings – among the only
meetings in history that people looked forward to. There'd be a
talk about a global or historical issue, a discussion on how to proceed in local campaigns, an animated argument about fuck-all
and a few beers. The branches organised collections for campaigns and coaches for demonstrations, they knew the trade
union rep at the post office and the slightly dope-addled lecturer
who could organise a fund-raising benefit as he knew every local
band. Those who ran them were often eccentric, or manic, or
would happily turn up at a funeral selling *Socialist Worker*. And
every branch had at least one beautifully crazy person, who
would eat cold baked beans throughout the meeting, or read out
a poem he'd written and sent to the United Nations. But they
had a purpose. You felt you should go if you could, firstly
because they were helping to organise a movement, and secondly
because they were fun.

Every year the SWP puts on a week of talks at a university in

London, which used to be an event that thrived and buzzed with optimism and youth. There'd be a thrill in the queue for many sessions as people fretted eagerly about whether they'd get in, while some passers-by must have joined the line, assuming it was to catch a glimpse of someone like Keanu Reeves and ended up disconcerted to find they were attending a talk about the General Strike. Every evening there was a frenetic scramble for the bar, in a crowd that steamed as if it was in the coolest venue in the centre of town on a sunny Friday afternoon – except the glasses were plastic and the arguments were about who was right in the debate on Ancient Egypt. Through the 1990s, however, this event gradually became smaller, until in recent years it's been possible to amble to the bar and order a drink as if you were in your local on a Tuesday. But never would anyone admit it had got smaller. Sometimes I had the most frustrating conversations, with one of the organisers telling me the figures certainly weren't down and more people than ever had come from Leicester and I must be imagining things, when I found myself almost banging my head on the table and shouting 'CAN'T YOU SEE – THE BAR'S EMPTY?' with the desperation of someone telling an anorexic that they're not fucking fat.

This attitude did lead to one of my favourite exchanges at the event, when the world of Marxism met the world of *Carry-on* scripts. I went to the toilet, and was standing at the urinal when a stranger came in and stood next to me. Mid-slash, he turned to face me and said, 'Well – it's definitely bigger this year.' I said, 'Thank you very much' and left feeling pleased with my little joke.

Around this time, when I was invited to speak or perform by groups such as People and Planet, a campaigning organisation for students, or local outfits with names such as Bangor for Peace, and they'd be packed with vibrant inquisitive youth. As well as being so much better attended, livelier and younger than the old Left's efforts, they were endearingly uncertain. Someone would ask a question and a number of people would try to work out the answer together, with no one assuming superior knowledge, the way a group of people might collectively figure out how to move a settee through a tight doorway.

In my experience, questions in political meetings were treated the way a maths teacher deals with a query from a puzzled student. A gentle explanation would clarify the correct way of looking at the issue, followed, if the questioner wasn't satisfied, by another attempt to sort them out, this time with a hint of irritation that they still hadn't got it. Then a series of hands would go up, and several other people would eagerly try to explain. If the questioner went as far as disagreeing, they could expect someone to get quite cross, splurting out something like, 'Because ACTUALLY, what you see in current-day Jordan is actually EXACTLY the strategy you're proposing which has led to the SLAUGHTER of the working-class movement.' And you expected them to carry on: 'So it's YOUR fault. The Middle East could be sorted if it wasn't for YOU, you ARSEHOLE.' And then the chair to add: 'But it's an important debate so I hope you can come back next week.'

One of the most terrifying challenges in the modern world must be to attend a national event advertised by a branch of the Left as 'a weekend of debate' and gently contradict the chosen line. A queue forms by the edge of the stage, and the succession of speakers blurs into one as the denunciations fly, each one angrier than the last, perhaps even using personal details such as 'That's a bit rich coming from someone who didn't even play an active part in the Norwich "Save our Swimming Pools' Campaign".' Presumably, someone must feel this is persuasive, and if at the end of the debate the person making the original faux pas still hasn't changed their mind, all the others must think, 'That must be because we didn't shout quite loud enough.' For many years I'd gone along with this, and even taken part in it. As the Left declined, however, a persistent nagging doubt grew that maybe this behaviour wasn't helping.

One of the most depressing gatherings I ever attended was a

row between the British and American sections of the SWP. For three hours, representatives took turns to rage and howl with unrestrained venom about how the other lot had lied, manipulated, abandoned principles, missed glorious opportunities and done everything wrong. Men who've written magisterial volumes explaining the finer points of the world economy stood and yelled furiously at each other about why the fact that the other lot attended a certain event in February but not one in January was an absolute DISGRACE. And for the life of me I couldn't work out what either side was on about, so it was like watching an episode of *EastEnders* written by the far Left. It wouldn't have seemed out of place for someone to get up and say in a threatening bass growl, 'Oy, accuse me of betraying the Marxist tradition, will you? I think we need to talk,' and for the reply to be, 'I think the comrade needs a little slap,' followed by 'Boom–boom–boom–boo–boo–boo–boom–boom–boom.' Then we'd have to wait until the following week to find out what happened next.

Not a single person could clearly explain what the disagreement was, and as far as I could fathom they'd simply fallen out but dressed it up in the language of revolution. I wish I'd proposed an amendment called 'Let's face it – we don't get on. So let's keep away from each other until we've all cooled down. It shouldn't be that hard as there's a fucking great ocean between us.'

The result of all this was the British and American wings of the organisation formally parted, so the British attempted to start up a new American party. After a few months someone told me excitedly, 'There's good news from America – we're up to eight.' Eight – in the whole of America – good news. When I relayed this conversation to someone else they said, 'And what he didn't tell you is that six of them are on Death Row.'

Perhaps it was becoming a parent that altered my outlook; if you responded to your child's thoughts in this way, you'd land yourself with a stack of behavioural problems. (Social Services report: 'The child revealed that when he suggested one Sunday the family might go to Brighton, his father replied, "The more we look at this proposal the more absurd it becomes. It takes NO account of the cost (but then resources never were Nathan's strong point), NO account of when homework should be completed, and flows from a complete misunderstanding, actually, of how the family should operate under current conditions." And furthermore, this response was then issued as a document and distributed to every other member of the family.')

Or maybe it was the declining numbers of the Left that made such attitudes seem even more absurd than before, or the growth of a new young movement, weaker theoretically but winning hands down on social skills, or it might just have been that with all the rowing at home I couldn't take another dose on top. Whatever the reason, it was making me doubt this whole project in a way that had never happened before.

4

IF I GO THERE WILL BE TROUBLE

For a while there was no issue the government wouldn't try to win by reverting back to the Twin Towers. For example, one year later when the Fire Brigade Union held a series of one-day strikes, minister of defence John Reid said they were providing a 'gift for terrorists'. Perhaps Bin Laden wandered round his Al Q'aeda training camps issuing his instructions, 'You – travel to Frankfurt to meet a sleeper cell and await details of your glorious holy sacrifice; and *you* – go to Eastbourne on a firefighters' day of action and set a chip pan alight.'

Between the ages of twenty and thirty, as an activist I attended dozens of strikes, but from thirty-five to forty-five they were hard to find, so the firefighters' dispute was quite nostalgic. Visiting the picket line I felt like a woman who used to be a dancer but gave it up to have five kids, then one day gets invited to be the lead in *Flashdance* for the local drama group and thinks, 'Oo, I wonder if I can still do this.'

This picket line wouldn't involve the irony of freezing while standing outside a power station with miners in donkey jackets. The firefighters were allowed to open the station, so we could all go indoors. This was handy, as I took my son who spent two hours being taught how to slide down the pole. And there was a huge pot of curry someone had donated. What a perfect picket line to visit in your forties – indoors, brilliant food and entertainment for the kids. Maybe these are the strikes to support as I get older, where instead of rubbing hands round a brazier we arrange a dinner party, and instead of shouting 'scab scab scab', you link arms and chant, 'The lamb needs a little more rosemary.'

Apart from allowing them to be childminders and eating their food, my other contribution to the dispute was to agree to appear at a fund-raising benefit at Acton Town Hall. A week later the organiser of the event called, spluttering excitedly, 'Guess who's agreed to do the show that night – JOE STRUMMER.' This was indeed brilliant, and I said I'd come along to watch. 'NO,' she yelled, 'You've GOT to go on for half an hour before, you've GOT to.' But why? It was sure to sell out and be packed with Clash fans eager for their hero; experience told me that trying to do half an hour of comedy would be a disaster. It was as ridiculous as if she'd said, 'Michael Schumacher's agreed to do a fund-raising Formula 1 race at Brands Hatch, but we still want you to do half an hour of jokes at the pit stop.'

This is often what happens with benefits – the people putting them on get so carried away with enthusiasm they're convinced all will be fine despite history being against them. 'We'll put you on late after the disco,' they say, 'because then they'll be really tanked up.' If you didn't intervene they'd be handing round free vodka until everyone was asleep in their own sick and then yell, 'Fantastic – go on stage NOW!'

Not only that but Strummer was *my* hero too. It had been lonely as a 16-year-old in 1976. Much of my parents' generation had little but disdain for us, especially when the post-war stability crumbled and was replaced with unemployment, fear and uncertainty. They seemed to think it was our fault, because we had no respect, and didn't we know they fought a war for us. We got angry in return, with a random and largely thoughtless rage, and then into so many teenage bedrooms exploded Strummer, legitimising the rage, screaming with a purpose. It wasn't just the lyrics, many of which you couldn't even make out; you heard the howls and realised, 'Yeah, that howl's just how I feel.'

So it *wasn't* our fault? It was like meeting a counsellor who tells you you're not the worthless human being you've been told you are by the person who wallops you. At last we were winning. We had Joe Strummer – they had David Owen.

Nor was he an icon for only an instant. Even in 2002 a Strummer gig wasn't just nostalgia, it was full of new songs and optimism, and he'd attracted a young audience. So he was a hero. But one that wasn't distant like the usual heroes. It's safe having a hero such as Dylan or Robert De Niro as you're never going to meet them. They live in another galaxy, as they should. But Strummer, despite being an international icon, you might bump into in a gloomy pub, playing the fruit machine and arguing with the landlord that he should be allowed a last round before they shut. It was an attitude that led him to Acton Town Hall, and I knew this was wrong in every way but a bit of me must have thought, 'I'll be on a bill with Joe Strummer.'

'Go on then, I'll do it,' I said, like a twat.

I arrived, carrying the first Clash album I'd bought from a record shop in Dartford in 1977 for Joe to sign. There were around 1,000 people there, jostling for the bar, spilling beer down their T-shirts, with the younger ones, who knew all the words to the most recent songs as they'd seen his last seven gigs, flitting about with an embarrassing amount of energy. Maybe this was a warming-up programme they'd been given by a physio so as not to pull a muscle when they started diving in all directions in the mosh pit when the band was on. How I wished I was a band, or even a folk singer, so when I was onstage I could strum away in my own world and be ignored with dignity. All the seats had been removed and the stage was bursting with drumkits and amps, so it would take most of my concentration not to trip over a cable and destroy the piano.

Occasionally one of the organisers would grab me. 'Mark – isn't it AMAZING? What a NIGHT. It's HEAVING, we could have sold TWICE as many.'

A DJ started playing a combination of reggae and hip-hop, loud enough to reverberate above the hubbub of anticipation. With every passing minute it seemed a new thing happened to make doing a comedy show more impossible. Maybe in a moment someone would bring in a bouncy castle for everyone to jump on while I was on. Or someone would tell me they were bringing in some horses to gallop around the room just as I was starting.

The room filled up with most people halfway between tapping and dancing to the reggae, muffled calls bouncing round the hall as they spotted their mates. The music stopped, there was a moment of confusion as about a quarter of the audience supposed this meant the band was coming on, the organiser tried to introduce me but the microphone wasn't working and I wandered on to a painful squeal of feedback, so that in the semi-darkness most people must have assumed I was a roadie.

'Joe Strummer,' someone yelled, possibly checking he was in the right place. And I started, every ninth word or so squeaking with feedback, to a background of 900 people talking and 100 at the front looking up in fascination, as if this was a social experiment and they were about to write notes on a clipboard. 'Fuck off,' shouted someone in a firefighters' uniform. 'Is that how you deal with people who support you, mate?' I asked. I attempted a routine wondering if movements in the past had employed this tactic – Martin Luther King, instead of saying 'I had a dream', telling all his supporters to fuck off? Now 950 were talking and fifty still watching, but with the puzzled expression of people at a zoo looking into a cage thinking, 'What *is* that? I've never seen one of those before.'

'Fuck off,' yelled the fireman. Then the lighting man turned the lights off and I was in total darkness. Half a dozen people yelled a noncommittal 'waheeeeey', and then the sound man cut off the microphone for a laugh. 'Despite this,' I shouted, 'I hope the firefighters win, but the agreement is thirty grand a year except for the bastard who shouted "fuck off" who has to work the rest of his life for nothing.' I think by the time I'd finished the DJ was playing Prince Buster.

Twenty minutes later the band came on. The front quarter of the room bubbled like a human volcano with heads and limbs frantically spurting in random directions. Strummer was as vibrant as ever, thrashing each chord with an urgency as if to ask, 'I've already *said* what's wrong with this world, do I have to tell everyone *again*.' Then Mick Jones turned up. Mick was the guitarist with The Clash, Strummer's colleague from the first days of punk, through the world tours and international acclaim until an acrimonious split fifteen years earlier. And now for the first time since then he was agreeing to get up and play. It was magical, the crowd were delirious and I was utterly fucking miserable.

Afterwards I decided at least to get my record signed, and went backstage, but a security guard was blocking the door. 'Can I get through to get my stuff, please?' I asked. The reply came back, 'Who the fuck are you?' Someone eventually persuaded him to let me past and I went into Joe's room where he was getting changed, still in his underpants, surrounded by fans who'd probably been backstage at every gig for a year. Thus the moment came to meet my teenage hero, and it coincided with my lowest point of self-esteem since I was twelve. 'Hello, Joe, er Joe, hello, er seventeen in Dartford with career opportunities I brilliant to support the firefighters I've brought my record,' I said. Joe looked sympathetic as I gave him the cover to sign, but as I fumbled for a pen I spilt the record out of the sleeve and it bounced on the floor, rolled between two roadies and spun to a halt by the feet of Mick Jones.

'Careful,' said Mick.

A few moments later I wandered through Acton to catch a night bus, but got on the one going north by mistake.

In his resignation speech Tony Blair dealt with Iraq by saying that, whatever the outcome, he did what he did because 'Hand on heart, I believed it was right at the time.' The selected audience of supporters broke into sympathetic applause, which suggests they were delighted this was the case, as they'd thought he might say,

'Do you know what – I *knew* it would be a disaster even when I started doing it. I just couldn't help it, 'cos I'm a bit mental.'

It was a remarkable series of events that led to this line, in which one after another justification for the war evaporated, leaving only this flimsy defence. It was almost like the moment at the end of a TV detective story when the murderer, faced with unquestionable evidence of his guilt, realises he's stuffed and resorts to saying, 'Yes, I did kill the professor, and so would *you* have done if you'd had to put up with him getting all the credit for your hard work all those years.' Except that, instead of handcuffing the murderer, the detective and all those assembled then break into applause.

At first, as the preparations were being made in 2002, the most common reason for supporting the US invasion was that it was an important part of the War on Terror. So it was back to the Twin Towers, and we were told by Blair that when we were reticent about the military action 'we should remember the victims that day'. So *that's* why so many people were against the war – now it was a year since the planes hit the Twin Towers, the whole incident had gone clean out of their minds.

Then the reason shifted to Saddam's famous weapons of mass destruction. Blair didn't just say he 'believed' Saddam had them, he told a select committee in the run-up to the war, 'I have no doubt that Saddam Hussein has weapons of mass destruction. No doubt – no doubt at all.' Even that doesn't do it justice, because he said 'no doubt' with the furrowed expression turned up to maximum, conveying the eager certainty of someone announcing the murderer in Cluedo when they're 100 per cent certain. And yet he can't in any rational sense have had no doubt at all, because the intelligence was doubtful and the weapons inspectors were highly doubtful. And because there weren't any.

Blair was aware that George Bush's entourage had been planning this for years, regardless of whether weapons of mass destruction were found or not. He'd seen the intelligence reports stating that an invasion of Iraq would increase the likelihood of

terrorism in Britain. And he said nothing to counter the persistent claims by George Bush that Saddam was linked to Osama bin
Laden, when the only link was that neither of them would have
got anywhere if they hadn't been armed and financed by the
British and Americans in the first place.

The war was sold on a series of lies. But there's another side to
the deceit which is that it must be doubtful whether any war in
modern times has been fought with such a wide section of the
population being *aware* of the lies. It's often forgotten, because of
the famous demonstration of February 2003, that already the previous September 300,000 people had marched against the war –
which was one of the biggest protests in British history. The
September march was the biggest I'd ever seen in Britain, bigger
than in CND days or the poll tax riot, and was part of the process
that forced the government case to unravel. At this point 71 per
cent of the country opposed the war.

Blair then produced the dossier on Saddam's weapons, with its
selective intelligence and Stalin-worthy fabrications, in order to
respond to this anti-war sentiment and anti-war movement. The
dossier's publication had been delayed several times, as if Blair
were a schoolboy who hadn't done his homework.

But why was there such cynicism about the reasons for this war
in the first place? Partly it must have been because the case for war
was so flimsy, but also, among the discontented there was already
a growing mood of dissent. Now the uneasy, the confused, the
disillusioned and let down saw a definite purpose in this issue that
they could unite around, which led to the formation of the Stop
the War Movement.

Yet somehow the achievement of the first vast protest didn't
hang about in the atmosphere for long afterwards. In the past,
smaller protests had a greater resonance with the wider population, as union leaders and prominent campaigners kept them in
the news, while Labour Party branches and left groups maintained
a connection between supporters of the campaign. But with that
network in collapse, the march slipped out of the national discussion

alarmingly quickly. Which was frustrating, because this was a record-breaking demonstration. If a protest attracts more than 300,000 people, there should be a law that everyone in the country should have to talk about it once an hour for a month.

At one point my partner and I were referred to a doctor who might be able to help us out, but he couldn't find the key to his office so we conducted our discussion sitting in the corridor as hobbling men and kids with broken arms walked past us. Without looking at either of us he muttered, 'Hmm, it may be depression' in a way that suggested that if you'd complained about chest pains he'd say, 'Ahh, the problem is you've got an illness.' After ten minutes of questions like 'What makes you angry?', he took me to one side and said, 'Do you have sex?'

'Now and then,' I told him hesitantly.

'Try to give her more sex,' he said, then walked off.

And I got the impression he'd prescribe a similar remedy for food poisoning or bee stings.

One problem when a relationship is fraying is that the words that come out are difficult to decipher, as both parties find it hard to articulate the underlying cause of their anxiety. I'd hear, 'The PROBLEM, as you well know, is what you KNOW it is and if you can't even KNOW what you've done, well then DON'T you think I don't KNOW.' This is a delicate situation for anyone, but a comic has the overpowering instinct to say something like 'That's the question for your philosophy exam – you may turn over your papers and begin NOW.' Which, I can testify, doesn't help.

Trying to answer the points raised, with however much sympathy, is just as useless because such anguish has its own language. Reassuring someone that you haven't done what they're crying you've done is worthless, because that's not what they're really crying about. It even makes them more frustrated, like when you present a yelling toddler with a bottle of milk when they really want their teddy but can't say the word.

If there was an immediate solution, I couldn't find it, so I entered one of the most negative phases of life in which despite having a house, a partner, children and middle-aged respectability, you find yourself sleeping every night on the settee. The fact that most separating couples first go through a period in which one of them sleeps on the settee proves that very few split up with the casual ease that's the stereotype of the modern age.

Once you're out of the settee phase of your life, it's hard to remember what you were thinking while you were in it. Somehow you get used to it and it becomes normal. In the same pedestrian way that classical sitcom couples put the cat out, emerge in their pyjamas and sit in bed grumbling about the neighbours while doing a crossword puzzle, I would grab the blankets, find a cushion for a pillow and lie on the settee that was a foot shorter than me. Each night I'd spend a moment deliberating on whether to bend, curl or leave legs dangling over the edge in order to fit on it, with the concentration of a golfer choosing his club for the next shot. Then I'd lie wide awake in front of all those channels.

Eurosport went through a phase of showing Icelandic buggy-racing, in which these half-tank, half-JCB machines would be driven up an almost vertical hill of volcanic rock, and the winner was the one who got up the furthest before tipping upside-down. I wondered how well one of them would have to do to become Icelandic sports personality of the year. There was a channel called GOD, to leave little doubt about the content, although it would be worth setting up a channel called GOD and filling it with Icelandic buggy-racing to see whether you could get the lowest ever viewer satisfaction ratings.

I grew to admire the Shopping Channel presenters, wondering if they had competitions to see who could be most enthusiastic about the most worthless heap of shit. One night they were selling tubes of tooth whitener, giving it everything, 'And it comes in this *wonderfully* compact capsule which is *so* convenient, you can be in a restaurant or at the bus stop and you know those moments when your teeth feel a little bit murky, well just pop out your capsule and with one quick wipe . . .' So I rang the number and said, 'I'm interested in the tooth whitener that's just been on. The only thing is, I'm not keen on that colour, have you got any in blue?'

'Hang on, I'll check,' said the bored clerk. Now I felt obliged to hang on until he came back and said expressionlessly, 'Sorry, sir, we only have this particular item in the one colour, I'm not sure if there are any plans to launch the item in other colours but you're advised to check in the future as we continually update our range of products.'

There was a programme on the BBC late at night in which women discussed their orgasms. I expected this to be a classic BBC treatment of the subject, all earnest consultants and smug therapists, but instead there was a series of women on settees, not unlike the one I was on, waving their arms and talking about their favourite shapes of penises. At one point one of them said, 'I think a cock can be TOO big, like, I had a really huge one inside me and it was actually quite uncomfortable. Do you know what I mean?'

'Hmm,' nodded the others in agreement, as if they were on *Gardeners' Question Time* and someone had just made a valid point about greenfly. Then the presenter conducting the discussion said, 'If I could turn to you, Laura, do *you* prefer big cocks?' And all in the intonation of Kirsty Wark asking the BBC economist if he thought it was likely there would be an imminent rise in interest rates.

In the morning my children would bounce into the room and call out 'Hello, Dad' cheerfully, having accepted this settee routine as normal. And somehow we'd carry on, living as a couple, sharing dinners and the bills and maybe we'd discuss whether the war on Iraq would go ahead if it wasn't backed by the United Nations, then out would come the blankets and I'd prepare the settee. But it isn't normal, it's crazy. What long-term prospects are there for a family trapped in settee-ness? For example, how could you go on holiday? You'd have to ensure the hotel you booked had a room with a settee in it so you could carry on as usual.

The question for any couple reduced to long-term settee status is how much bitterness must there be to make the settee preferable to the bed? When I was hitch-hiking across Europe I once slept in the same bed as a Dutchman taking me from Florence to Luxembourg, who'd spent all day telling me he was an international terrorist who'd formed the Amsterdam branch of the Red Brigades. I woke up a few times and clung to the furthest margins of what kept me horizontal, but even then it never crossed my mind to go in search of a settee.

Settees are uncomfortable. You sleep at best fitfully and every morning a different bit of you is crunched and twisted. You wouldn't choose to sleep there when there's a specially designed piece of sleeping apparatus a few feet away, just because you'd had a row or were in a sulk. You'd have to feel as if you were two North Poles on a magnet, so that even if you were pushed into the bed, you'd ping backwards, twizzle round and land on the settee.

And somehow you get used to it, the journey from overwhelming love and passion to repulsion happening in such gradual increments that you accept it as normal. Which must be the same for all manner of routines that accompany a family life that's gone sour, but no one can find a way of resolving; secret affairs, visits to prostitutes, weekly sessions with strangers behind a bush on the common, are probably all arrived at bit by bit. And as someone wipes themselves down by a broken wooden fence they think, 'At least I'm not breaking up the family.'

Each morning I'd return to the same world everyone else inhabited, one in which they mentioned what they watched, did or talked about with their husbands, wives or partners as if they still held sufficient affection for them to sleep in the same room. Occasionally I'd join in, saying, 'We went there once,' or 'My missus can't stand him either,' without adding that I now slept on the settee, because it's easier to pretend things are still OK. I suppose it's a tiny version of the pressure some gays feel that leads them to reply to 'Did you and the missus do much at the weekend?' with 'We decorated the bathroom' without mentioning the missus is a bloke.

The toughest nights were when I'd been somewhere posh. My radio show was nominated for a Sony award, so I attended the ceremony at the Dorchester. There was a toast to the Queen, and I had beef followed by profiteroles sitting next to Nicholas Parsons. One of the awards was presented by Meat Loaf, there were carriages at midnight and then I went home and slept on a settee.

Eventually you reach a phase when it seems this impasse will never be resolved – it's a constant feature of the world like turmoil in the Middle East. But then comes a moment, a look, a glint that reminds you of how you once were and you both pledge to try something, anything – and so we booked a series of meetings with the marriage guidance people, now called Relate.

The theory is, I suppose, that in the presence of a neutral observer you're more likely to express your real concerns. But it can go the other way. I'd listen to complaints such as 'Well, if I can bring up an incident last Wednesday, I felt that, well, again there was a problem with communication, in that we weren't able, and this applies to both of us, to talk constructively, which I found disheartening.'

'Hmm,' the Relate woman would say carefully, as if she was dismantling an unexploded bomb, 'I see.'

And I'd be thinking 'Hang on – you came in and stood in front of the fridge screaming "Fuck you and your fucking attitude, *fuck, fuck, fuck*!" And then you smashed a milk bottle.'

Soon it was Christmas. However flippant you are about it, you'd still think, 'Oh no – I can't sleep on the settee at *Christmas*.' One morning, just before Christmas, I listened to a phone message while I was sorting out some papers. The stunned voice of a friend said almost robotically, 'Joe Strummer's dead.' And I carried on, thinking, 'I wonder what he meant by that?' He couldn't have meant Joe Strummer was dead because that wasn't possible. Eventually I rang back. 'What do you mean, he's dead?' I asked, but what he meant was that he was dead.

I turned on the news and saw a reporter detailing Strummer's life in forty seconds, in front of his picture, before 'going over to Andrew for the sport'. I ran outside and sat on a wall, rang random people who were likely also to be sitting on walls, and said to a neighbour, 'Joe Strummer's dead.'

'Did you know him?' she asked.

'No, well, I met him once, a few weeks ago, but no.'

'Ah,' she said, picking up loose twigs from her garden, 'Did he have any kids?'

'Yes, er, yes,' I said.

'That's a shame then.'

Musical heroes are supposed to die young, for full pyrotechnic dramatic effect, or survive the chaos and become wise and for-givably embarrassing. They're not meant to go at fifty in Dorset. Now I was thankful I'd met him, and in such a low-key fashion. In the age of monumental entourages flanking rap stars to shield them from the bacteria of the population, Strummer had been signing records in his underpants, bantering with whoever came in with an ease and humility politicians practise all their lives and never understand why they can't accomplish. Now they had David Blunkett and we didn't have Joe Strummer.

I took my son to the pictures as I'd promised, and on the way stopped the car for a moment. 'Are you crying, Dad?' he said. That night I shared some beers in the gloomiest pub in my area with some fellow mourners, and spent all night lying on the settee playing Clash albums.

5

MOSH THROUGH THE MARSH

Joe Strummer had written the soundtrack to the months after his death. The Project for the American Century was hurtling towards its grand moment, shipping out entire cities' worth of people and equipment to overthrow Saddam. Bush and Blair maintained the war would be called off if Saddam complied with the inspectors. As if there were any chance of Bush saying, 'Well, he's let the inspectors in now, and they're doing a thorough job so fair's fair, we're all going home.'

It seemed obvious that the United Nations, the governments of Europe, the weapons inspectors and official bodies would crumble under American pressure. An anti-war leaflet for one rally I spoke at had the headline, 'If the UN backs the war it's still wrong' in expectation that, of course, the UN would back the war. An article in *Socialist Worker* began: 'Hans Blix shows every sign of caving in to pressure.' What no one I knew expected was that all these organisations would become even more strident against the war, but it *still* wouldn't make any difference. The novelty was that the anti-war case became so mainstream that the arguments about oil, and the West having armed Saddam, became central parts of any discussion on the matter.

Every debate on the radio or television acknowledged the frailties of the case for war. And this only reflected the discussions in every office, college and bar. The next anti-war march, held on 15 February in conjunction with marches around the world, attracted support from such extraordinary sections of the population it was disconcerting. In my genteel road, in which the residents of four different houses were members of a golf club, they all knew about the march and some took it as read they'd be going on it. This couldn't be right! When you live in a road like that, your neighbours are meant to think, 'He seems reasonable enough, but he goes on those marches,' not necessarily out of disapproval but because you're an oddity, in the same way they'd react if you ran a society of people who collected barbed wire. Your neighbours going on the march with you, it was like being nineteen and telling your Gran you're going to a drum 'n' bass night, and have her say, 'Well, I'll come with you, dear.'

Not this time. One report from Stop the War carried a series of reports from round the country, such as this one from North Devon: 'As well as four coaches from Exeter we know of coaches going from Crediton, Barnstaple, Exmouth, Bideford, Newton Abbott, Totnes, Instow and possibly Chagford.' It might be uncharitable but my first thought when I read that was, 'What's wrong with uncertain shitty Chagford then?'

This couldn't be dismissed as just the usual malcontents. The Stop the War office reported dozens of calls each day from people declaring their intention to come on the march but wanting to know where they could buy the tickets. There was a group from Eton school, calling itself 'Eton for peace' and another contingent claiming thousands had enrolled on their website, who called themselves 'Masturbators against the war', with the imaginative slogan 'Whack your sack, not Iraq'. They told of a rugby player who wrote a letter informing his club he wouldn't be attending the annual dinner as he was going on the march instead, only to discover several others were planning to do the same. To prove the breadth of the support, a friend who has always been told off for her participation in protest marches by her strictly Catholic mother, told me her mum was coming from Hampshire on a coach organised by her church. If only the organisers had the time and the right sense of humour they could have ensured the Catholics were forced to march side by side with the masturbators for peace and encourage a whole new unlikely friendship.

One impact of such a mass movement is that it frees those who feel strongly about an issue but are reticent to make their views known. The first person in a crowd to question authority makes it easier for the second, as in *Twelve Angry Men*. But the millionth makes it considerably easier for the million and first.

This process was evident within the murky world of celebrity. The little photos of TV presenters and sportsmen printed in newspapers above captions saying why this person thinks we should all eat more fruit, or why they support buying British cheese, appeared every day alongside a synopsis of why that celebrity was going on the march. Chris Eubank, Joanna Lumley, Jerry Hall and so on, until one day there was Jimmy Hill. This would be like one of those weird dreams that you can't stop analysing for a month: 'I was on an anti-war demonstration and next to me with a placard there was Jimmy Hill. Does this mean I'm gay?'

A television producer told me the owner of his production company, who lived in Pimlico, had sent out invitations to his esteemed friends to meet at his home, attend the march and then 'return to my flat where drinks and supper will be served'. One afternoon on XFM, I heard Zoe Ball announce all the records played that day would be anti-war songs and would afterwards be sent to Tony Blair in time for the march. Never was anti-authority so mainstream. The *Daily Mirror* rang me to ask if I would write an article for page 2 on the day of the march 'to persuade any last-minute waverers that they must come'.

The organisers claimed they were expecting a million, but I kept running this figure through my mind forensically. Given that Scotland had its own march, 1 million would represent 2 per cent of the entire population. So an average of 2 per cent had to come from everywhere. If a hamlet near Cockermouth with a population of 200 didn't bring anyone, another similar-sized hamlet near

Oswestry would have to provide eight to make up. Oswestry itself, with a population of 20,000, needed to turn out 400. Obviously the figures would be uneven, but Manchester would have to send around 40,000, and in London every road with twenty houses would have to provide a few marchers, if it was going to be a million.

And then the government in a wonderful display of angst and pettiness declared the march wouldn't be allowed into Hyde Park 'because it may damage the grass'. What a magnificent excuse to disrupt it – grass. And the concern that the park could become 'very muddy', creating health and safety problems. Oh such joy to be older and understand that when someone throws a fit like that it's because they're boiling away with helpless fury. When cabinet member Tessa Jowell made the announcement she might as well have assembled the press and said, 'Here is my statement – will you STOP going on about this BLOODY march. It's ALL I bloody hear about.'

An added artistic flourish was that, for two weeks prior to the march Hyde Park was occupied by an enormous Star Trek convention with no grass-related worries, though presumably if they found themselves getting 'very muddy', they could beam themselves up and head off for a firmer frontier.

Could there be a million? That would be five times the number on the poll tax march. You just didn't get a million in Britain. But it felt as if there *was* going to be a million. And there were similarly gargantuan numbers marching all round the world. There was even a march in the Antarctic, which was included in the *Socialist Worker*'s 'Where to join the worldwide protest' list. Maybe they had to have a meeting with the police to discuss the route, and the South Pole government tried to ban it on the grounds it might damage the snow.

So compelling was the sense of unity that I was going on the march with my partner. This meant that throughout the morning my thoughts were divided between welcoming this historic day and wondering if we'd get from Trafalgar Square to Hyde Park without descending into ear-splitting vitriol for a reason such as one of us bringing the wrong flavour of crisps. Maybe there'd be a row and other marchers would assume this was a particularly cryptic pacifist slogan that went 'It's all right for you, I had to take the MINCE out of the freezer or there'd be nothing for fucking DINNER.' And by the time we passed Green Park there'd be hundreds of thousands of protesters chanting, 'What do we want?' – 'It's all right for you, I had to take the MINCE out of the freezer.'

Our son was six and had anticipated the event with great excitement; he even invented a slogan: 'Ducks say quack quack, not Iraq', which although it doesn't quite scan, or indeed even place ducks as an unequivocally anti-war bird, nonetheless caught on with other kids and for the last half a mile drowned out all other slogans in our section. The children may have understood the concept that it was wrong to bomb a place to grab its resources, but mostly they could sense that a protest of that size means authority can be challenged, that you can be legitimately naughty.*

At one level there was nothing different about the march itself from previous large marches. Walking slowly in the middle of a million people doesn't feel different from walking slowly in a crowd of 80,000, as you can't see a million. But somehow you could sense it. Partly it was the endless rows of coaches parked on every space in every street. And the crowds packing on to the

---

*When my son was three, I took him on a demonstration against low pay, which he loved, mostly because of the slogan of the day: 'You can stick your three pounds eighty up your arse.' The following day I was driving him through Central London when traffic policemen stopped us and said we'd have to wait for a demonstration to pass. Accompanied by the familiar whistles and chants it turned out to be a protest by sado-masochists, in full regalia – nipple clamps, rubber masks, the lot – and one of them was chained to a wooden trolley which was being pulled along by a man in a rubber suit. My son called out excitedly, 'Can we go on *this* demonstration, Dad?' As it passed, I have to confess, a traffic cop and I caught each other's eye and we both smiled. See, when you get to forty you can even find common cause with the police.

train at Crystal Palace station with self-made placards, mostly unable to find a seat. But instead of bearing the weekday frown of the standing commuter, or escaping into a trance, they joked with their fellow travellers, swapping comments on what they'd packed for lunch or *how* muddy the park would be. And the disconcerting feeling that Central London was packed with demonstrators an hour before the march was due to start. That's not supposed to happen. An hour before there are meant to be a couple of hundred lefty activists trying to sell their papers to bemused tourists and hot-dog salesmen.

But mostly it was the eerie quiet of the vast crowd. Because this was a mass who had never imagined they'd be at such an event; they weren't used to marching culture, they didn't know about chanting or standing behind specific banners. They were people who'd made sandwiches the night before, and checked the weather forecast to decide whether to take an extra jumper. And this made it the most earnest march I'd ever witnessed. For those who are used to protest culture, a march is not necessarily a huge event in their lives. But for most people that day it was. They'd thought about it deeply and made a serious commitment to act in a way they'd never done before. They were making a statement, that this war shouldn't be embarked on, and if it was it would be not in their name. The Left, the jihadists, the whistle-blowing crusties who can seem like a large proportion of many protests were drowned out by the determined quiet of all those who were doing something unique and courageous by turning up at all. That's how you knew it was a million.

The size of the protest was also testimony to the logistic abilities of activists: the mass organisation, the coaches, the trains, the media, the screens, Jesse Jackson, the police – all of which needed handling with delicacy. Anyone who's got in a flap before holding a party for forty people can imagine what it must be like to ask how many are expected at an event you're putting on and be told, 'About a million.' And what a testimony to the ability of a mass movement to draw people together, that my partner and I made it from start to finish in harmony, all in the name of unity.

But now what? How do you top that? Blair said he understood the marchers' concerns but it wouldn't make any difference. Anger spread among the million and many more because not only was the war wrong but 'we're not being listened to'. I had a book detailing the marches through London at the time of the French Revolution which stated: 'If that percentage of the population marched today there would be a million people on the streets, which no government could survive!'

And there *had* been a million but the government had taken no notice. I was interviewed on a news programme, alongside a man from Bedford who'd been on the march. At one point he fumed, 'This government'd better understand, if it doesn't listen to over one million people who marched, I'm going to *sit down in the road.*' And he had a point. You wanted to say, 'Oh come on, a *million*, you've got to take notice of that many or there's no point in playing.'

For weeks after the march everything seemed dramatic, like the last moments of a prestigious sporting event that's closely fought, when every little move takes on a huge significance. The Turks wouldn't let the Americans use their country as a base, the United Nations wouldn't back the war. The Americans even said they could go ahead without Britain – but it made no difference.

Robin Cook made the anti-war case with a forensic account of the deceptions that had been perpetrated and resigned in spectacular fashion. But most Labour MPs backed Blair. So there was the Labour Party, set up to further the cause of socialism, now, on the defining issue of the age, militantly, defiantly to the right of one million marchers, the Pope, an ex-president of the USA, the President of France, the President of Germany, 90 per cent of Spain, the weapons inspectors, the United Nations, Turkey, every country in Africa, Zoe Ball, marchers in the Antarctic, the Liberal Democrats, 90 per cent of South America, Cat Stevens, a bunch of students from Eton, virtually every living Arab and Jimmy fucking Hill.

One night George Bush announced on television that the war had begun, reportedly after saying just before the broadcast, 'Hey, I feel good.' The next morning I took my daughter to the local park. Occasionally, in the background, on a fisherman's radio leant awkwardly against a tree by the tranquil South Norwood lake, there was the news of the 'shock and awe' the planes were proudly depositing on Baghdad. It was severely depressing, but not just because of the gruesome human consequences of this shock and awe. It was the depression of immense frustration. It's one thing to be dismayed at how everyone's fallen into line behind a patriotic call for war, as happened in 1914 or with the Falklands War. But that hadn't happened. An unprecedented movement had taken place against it, the majority of the country and the vast majority of the world was against it, and still they were flattening the place.

The next inevitable source of irritation was the round-the-clock news coverage, involving presenters trained to look just serious enough but not overly concerned, reporting on the coalition's successes and the accuracy of their bombs.

One night, on the BBC news, a reporter informed us that the anti-war movement had 'literally melted away'. As evidence he stood in Parliament Square, saying, 'The night before the war began, this square was packed with demonstrators. But tonight there's just one lonely man with a placard.' Which may have been true, but he hadn't considered one possible explanation, which was that on the night before the war began there was a demonstration, but on this night there wasn't one. I suppose if he ever becomes a sports reporter he might go to Old Trafford on a Tuesday afternoon and say, 'Support for Manchester United has, quite literally, melted away. On Saturday afternoon, 67,000, but today – just the cleaners.'

And you feel so helpless. Even a section of those opposed to the war started arguing that now it had started, our job was to 'support our boys'. Which is to say it's all right to oppose an atrocity when it isn't taking place, but once it is you have to back it. 'Our armed forces can't do their job without our support' was a common argument against anyone who publicly disputed the merits of the war. As if, when a tank commander's about to incinerate some target, his hand hovers over the button as he thinks, 'I can't seem to do it because there was this letter in *The Independent*.'

The meetings during this time were even bigger than they'd been before the war began, especially among students. On the day the war started, thousands of students left their schools in protest, often defying threats of expulsion. Every day and evening there were gatherings as big as anything that hall or community centre had ever seen, in opposition to this war. And the people who came knew they weren't going to stop it through their campaigns and stalls, so they were coming to express their outrage. They weren't meetings in which seasoned campaigners would make rehearsed speeches, but were representative of those on the march, many of them slightly bemused to be there at all. An imam would speak about peace, then froth with fury about the necessity of driving the local war-supporting MP out of a job, often reaching such a state you couldn't tell if he was still speaking in English or had reverted to Urdu. Someone would suggest we give more power to the United Nations, or demand a written constitution, or raise money to arrest Tony Blair for war crimes, and the Left would say we had to keep demonstrating. And always the subtext was: 'I don't really know *what* to do but we've got to do *something*.'

It was also obvious this was a rage that wouldn't go away. These people, and a much greater number besides, were furious, not just about the war but because they felt Blair had taken the piss out of them. Blair's henchmen calculated that as time went on the wrath would subside. They should have sent people to those meetings. They should have witnessed the man in a cardigan with a suburban moustache and a John Major voice waving his fist and shouting, 'This man is a BLOODY CRIMINAL.'

The government insisted it wanted good relations with 'moderate' Muslims. Perhaps they're referring to those like Hassan, who had been a member of the Labour Party for thirty years and works in the ticket office at my local railway station. He seems to know everyone who buys a ticket, so that a static queue builds up while he nods his head and says, 'Aaah, I saw you yesterday with your baby – not such a baby now, eh? How old – three? *Four*, oh my goodness. Believe me, when they have grown up and left home it is much easier. Maybe lonely but easier, ha ha.' And he reels off an appropriate and personal spiel for everyone, like the Queen, finally handing over a travelcard, which he must see as the boring formal bit, just as maybe the Queen feels about finally knighting someone after a cosy chat.

He's so sincere and delightful, so engaging and humble that, despite the fact he's at the critical point of the most frantic urban time-conscious moment of stress for the people he's serving, no one seems to mind that he's made them miss their train. There must have been times when, at the end of a chat about where someone's going for Easter, he's asked which ticket the person needs and they've said, 'It doesn't matter now as I've missed the meeting I was going to' and gone home. I've missed about a dozen trains from there, because Hassan once saw me on the telly talking about the war in Iraq. 'Mark – MARK. Ha ha haaaa, have you seen what he's done now, have you? Our friend Mr Bush, now he's blaming the insurgency on Iran and Syria. But he was *allies* with Syria, I'm telling you. Look here, I've kept this from *The Times*, a report of Dick Cheney's dealings with Halliburton who make *millions* from the war . . .' Then he'll slide the perfectly cut out article through the tray for giving people their change, while seven people behind me ponder whether to walk to work or ring in sick.

Sometimes, if I'm not up to the minute, he'll catch me out. 'Mark, MARK. What about that idiot Geoff Hoon, you see what he said?' And I don't know. So I look blankly and he says 'On Radio 4, you see?'

'Er, oo, no, I don't know,' I confess, feeling I'm owning up to not having done my homework. And these conversations always end with, 'They're LIARS you know, DIRTY LIARS, they don't CARE how many they kill. There's your return to Charing Cross, bye bye.'

It was a time when the mass confusion that would crystallise later first developed. So many people were so disenchanted, and wanted something to be done, but so few had a clear idea of what to do.

As the Americans approached Baghdad, I was asked to appear on BBC1's *Question Time*. There's something splendidly British about being on *Question Time* as the panellist who is not a professional politician. The viewing audience gives you no points for being an actor or a comic, even a well-known one. Tom Jones could be on, and his reply would be studied with the same weight as the agriculture spokesman for the Liberal Democrats. And if Tom gave an incoherent reply to a question about House of Lords reform he wouldn't be able to rescue the situation by belting out a chorus of 'What's New, Pussycat'.

So when you say the words 'yes, that will be fine', agreeing to be on *Question Time*, your stomach immediately tightens and you feel a fizzy anxiety as if you've drunk a dozen espressos. I was aware of the pressure of being the voice of the Left on the week's programme, because I'd watched it often enough while either cheering 'Go on, yes that's stuffed them' or wailing 'Oh no-o-o-o you idiot, don't say there's some good things about North Korea for fuck's sake.' When the panellist representing your views starts gibbering nonsense, you feel the despair of watching your football team give away an unnecessary penalty.

And it's never like an informal conversation in a café, when you're on a programme like that. Because if you start an answer with 'Well, this can be complicated, because it's true, right, that you can't, well you can but in a sense you can't, er, sorry let me start that again,' two million people think, 'Who let this twat on?' And what if they started discussing something I hadn't seen?

Imagine that. Sitting there when Dimbleby says, 'Yes, this is a question about yesterday's announcement that the Germans are no longer to recognise the part of the GATT agreement that relates to British cauliflower. What do you think, Mark Steel?'

This week, however, the programme would obviously be dominated by the war. Then an hour before we went on air, the Americans took over the main square in Baghdad and pulled down the statue of Saddam standing there. Immediately it was portrayed as a glorious event, a day of universal joy that you could no more oppose than you could an announcement that someone had found a cure for cancer.

As my heart thumped, the audience in Southampton fidgeted, all of them eager to speak, or clap or call out abuse. The timing was perfect to cause maximum nerves. It was as if the Americans had deliberately scheduled their arrival in Baghdad town centre to ensure high viewing figures for that week's *Question Time*. As the sound man attached my microphone, I ran through my arguments in my mind. David Willetts, Conservative spokesman for something, sat next to me. 'No need to be nervous,' he assured me. 'Once it starts it will fly by. You just make sure you get stuck in and enjoy yourself.'

Even in their brief moment of triumph, the supporters of the war were on the defensive. Mike O'Brien, a minister in the Foreign Office, was Labour's representative, and at one point he was asked why, if Saddam possessed these terrifying weapons, he hadn't used them. And O'Brien said, 'Because it was made very clear to him that if he did use them there would be very serious consequences.' Right. So, as the Americans circled Baghdad, Saddam was sitting there with weapons of mass destruction he could launch in forty-five minutes, thinking, 'Hmm. I'd better not get those out or I'll be in *real* trouble.'

As the recording went on, the audience seemed to cheer every statement against the war, while supporters of the war remained hesitant. And this was supposed to be their night of glory. They weren't helped by David Willetts, who insisted Saddam was a threat because of the weapons programme he'd been nurturing. What an open goal. His party, in its last years, had been shamed by an inquiry that revealed they'd spent years selling piles of weapons to Saddam Hussein. When I said this to him he actually blushed. It was almost enough to change the balance sheet of the war: on the one hand, an entire country was subjected to horrific carnage, but, on the other, I got to make a Tory go red.

At the end, as the signature tune was playing and the sound man arrived to take off our microphones, David Willetts said to me, 'There you are. I *told* you there was no need to be nervous.'

'Sorry,' I said.

'I *told* you. I said if you just got stuck in you'd enjoy yourself.'

'I just called you a Tory idiot in front of millions of people,' I said.

'Yes, that's the spirit,' he said, like a public school rugby coach. Then he added, 'Well, I think we jolly well deserve a drink after all that hard work.'

So we went into a hospitality room, where there was a bucket full of bottled lager. I handed him a bottle and looked for an opener but couldn't find one. He placed his bottle by a shelf and shoved off the top with the bottom of his hand. I've always been useless at that, and tried opening mine by a ledge but it kept slipping; then I banged it to no effect except causing me to yell, 'Ah bollocks!' as I jarred my wrist. I made a pathetic Stan Laurel-esque effort to use my heel, and Willetts said, 'Come along, give it here.' He took my bottle, expertly banged off the top and handed it back to me.

'Look,' I said, aware I was becoming dangerously jovial, 'promise me you'll tell no one. Because if word gets out that I relied on a Tory shadow minister to open my bottle of beer with his wrist, I'm fucked.'

'Yes,' he said, 'I rather see your point. Cheers.'

6

EVERY LITTLE HELPS

I used to distrust big business mostly for traditional reasons – it is dedicated to robbing us of our labour or our money. But in the twenty-first century they've earned a more fundamental reason to be distrusted: they're robbing us of our soul.

At one time the Left was accused of wanting to make everything everywhere the same. But look what THEY have done. Now you could go to a shopping centre in Croydon, Penzance, Lincoln or Dundee, and guarantee there'd be a Body Shop, Clinton Cards, Going Places Travel, HMV, Waterstones, fake Irish pub, Wetherspoons, Pizza Hut with a little glass screw-top jar of Parmesan cheese, JJB Sports, Burger King, a bloke in a green pullover trying to recruit you into the AA and a bunch of Peruvians playing 'I Just Called To Say I Love You' on the poxy pan-pipes.

If there's room, there'll be a shopping mall, a sterile shiny structure crammed with oblong units such as Next, River Island, Vodafone and Thorntons Chocolates, in which every plug, coat hanger and sheet of gold-coloured wrapping paper is in the exact place ordered by the chain's marketing manager from head office in Basingstoke. If there's a rubber plant in the left-hand corner in the T-mobile shop in Ipswich you can guarantee there'll be one in the same spot in the branch in Hereford. There'll be a fountain, in front of which two actors demonstrate a gadget for cleaning

windows now on sale in Debenhams, and an area where you can
sit on a metal chair and eat a panini that's so expensive you go
through with the purchase only because you've queued for twenty
minutes.

Wander away from the centre and you'll pass the street with all
the building societies, the All Bar One, Nandos and eventually a
Harvesters, followed by the wide road flanked by PC World,
Dixons and a carpet place, until you've forgotten whether you're
in Kettering or Clacton, past the Big Yellow storage place to the
Tesco, with its vast car park, symmetrical shrubs and slightly
wrong clock. Maybe modern town planners have nightmares in
which they wake up shrieking, 'Oh my *God,* I dreamt I'd built a
town with the Kwik-Fit on the *left* after the Esso garage instead of
on the right. It was horrible, so horrible.'

Such practices led, by 2005, to 42 per cent of towns in Britain
being categorised as 'clone towns', those dominated by these
chains, with another 28 per cent described as 'border towns',
retaining some local character but heading in a cloneward direction. The champion was Exeter, which boasted a town centre in
which fifty-nine out of sixty shops were part of these chains.
Exeter – where the planners must have said, 'We live in a beautiful city, in which the medieval cathedral sparkles above the cattle
markets, that in turn blend with the family businesses selling local
produce, and tea shops full of scones and lace tablecloths. It needs
just one more thing to make it absolutely perfect – a fucking
great pedestrianised precinct full of shit like The Link to make
it exactly the same as everywhere bastard else.' When they survey
what they've done they probably think, 'We must admit it isn't
right. The problem is that one independent shop that's left. Once
that's turned into Specsavers it'll be perfect.' Maybe that last
beacon of independence is the cathedral; soon it will be replaced
by a warehouse with automatic sliding doors called 'Holy Ghosts
R Us'.

Tesco itself is terrifying. It's unstoppable, like bindweed. You
couldn't even organise a guerilla army against it because if you

blew one store up, two would spring up in its place. They must land in the night, like triffids. Soon Tesco will have permission to set up mini-stores in your house, so you'll get up one morning and there it will be in your bedroom. And a PR spokesman will issue a statement that 'Our customers have indicated that any lack of privacy that may result from having a shop by their wardrobe is compensated by the convenience of being able to purchase our pop-in-the-oven lasagne in the middle of the night without getting up.'

There's hardly anything left it doesn't dominate. The company will launch their next new line with an advert in which Prunella Scales says to Jane Horrocks, 'Don't expect me to do any housework tonight, dear – not while Tesco is offering springtime savings on a quarter ounce of top quality Afghan skunk.'

Tesco isn't just a symbol of how big business wants everything the same, it's a symbol of how it wants everything inhuman. They claim customers choose to go there, but no one in Tesco ever seems happy. People are lured by cheapness and convenience, but they pay for that by spending their time there, staring aimlessly into the despotic white light in a vegetative trance, maybe drifting back into consciousness for a moment to whack their kids on the back of their legs for climbing on the trolley, before the regular beep-beep of the bar code machine returns them to their hypnotic dreamy half-life. Maintaining your faculties in a queue at Tesco is almost impossible. Once you're stuck behind six families with overflowing trolleys, you could be a multilingual biochemist and you'd struggle to remember the capital of France. These conditions could be used for training people who need to be able to think clearly in extreme circumstances, because if you can keep your thought process working at 90 per cent in a Tesco queue, then repairing an oxygen mask while in space must be a piece of piss. And you have to hire the trolley for a pound – the bastards. Even in Abu Ghraib they don't make you pay for use of the electrodes.

That's why it's wrong. Every boast they make is actually the crime. Each store is horribly, irredeemably, joylessly functional. Every tin of custard powder is placed at an angle designed to entice you to chuck it in the trolley. Every tomato is perfectly spherically fluorescent. Occasionally they might decide customers have indicated they appreciate conversational check-out staff, so the cashiers will be ordered to say, 'Hope you enjoy your afternoon.' But that's worse than if they stared into space. Soon we'll all be fitted with a chip in our arm, so our interests can be recorded and pop up as we're paying, enabling the staff to make an appropriate comment. So if you're a carpenter, they'll say, 'Enjoy your dovetails this week, sir,' while if you're a racist, they'll say, 'Good to see you've bought British shampoo. Send 'em all back, I say. Can I help with your packing?' And so on.

There's usually some 'new' thing they're doing that's pointless, such as pre-packed diced pyramids of rhubarb, or bananas in balloons, so 'Now you don't have to pick your bananas off the shelf, just pluck them from the air as they float round in balloons that keep them extra-nana-fresh!!'

For example, Sainsbury's launched a product called 'Kids Snack Pack Carrots' which differed from the boring old-fashioned adult carrots in one respect: they were thirteen times more expensive. They also came up with packets of 'Fully Prepared Apple Bites'. Thank God for them. Because up until then, for thousands of years mankind has surveyed these objects dangling lusciously from trees and thought, 'They *look* as if they'd be tasty, but they're all stuck to branches so how can we possibly get to them?' For fuck's sake, according to a huge chunk of the world the apple is the first thing a human being ever bloody well ate. Or maybe the original version went: 'And Eve looked upon the apple and said unto the serpent, "I am tempted not. For while the juices would nourisheth me, the fruit is too cumbersome and unwieldy to biteth." And so the serpent did holdeth a meeting with his executives and return to Eve with the Fully Prepared Apple Bite.'

'The free market has spoken' is the usual defence of the modern city centre. In a competition with local stores chains stores have won, because most of us prefer to shop in this modern way; but it's a competition the chains can't lose. A new Tesco only has to swipe one-third of the local custom for meat, and the butcher in the area is stuffed. So he struggles for a bit, shuts down and then almost everyone goes to Tesco. Somerfields declared in a strategy document its plan to run extra promotions 'where there is strong local competition', to drive the locals out of business. And economic clout brings political power. The director general of the British Retail Consortium declared, 'We are no longer an organisation that simply reacts to Government's proposed legislation or White Papers but sets out to help shape them. By creating significant links with special advisers, policy specialists and the leading think tanks . . . we are involved at the beginning of any legislative process.'

This method probably isn't open to their competitors. When a government committee meets to discuss new legislation on planning permission regulations, I doubt whether the minutes begin: 'Those present: Secretary of State for Trade, Sir Terry Leahy, managing director of Tesco, Lord Sainsbury and Ken the fishmonger from Hastings.'

Nor would Ken be knighted, as Terry Leahy was. Nor would Ken expect to receive the help of a government adviser for his business, whereas Philip Gould, Tony Blair's key strategy adviser, was hired by Tesco to reorganise their media operations. And to make the point, a government paper on the direction included Planning Policy statement 6: 'Farm shops shouldn't inconvenience supermarkets.' Absolutely. Those arrogant farm shops are moving into every pedestrianised precinct and making it hard for traditional Tesco to struggle on.

Anyway, all that driving and jostling can't make it much quicker or cheaper than going to a local shop, except the local grocer's probably shut down because of Tesco. Then they claim they've turned ecological, having set up a 'green fund', when in truth they're responsible for so many car journeys they'd be more green if they spent all day melting icebergs with a blowtorch.

Even the claim that shopping in Tesco saves time is mostly a con. People say, 'At least I can get everything in one place,' but the place is bigger than an average High Street. You might as well say, 'I go shopping abroad because at least you can get everything in one place – France.'

But nothing I had experienced so far prepared me for IKEA. The aim was to emerge with a cupboard, so with my children I ventured forth into the maze of self-assembly that lay ahead, and wandered with increasing bemusement through angle-poised lamp after CD-rack, occasionally spotting an assistant and running after them through the crowd like in a film where a detective chases the suspect through the busy back streets of Hong Kong, catching the odd glimpse but eventually arriving at a crossroads and desperately peering left and right before giving up and slumping on to a display of bread bins. At one point we were told, 'Just follow the blue lines on the floor,' which cross backwards and forwards across several other lines, like a puzzle that goes 'Freddie the fisherman has got his line tangled with those of all the other fishermen. Can you help Freddie figure out which line leads to his prize Catch of the Day?'

The three of us followed the blue lines up and round and across, past wine racks and barbecue sets and twenty minutes later to the place where we'd asked the assistant in the first place. All around stood huge boards telling you how helpful and modern and splendid everything was, with no more justification than similar claims made by King Abdullah of Saudi Arabia. The increasing sense of panic and loathing that grips you is not a result of the inconvenience; it's the overwhelming soullessness that gets to you. Everything's the result of a study group, a promotions plan, a marketing initiative.

It took just over an hour to find the cupboard, but then we were told we hadn't found the cupboard at all. What we had found was the fully assembled version of the cupboard. On it was the reference number you need before proceeding to the storeroom – following the blue lines – where you can pick up the pack containing the bits of the cupboard. But the pack wasn't there, so we asked someone and they told us to wait but didn't come back. Eventually it turned out to be on the wrong shelf and we reached the next stage where we queued for a cashier. And you're left wondering whether you're trapped in a quest to pursue the holy grail, so that each solution merely provides a further clue. Maybe the cashier will say, 'Ah, you have found the pack. Now travel to the place where a fool may drink vinegar but the eagle will flee.'

And there's no way out. Any attempt to go backwards steers you into barriers and culs-de-sac, and if you jumped over them you'd encounter a rabid three-headed dog. So we queued and queued with no prospect of forward motion, until I yelled, 'SOMEONE HELP US TO ESCAPE. SURELY WITH ALL THIS WOOD, BETWEEN US WE COULD BUILD A GLIDER.' And no one laughed, they just looked at me as if I was mental, which was fast becoming true. I dropped the pack on the floor, lifted the kids over the cash desk and clambered over it to freedom, feeling like the chief at the end of *One Flew Over the Cuckoo's Nest*.

As these monolithic institutions came to dominate the environment, I started to rethink certain attitudes. These monstrosities seemed to be doing more than exploiting their staff and their customers, they were stealing our spirit. Perhaps this is how Aborigines feel when someone takes their photo.

When Marx wrote about 'alienation', he was referring to the outcome that results when the workforce feel removed from the product of their labour: the garment or pot they're making ceases to be a garment or pot and becomes a commodity they must labour on in return for a wage. My friend Linda Smith used to tell a story about the time she worked in an apple pie factory. The pies would travel along a conveyor belt, she said, then into a super-hot oven where they'd be rapidly cooked. Then the oven door would pop open and the boiling hot pies would come back down the belt, where Linda and her colleagues had to pick them off (leaving those that seemed slightly too crumbly or burned) and place them in tinfoil cups. And every time the oven door opened and the hot pies began their journey, there was one bloke who'd snarl, 'Here come the little fuckers.'

The modern practices of chainstores and supermarkets also alienate their workforces from the object of their labour, the difference being that now that object is the human race. Because it's not stockings, flowerpots or apple pies that travel along the assembly line to be dealt with, it's people. Each person that comes into Caffè Nero or Gap or TGI Fridays becomes an object that has to be routinely smiled at and asked questions in an identical way following the procedures learned on the training course. The writer Joanna Blythman got a job in Asda and described how the staff had to make written declarations 'in an almost Maoist spirit of self-criticism', to 'go the extra mile' in helping customers. And on one wall were 'cheery photos of memorable Asda days, such as the "Pocket Tap Day", when customers and colleagues were encouraged over the tannoy to have fun by simultaneously tapping their pockets, as in the Asda TV advert'.

Of course, if someone gets up one morning and spontaneously pledges to be extra helpful to customers, the world benefits from this attitude, but enforced corporate friendliness is demeaning to both staff and consumer. To the checkout girl, the queue of people she's obliged to ask, 'Have you got a loyalty card?' and 'Can I help with your packing?' is not a series of individuals – a stressed mother followed by a man who is probably stocking up for a party and so on. It's just a line of little fuckers.

When the bored lad in the coffee shop stares into the middle distance and asks, 'Would you like a pastry with that?' it's both annoying and depressing. It's so obviously what he was pro-grammed to say as he hands over your unfeasibly expensive corrugated cardboard container that even if you replied, 'Guess what? I went to the doctor today and it turns out I'm allergic to pastry. One flake of the stuff and I'll immediately die,' he would continue to stare and repeat, 'Do you want a pastry with that?'

All these questions we're asked allow these franchised companies to present this mechanical sterility as greater choice. For example, I spent a harrowing few minutes in a Subway sandwich bar trying to buy a sandwich for my son and daughter. I joined a queue, and shuffled along to face four men with latex gloves all rapidly buttering and firing off questions with such efficiency their training must involve running across moors while a sergeant calls, 'Cheese and bacon crusty bake' and they all sing back, 'With apple juice or yoghurt shake?'

'Bacon sandwich,' said my son, but by about the 'd' of 'sandwich', the latex man called back, 'Which bread?'

'Eh, brown,' he said. But before the 'r' of 'brown' the sandwich man said, 'Maltedcrustyryegrain.'

'Eh, sorry, what?' I asked, feeling the pressure of all four latex men plus the queue behind urging, 'Hurry up, you idiot,' as if I was one of these old people who stands at a station ticket office during rush hour and asks for the times of the next eleven trains to Chester.

'Maltedcrustyryegrain,' he repeated, even quicker.

'Eh, malted,' I stuttered. Then came an avalanche of quickfire questions involving cheese, mayonnaise, butter and crispiness requirement, until I expected him to continue, 'Served with left hand or right hand? Square napkin or rhombus? Added spit or no spit? Chewed by a dog? I said, "DO YOU WANT IT CHEWED BY A DOG?" Come on, there are customers WAITING.'

I tried to keep answering the questions but in the end the brain can't keep up and for a moment I thought I should say, 'A consonant, a vowel and another consonant please, Carol.' After each answered question, the speed at which the next one flew back increased, until it was like the last five minutes of *University Challenge*. Eventually I was worried that after a question about salad dressing he'd ask frenetically, 'The compound lithium nitrate was discovered in 1837 by *which* prominent Austrian chemist? Come on, I'll have to hurry you, come on, hurry hurry quickly.'

My daughter asked for a 'Kid's Pack', which provoked more questions, leading to the poor man shouting what sounded like 'cookyercrisps' several times right at me. 'I'm sorry, I don't understand what you're asking me,' I said in panic, feeling like Dustin Hoffman in *Marathon Man* when the mad dentist keeps asking, 'Is it safe?' Whereupon he turned to his colleague and said, 'I think this one must be Greek.'

'Kid's Pack,' he said, exasperated. 'Comes with cookie or crisps.'

My daughter was outside so I said, 'I don't know. You decide.'

'I can't decide for your child,' he shouted, so I said, 'Cookie.' And he said, 'Which one?'

I said, 'Whichever one is the third one along,' and he said, 'We've only got two.'

The last people to get cross with in this situation are the poor latex people, because as they shuffle you through the system, you become aware you're on that assembly line, an item to be dealt with and dispatched. If you stopped for a chat you'd be as much of a nuisance as a custard pie on an assembly line stopping to ask, 'How was your Christmas?'

There are, apparently, 28,580 of these Subway places around the world, in eighty-six countries. Right now someone in Uruguay will be sweating as they're asked, 'Cookyercrisps?' And the irony is that it hardly matters which answers you give, because everything in the metal trays looks utterly rancid, the implausibly thin bendy slices of fluorescent ham looking less like something that originated from a pig than any other object you could imagine, including lawnmowers and hot air balloons.

As the chains multiply, their corporate manner pervades almost every area of life, eroding genuine human interaction and replacing it with this automated insincerity. Imagine a love affair conducted on this orchestrated basis. Each morning you'd have to dress in the same uniform and say out loud, 'Today I pledge to be not just a boyfriend, but a joyfriend.' And later on greet your partner with 'Good evening lover, can I interest you in a kiss? Would you prefer formal, affectionate, lingering or dirty? How about some conversation with that?'

Even that would be welcome in certain modern chains of pubs. For example, who knows how much research and psychology has gone into creating the carefully cultivated ambience of forlorn misery that wafts through a Wetherspoons? The shiny soulless wood, the gloomy air that would somehow be fresher if everyone was allowed to smoke, the huge menus in laminated plastic, everything spotlessly sterile, unsullied by the dirt of human life. A manageress in a Wetherspoons pub told me she'd been trained *not* to engage the customers in conversation, as this encouraged the wrong sort of atmosphere. Too much informality is bad for business. And with most branches of Wetherspoon pubs, from the screams of 'NO, NO, YOU CAN'T BRING HIM IN HERE' if you try to go in with a child, you wonder if just behind you there's a Vietnamese pot-bellied pig they mistakenly think is yours.

After one local pub was bought by the O'Neill's chain, they banned all children at all times, even from the garden. When I rang the head office of Mitchells and Butlers, who own the chain, I was told by a polite press officer that 'Children don't fit our brand image.'

Nothing is real. Every mirror, every smile, every trinket on the wall and flourish at the top of a Guinness is the result of an operations document approved by a board meeting.

Frighteningly, the British chain pub has spread overseas. When you're in an aircraft about to land abroad and the captain makes that announcement about things you're not allowed to take into the country, he should add 'As well as meat products, live animals and tropical plants, passengers are reminded you are not permitted to import any chain pubs through customs.' On a trip to Greek Cyprus, I naively expected the village we were visiting to be lined with Greek or Cypriot bars, with the odd vine leaf. Instead there were countless British chain pubs, each with Sky Sports beaming out from at least four screens. By the time I came back I'd never been so well informed about Port Vale's injury crisis. I began to wonder whether one consequence may be that a new dialect, half Greek and half Sky Sports, will develop. So you'll ask someone in a Cypriot bar how he is, and he'll reply, 'Not bad, ah cod be worse, ah cod be Crewe Alixandra, nine home game withaht win, more on this story coming op after break.'*

Leaving no stone unturned in removing humanity from our lives, twenty-first-century capitalism relishes the ultimate triumph: the automated telephone system. How many gigs, films and plays have people missed, how many objects have been discarded when they could have been repaired, because after twenty minutes of Celine Dion and assurances that your call IS important, people have yelled, 'Oh fuck it' and given up. Or, as you're desperately pressing 1 and 2 to get to the next stage, palms sweating in the knowledge that at any moment the phone could go dead and you'll be sent back to the start as if you've dropped the egg in an egg-and-spoon race, there comes a question you simply don't know how to answer, such as 'If your query was a colour, press 1 if it would be green or 2 for turquoise.'

Yet my frustration on these occasions is only partly due to the inconvenience, it's mostly a longing for a human reaction. If you actually succeed in being 'put through to an operator', it is slightly bewildering. When I hear, 'Hello, my name's Naomi, how can I help you today?' my initial comment is usually, 'Er, oh, hello? Oh sorry are you real?' I feel I've accomplished something simply by making contact and have a brief urge to say, 'Thank God you're here,' as if I've been discovered on a desert island, and then put the phone down.

It's as if the corporations that control modern life have no concept of the joy of genuine human interaction. They can't grasp

---

*Such is the dominance of English in southern Cyprus: returning home from taking my daughter to the bird sanctuary, it suddenly dawned on me, 'Hang on – even the fucking parrot spoke English.'

that any meaningful relationship, even a casual acquaintance with the lad who works in the shop, depends on being unpredictable. Joanna Blythman reports the ASDA training course insisting at all times the staff should 'inject enthusiasm into their voice' with a tone that 'reflects sincerity and confidence', while at Tesco each new recruit is taught 'Don't bring your problems to work' and 'If you need to cry, cry at home.' As if that attitude represented the relationship we prefer with our fellow humans. So the ideal friend is one who, having found out they're terminally ill, rings up to say, 'I've got some news. We've just brought out a new range of blue-berry-flavoured mild Cheddar slices.'

Music halls and early cinema, local pubs, transport caffs and village fishmongers were all, to differing degrees, motivated by the desire for a profit. I used to be somewhat uneasy when politicians emphasised the necessity to 'boost small businesses' as if small businessmen were the most wholesome of citizens. But now, if there's a local independent bookshop or butcher's or record store, I want to run in, give them my spare change and a hug and implore them to stay open even if every item they sell is being given away in Tesco free with each box of Rice Krispies.

In All Bar One I long for a grumpy independent pub landlord, because at least his grumpiness is genuine and not choreographed on the 'How to Look Grumpy' course in a conference room at a Jury's Inn hotel.

When my son was upset after getting in a fight at school, the first people he ran to eagerly to tell the story were the Colombians who own the local shop and always chat to him about video games and hip-hop. They calmed him down and gave him lemonade and by the time I arrived he was laughing. Whereas, if he'd run to Tesco and approached the checkout with a similar story, the poor robotised cashier would probably fizz with confusion and explode, or at best press the little button and say in a monotone drawl, 'Mr Fredericks, traumatised boy at checkout number 6 please,' before returning to pack the next customer's Apricot Stilton.

At the remaining not-too-distant butcher's, the pungent aroma of offal is like fresh sea air because the woman who serves me says 'sweetheart' in every sentence. 'Hello sweetheart, what d'you fancy sweetheart, lovely chops in today sweetheart . . .' I'm sure if someone swiped a tray of sausages and ran off she'd call out, 'Bring 'em back sweetheart, or you'll get this meat cleaver in your head sweetheart.'

The small retailer was once someone driven by a desire to be independent from, and more financially secure than, the local working class. That may still be partially true, but they have now become a barrier against the onslaught to robotify human relations – an ally on the side of humanity.

There is a deep sadness at the heart of the anguish of anyone appalled at the artificial nature of our modern environment. Because we know that it's true that if no one used these places they'd pack up; unfortunately enough people, because it's simpler, or easier to park or they believe it's cheaper, patronise them and keep the shareholders happy.

This, it's claimed, proves the superstores and pedestrianised precincts have won a democratic battle. But remember that, as well as the huge advantages they enjoy in planning, legislation, advertising and having billions of pounds to cushion themselves against anything going wrong, they also hold the crucial card of being so dominant that it takes an effort of will to *not* spend money there. As the alternatives dwindle, you almost have to boycott these places on principle to stay away. Which is different from saying that most people prefer it that way.

The evidence for saying this seems to be the growing number of campaigns against the chains, and the way each one quickly attracts a large part of the local area. For example, in Newham, East London, residents and market traders set up a campaign which started with a demonstration by 120 people, led to a petition signed by 12,000 and culminated in the election of local councillors opposed to the new store, so the development was cancelled. They issued a leaflet advising other areas on how to campaign, ranging from how to hold open meetings welcoming everyone in the area to the touching 'Tip number 5': 'Be patient with fellow campaigners because the bigger the campaign gets, the more likely that some of them will drive you crazy.'

In Inverness a campaign against a fourth Tesco was launched by one woman, Anne Walker, who drew up a petition and put it in the local store. Three hundred and fifty people attended a public meeting and following a series of events Tesco consoled themselves with sticking to three stores in Inverness.

At one point in 2007 there were over 100 similar campaigns against plans for new Tesco sites. Once again, every official body and political party describes Tesco as a huge success, and unstoppable because it's played by the rules of the unstoppable free market. But a vast chunk of the population finds this utterly distasteful, though their discontent remains buried until a credible local campaign pops up to tap into it.

For example, while writing one series of *The Mark Steel Lectures* at BBC Television Centre, we depended for refreshments on a tiny tea bar just outside our office, run by two dedicated Jamaican women. It was unusual because almost every other tea bar in the building, at which there are 4,000 employees, had been franchised out to Costa Coffee.

At our tea bar there was all the jollity of a bygone pre-twenty-first-century age. Whenever the 25-year-old tall Scouse writer on the show ventured in there for a tea, they'd howl, 'When do I get to take you away my dear – ahoooooeeeeeooooha ha ha.'

Occasionally, if we were stuck on a surreal moment in the script that required choosing the right vacuous celebrity to fit a particular joke, we'd yell into the tea bar, 'Shout out some pointless celebrities.'

'Jennifer whatsername, Lopez, ha ha haoooo,' they'd laugh.

'Hmm, she's more annoying than pointless,' we'd call back.

'Simon Cowell.'

'No, he's more horrible than pointless, and too much of a cliché.'

'Oh, what about Anthea, um, oh is it Anthea?'

'Turner, Anthea Turner – perfect.'

'Now do we get some money for writing your script – aaaaha-haaaa haaaaawoooooaa.'

One Monday morning I went in for tea and biscuits, and instead of greeting me with a shriek and a squeeze the two women stared tearfully in the direction of the crisps. One of them showed me a letter from the hived-off section of the BBC that deals with catering, informing them the tea bar was losing money and was therefore being shut at the end of the week. What a classically callous, mean-spirited and illogical way of looking at a tea bar, I sympathised. This tea bar was part of the structure of the working environment, as everyone needs tea. You might as well assess that the toilets are losing money and shut those down too. Anyway, I was sure this was illegal, to sack employees at this short notice, and to start with, I said, maybe we should draw up a petition. But as I suggested this, a woman who worked across the corridor came in with a petition she'd already drawn up and printed, and stuck it on the wall.

Over the next four days, 400 people signed the petition to save the tea bar, which must have been everyone who worked on that floor plus some visitors. In the tea bar people were constantly discussing the injustice of the proposed closure. At one point I stood behind a young black cleaner who seemed to have entered a contest with a chief accountant to see who could be most angry about it. 'It's an absolute bloody disgrace if you ask me,' said the accountant to the cleaner. 'Yeah, man, it's bear out of order you get me,' said the cleaner. The only person who didn't seem concerned was the trade union official, who said he didn't have time to meet the women until after the date they were due to be sacked.

Not everyone will have been aware of it, but they were all defying the spirit of the age. So we contacted the BBC magazine,

Ariel, and explained the campaign, and they said they'd like to take a photo of the tea bar filled with its supporters. The next day we packed into this tiny space, and as the photo was being taken, marching down the corridor with high-heeled urgency came the executive who'd ordered the closure, in a grey suit and carrying a clipboard with an angry authoritarian gait reminiscent of Hattie Jacques when she was a hospital matron in *Carry On* films.

'*I* will present you with some facts concerning the operating costs of this tea bar,' she announced sternly. But as she did so, several women began to present some alternative facts. 'Is that all life is to you – profit and loss, profit and loss, I bet you *dream* in profit and loss,' said one. 'Do you go *everywhere* with that clipboard to see what else you can shut down?' snapped another. And this went on and on, with people almost queuing up to take turns at this symbol of modern priorities, until she was visibly shaken, her hair in disarray, her glasses slightly skew-whiff on her nose.

Half an hour later she rang me: 'I have to say I was unaware of the strength of feeling surrounding this issue, and have decided to reprieve the tea bar for a further two weeks while we investigate its viability.'

As the word went round the whole floor buzzed. It was the tiniest of victories but people felt buoyed up. They pledged to spend the next two weeks haranguing the Hattie Jacques woman until she guaranteed the tea bar's future.

Without the union's assistance, we bombarded the catering manager with e-mails and letters, but this time they stuck by their decision, although they did at least give the two women jobs in another canteen, rather than sacking them as they'd proposed to start with. In the global framework in which entire villages are destroyed to make way for oil pipelines and whole provinces are left without clean water as the supply is privatised, the tea bar incident seems to be at the trivial end of the spectrum. And yet it's the same philosophy as that which wrecks the African village and ruins the Mexican landless labourers. The people with the clipboards see the world from a different angle from the people who pour the tea. They don't have a space on their balance sheet for the jokes, the warmth, the humanity that is the essence of life. They simply can't comprehend why the rest of us can't see that every corner has to be thoroughly searched for errant items that aren't justifying themselves with profit, so that anything left alive simply because it brings a spark to its neighbours has to hide in fear from the clipboards, like an economic Anne Frank.

It was a typical tale for our times because the traditional organisation for protecting the vulnerable against the bully, the trade union, was useless. It's as if *they* believe nothing can be done to halt the march of profit, so they see anything that is being done as a nuisance. And it's still true that without a vibrant union, success against the onslaught of the clipboards is a much tougher prospect.

But the story also displays the obstacles to the clipboard. Most people are appalled at this way of operating, now more than ever. Most of the time they're quietly and abstractly appalled, but when confronted with it in their own life, many feel they have an opportunity to shout back. So they draw up the petition, scream at the manager, organise the meeting and confront the apparent invincibility of Costa Coffee or Tesco.

And there lies the defence against the transformation of every space into a soulless corporate monument. The crowd in the tea-bar photo had something in common with Gertruida Baartman, a fruit-picker in South Africa on a farm that supplies Tesco. She earns 30 pence an hour, and the pickers are obliged to call the farm owner 'Master'. Through the anti-poverty group Action Aid, she bought a single share in the company so she could attend Tesco's annual general meeting and speak about the outrageous conditions on the farm. One year later she was asked if this had had any effect. She said one thing had changed for the better – the pickers were no longer forced into the orchards immediately after the crops had been sprayed with pesticides, which meant handling wet dangerous chemicals. But her stand had led to victimisation. She was sacked, though a campaign (this time led by the union) won back her job. And she said, 'In the past the farmer provided transport for my brother, who is in a wheelchair, when he needed to go to the doctor. But when I spoke out they took this away.'

Robbing us of our soul is a new reason to distrust big business. But that's not to say the traditional reason for distrusting them, they're a bunch of vicious bastards, isn't still as valid as ever.

7

WHERE DID YOU SLEEP LAST NIGHT?

I realised my life was in trouble when I started envying couples who had normal ferocious rows. They would be sitting opposite each other on a train, he fuming ahead, lips tight together, breathing heavily through his nose, while she turned each page of a magazine with a violent flick as if swatting away a strange green insect, when without looking up she would snarl, 'I can't BELIEVE you're going to Dublin on my mum's sixtieth, Sean, you bastard.' He'd give it two more snorts and a fume and splutter, 'He's my mate, right.' And I'd think, 'Aah how sweet.'

Because my rows had no logic and no plot, if anyone had overheard them, they'd have complained 'I didn't enjoy that, there was no beginning, middle or end.' They'd get going with an abstract complaint, such as 'Oh yes, that's TYPICAL' and move rapidly on to random complaints such as 'How DARE you? You couldn't even stand my CAT.'

Worse, there was no discernible pattern. A row was as likely to kick off in the midst of a jolly afternoon as any time I'd been disgraceful. For example, I discovered a local pub that boasted the only lock-in that truly lived up to its name. Around half past eleven, the bulky corrugated curtains would be ceremonially drawn across every window, hefty bolts would be shoved across the door as if we were expecting a medieval siege, and you were locked in. One night, around 3.00 a.m., in the flickering dim orange light, I staggered to the door with a friend, where we hovered, waiting to be let out like dogs. And the huge Irish landlord grabbed us both round the waist and with mischievous anticipation asked 'Will you not have one last little whisky before you go, boys?' My friend looked in his eyes and said, 'This is the only pub I've ever been to where *I* have to say to the landlord "Haven't you got a home to go to?"' 'Araaa haaa eeeee,' said the landlord, and reluctantly released us.

On these nights I'd arrive home, do the drunk's trick of locating the only metal object in the house and clattering into it, and be greeted with 'Oh hello, what time is it? Blimey, that's a late one, did you have a nice time?' And I'd think, 'No – NOW you're supposed to be surly, then sulk all day tomorrow before ending with a flourish of invective, while I pout with shame like a 1960s schoolboy who's been caught wanking in the sandpit by the headmaster. Go berserk NOW while you've got reasonable grounds. Throw one of the records I never play such as the second Arrested Development album out of the window as a gesture. Burn my socks, throw a chunk of cheese at me, but do it soon when there's a discernible reason.'

Instead all would be calm. And it would stay calm, so I'd begin to wonder whether I'd exaggerated our rows in my mind, the way you see the innocent-looking birds at the end of the Hitchcock film, and think 'They CAN'T be the same ones that caused havoc a few hours ago.' Then somehow we'd dissolve into a cacophony of snarls concerning an issue such as car parking or a lost piece of toast.

However you seek to cope with this situation, it's hard to find a method that doesn't involve drowning in animosity until all parties are exhausted. Sometimes a session would start about ten at night, so that during the odd gap I'd catch a bit of *Newsnight*. As such, I must be the only person who's ever found Charles Clarke or Ann Widdecombe a spot of welcome relief. One night, when we'd rowed and rowed until I was drained, I threw the towel in and drove off in submission to the Purley Way in search of a hotel.

The Purley Way is another symbol of twenty-first-century Britain, engineering plants having been replaced with a row of vast oblong stores where people spend their Sundays trying to buy settees or inkjet printers from overkeen young black men in their twenties wearing crisp red shirts. During the day the functional nature of the place is offset by people pushing vast shopping trolleys containing one huge box, but at night there's nothing moving, nothing human or unpredictable to distract from the still, soulless, franchised presence of this creepy stretch of road. At the far end, opposite the site of the old airport, there's the Jury's Inn, a hotel version of the stores lining the rest of the road, that ought to be called 'World of Sleep'. I parked in the drizzle and walked past a man with a red face slurring into his phone, the last survivor of a reception for a conference of carpet designers. And I'm thinking, 'I shouldn't be in the middle of this sort of turmoil, standing in the foyer of the Jury's Inn as a refuge from nocturnal yelling, I'm FORTY. And I'm sometimes on the telly.'

'We're fully booked, I'm afraid,' said the girl in the dark blue suit, without looking up from her papers. So I got back in the car and set off for the hotels at Gatwick.

Somehow this is all so much worse once you're in your forties. Firstly, because you feel by now life ought to be calm. Surely this sort of scenario doesn't happen once you've got a mortgage, and certainly not if you've been on *Question Time*.

Television Centre can be a surreal place to work. For example, one day I found myself having a slash next to Peter Snow. For a moment I was tempted to shout 'Bloody hell, it's Peter Snow' or do an impression of him excitedly gesticulating and exclaiming, 'Let's see what might happen to this slash over the next few seconds – ALL this side of the urinal should stay dry but LOOK AT THIS BIT IN THE MIDDLE – ABSOLUTELY SOAKED.'

One morning there were two workmen in brown overalls,

acting as if they were doing the most normal bit of labouring in the world despite the fact they were carrying an eight-foot pepper pot. Occasionally they'd stop for a cigarette and a chat, then off they'd go with a 'Got it up your end, Steve?', probably to deliver the prop to a French and Saunders sketch about Gulliver's Travels.

More freakily, I was once on a programme with Joan Collins, and as we chatted afterwards I kept thinking, 'Don't ever get to a point in life where you think being in a room with Joan Collins is normal.'

But all that was put in the shade compared to the evening I left the building and spotted the figure of Bob Monkhouse. The epitome of all that my generation of comics had tried to replace, a permanent eruption of false showbiz cheesiness, supporter of Margaret Thatcher in the 1980s – there he was, just twenty yards away in the car park. It seemed odd that he could be there, in person, existing, the way other people do. Then he looked across and came towards me. Five yards away he smiled, as if he was about to say, 'And up against the Davies family this week is Mark Steel's family. Welcome to the show.' Instead he said, 'Mark Steel, I'm *so* pleased to meet you.' While I tried to figure out a response he added, 'I *loved* your book *Reasons to be Cheerful*. It was given to me as a seventy-fifth birthday present by Jeremy Beadle.'

What was he going to say next? Would he tell me he was planning to sing my article about the war in Yugoslavia as a duet with Bruce Forsyth? Actually he asked me about the miners' strike while I asked him about *The Golden Shot*, and at one point he said, 'I know we disagree about politics, but I'm afraid that was all down to a condition that made me find Margaret Thatcher sexually attractive.' And he delivered the words 'sexually attractive' as a punchline, turning his head to one side, as if he were completing the joke into a special close-up camera, the way he did on *Celebrity Squares*.

There's something undeniably flattering about being acknowledged by someone so well known, no matter who it is. I'm sure if Robert Mugabe sent me a letter saying how much he'd enjoyed a programme I'd done on Radio 4, my first thought would be, 'Oo that's nice.'

But there was something more than that with Bob. He was interested in the French Revolution, especially the motives of Charlotte Corday,* and he was fascinated by the modern comedy scene. So we met up again, and he talked at length about his worst gigs, and New Labour, and the impact of Richard Pryor. Later I saw him do a talk in the back room of a pub in which he started by listing all the shows he'd presented, then said, 'In other words I've been responsible for more shit on British television than anyone else.' He knew he was in the advanced stages of cancer, but cheerfully told a joke about the ego of a comic being such that he was delighted when he passed an undertakers' and saw a poster of himself on the door under the words 'Coming soon'. And eventually I had to own up to myself that I *liked* him.

This was slightly disconcerting, maybe similar to when someone first comes to terms with the realisation that they enjoy being beaten with a broom. Where would this end – a weekend of scuba-diving with Jimmy Tarbuck? I don't think it was that I forgave Bob's support for Thatcher or his sickly false quiz show bonhomie, but that I realised there was much more to him than that. He was clearly fascinated by history and philosophy and gloried in the darkness and mischief of comedy, therefore must have felt compromised to some extent by his public persona. His amicable nature seemed *so* genuine, it was as if he was making up for all those moments of 'Oh Elsie, I want you to get that new kitchen, I really really do.'

The gradual realisation that humanity is nowhere near as black and white as you once thought, and that the unlikeliest people can surprise you as he did, adds an inspiring element to the process of getting older. But it also makes it even more confusing. Maybe subconsciously I was wondering, given that someone I'd derided

---

*She murdered the revolutionary hero Jean-Paul Marat. I'd suggest a book that could give you more information, if only I could think of one.

so comprehensively as Bob Monkhouse turned out to be a welcome companion, who else I had prematurely written off in the past. We pledged to get together again soon, but a few weeks later he died, and I was genuinely sad, to the point of feeling I should shed a fake tear in his honour.

One of the shocking aspects of becoming forty that I hadn't fully appreciated was that once you get to that age it doesn't stop. You carry on getting *even older than that*. There follows another age, called forty-one, then forty-two and each one comes round quicker than the last. You talk to a friend about the day you all went to Southend and played cricket under the biggest pier in the country, saying, 'Blimey, that must be five years ago now.' Then you work it out and realise it was in 1989. There are endless shocks, such as the fact that the bloke who presents the news is younger than you. Which can't be true. He's middle-aged and grown up and says grown-up things like 'That's all from us, there'll be more on our evening bulletin at ten o'clock. Good night.' I can't be *older than him*. And the same age as people with jobs like secretary of the FA and economic spokesman for the Liberal Democrats.

If you have kids you're also *forced* to be sensible. When my son was thrown off a bus by a grumpy driver and plotted a revenge that could have been a screenplay for *Die Hard*, I found myself saying, 'The best revenge is to forget about it. Remember, you only have to put up with his grumpiness for one moment, but he has to go around with it twenty-four hours a day.'

And then there's the logistics of it all. Kids are life-affirming, life-defining conveyors of all your hopes but they also make life relentlessly complicated. It is not primarily the effort to raise them with a decent set of values, but simply the problem of what to do with them. Every morning outside most schools parents are involved in intricate negotiations. 'If you pick up Jenny and keep her until half past four, Tina will pick up her and Oscar and give them and Nathan some pizza while taking her aerobics class, then my mum should be able to have them from six because the hospital says she should be out of her coma by then and she'll drop them off with Eileen at the brothel as she gets an hour off between seven and eight, then David should have finished at the site and can bring them all back in his wheelbarrow.'

Even after you've dropped them at school in the morning you dread getting a call that goes, 'You'll have to come and collect your son as he's been sick in the corridor.' And they take no account of the fact you might be working. You could say, 'But I'm flying a Boeing 757 full of passengers to Manila' and they'd reply, 'Well, you'll have to make an emergency landing, we do have a strict "sending home" policy following vomit.'

What are you supposed to do with them? Most workplaces act as if having children is a peculiar hobby. If you say, 'I've GOT to leave at five to pick the kids up,' you might as well have said you've got to get back to feed your octopus or 'I HAVE to get home by six because that's when I have my wank.'

Somehow we've arrived at a culture in which children, which define and shape more people's lives than anything else, are treated as an irritating intrusion. They're hard to find a place for in a culture driven by profit because they really aren't very profitable. When an individual's success is measured by wealth and status, kids can only be a drawback. Perhaps it's a similar accounting of everyone's value as if they were a share price that's inspired the tsunami of vitriol hurled at the modern teenager.

Historians of the future might come across the complaints made about today's youth and conclude that the country was under siege from marauding gangs of 'hoodies', probably descended from the tribes of Genghis Khan. To prove the connection, someone will declare they've found evidence that the Mongol warriors terrorised Asia by sweeping into villages, then leaning on mountain bikes by the fountain in the Arndale Centre and mumbling 'I'm bored bruv' at which point the entire local tribe would flee.

Their chosen weapon, the hood, must be one of the most

harmless objects ever to cause mass terror. It's made of cloth. It's true that some young people in hoods are rude and intimidating, but it would be just as easy to generalise about old people in caps. Who hasn't been a victim of these 'cappies', blocking up post offices, driving in the exact middle of the road at fourteen miles an hour, then pulling out without looking, on their way to sit by the window in a Wetherspoons pub from half past ten in the morning – haven't they got anything useful to do? Their dogs mess in the park, and if you kick a ball into their garden they don't let you retrieve it, probably so they can sell it and buy bottled Guinness.

The most tragic side to this issue is that the people most venomous about hoodies seem to be my own generation, we who had exactly the same cobblers said about us during the punk years. I never even dressed as a punk but I remember older people growling 'tut, tut disgraceful' loudly as they walked past, while staring in horror as if I was eating a live cat. It was as if they were saying, 'We fought in a war and they have the cheek to be sixteen. When we were that age we had to be thirty-five, otherwise we got a belt off our dad.'

Now it's my generation's turn to grumble like that: 'We may have sung "Anarchy in the UK" but we always respected our elders – not like the yobs of today.' I'm sure one day I'll hear an old punk say, 'This hip-hop they listen to isn't proper music, you can hear all the words.'

This is why I felt uneasy one day when about twenty men were sitting in that midweek slouch in my local pub, occasionally breaking the silence to fire jokey insults at each other through the gloom, and Pretty Vacant came on the jukebox. Suddenly there were fists pounding on the tables, rattling the pints of Adnams, as the bald and the paunched yelled in unison, 'We're so pretty oh so perrretty – a-vaya-cant.' It felt awful, because whereas this had once been a scream of defiance to the future, now it was a yearning for a lost time. Of course we should cherish the culture of our youth, especially the rebellious stuff that ignited our hopes, but once the subplot is 'those were the days' it becomes conservative, whatever the content.

There's even a trend among some punks and rebels of old to add to the sneering against modern youth, lamenting that 'youngsters of today don't rebel like we did.' Yet the number of young people who have marched or protested in some way, who engage with the ideas of figures such as John Pilger and Michael Moore, who abhor bigotry against foreigners or gays, is far greater than in the 1970s. The problem, beyond the cycle of youths turning into their parents, may be that while a smaller percentage of my generation may have thought rebelliously, those of us who did were *organised*. From 1970 to the end of the miners' strike, youthful dissidence formed organisations such as Rock Against Racism that met, campaigned, produced papers and put on bands, creating structures that, even if they didn't change society for ever, often transformed the people in them for ever. Today the rebelliousness of youth is scattered and sporadic, making it less effective and giving the false impression that it is not there at all.

And while it's true they've now got Ipods, X-box 360s, Facebook and a choice of ringtones, the young of today also have tuition fees, interviews almost every day if they're on the dole more than a fortnight, homework from the age of eight, SATs and ASBOs.* Maybe when they're sitting by the fountain in the Arndale Centre, they rub their hoods and snarl, 'Kids of the seventies, they didn't know they were born.'

---

*I don't wish to dismiss the unpleasant effects of teenage crime – obviously if a truant schoolboy burns your house down that is a nuisance – but it's becoming increasingly clear ASBOs are not always helping. For example, a lawyer told me he'd been approached by a teenager who'd been issued with an ASBO for 'being sarcastic'. Now, apart from anything else, surely a conversation between the police and someone being illegally sarcastic would go on for ever, wouldn't it?

'Ah, think we're clever being sarcastic, do we?'

'Go on then, officer, arrest me for it, *that* should keep the streets safe.'

'Oo doing it again, *like* spending the night in a police cell, do we?'

'I do as long as I'm in there with *you* and your sparkling wit, officer.'

8

THERE IS A GREAT DEAL OF MONEY TO BE MADE, SIR

One essential requisite for politicians is to revere new technology, to be seen beaming as they test a revolutionary piece of software that will enable schoolkids to actually experience being Alexander the Great as he burned down a village. In one of his conference speeches Tony Blair concluded a section on 'rapid technological progress' with the words 'because the world changes, we have to change with it' – whereupon the audience clapped and cheered. As if there was ever a chance he might have said, 'I never worked out how to use the video, so I'm buggered if I'm bothering with a DVD.'

Drifting through your forties you're tempted to become sceptical about this rapid progress, and despair at the use it's put to. E-mail seems to be mostly a means whereby office workers can send out messages like 'In future can people PLEASE take only one Malteser at a time' or 'Does anyone know where I put my elastic band?'

Similarly, You Tube could have a million uses, but the most common one appears to be to enable schoolboys to shriek, 'Have you seen "Man gets leg eaten by piranhas"? It's *jokes* man, 'im WELL mash up.'

Internet forums can be compelling, but often in the same way as cable TV, a constant source of pointless amazement. Sometimes

I've had the disconcerting experience of trawling through a discussion to find people talking about me. One day I saw someone had written 'The only way I'd ever find Mark Steel funny was if he was being stabbed to death with shards of AIDS-infected glass.' Which shocked me for about three seconds until I became immensely proud. Imagine annoying anyone that much, that if they saw someone about to stab you to death with glass, they'd shout 'Have those shards got AIDS on them? NO! What are you, his FAN or something? Now go away and don't come back until they're covered with AIDS. I want him to be stabbed to death and then catch AIDS after he's dead, so he won't even be able to go to the doctor's to get drugs for it.'

Almost every one of these forums, whether run by football supporters or political activists, tends to degenerate into reams of abuse between the same twenty people who never seem to sleep. There's probably an astrophysicists' forum in which every thread ends with someone calling themselves Collapsed Star posting. 'So – Quantum Boy upholds the possibility of string theory in a parallel universe. Why aren't I surprised? Face up to it, your theories are anti-matter, you tosspot sub-atomic loser.'

But the internet was adopted in its early days by a certain type of radical. It provided an unprecedented freedom to exchange information, they enthused, so we'd be in the best position ever to know what was really going on in governments and corporations, or among groups we'd previously no knowledge of. There was the potential, apparently, for rapid contact across the world, so protests could be coordinated like never before. I was utterly cynical. I argued this technology couldn't be a substitute for the face-to-face contact, the 3-D discussions and debates of real life. To organise or even simply launch a campaign, or sustain a movement you had to have meetings of real people in their human and not virtual forms.

But then I'd meet students, or indeed postmen, who in the midst of a conversation would say, 'You know this new plant in the Philippines . . .' I'd try to look as if I did indeed know, though I didn't have a clue. 'You know,' they'd reiterate, the way you might if someone looked puzzled when you mentioned Elvis Presley, 'the nuclear plant backed by the US import-export bank by the side of a volcano.' I wasn't used to this, bumping into random individuals who were reading stuff I didn't know about. What were they thinking of?

Towards the end of the 1990s thousands of people became familiar with Subcomandante Marcos, the poet and spokesperson for the Zapatistas in Mexico, the group that sparked an uprising against the sale of rural land jointly owned by the people of the Chiapas region. Marcos posted his poems and articles on the internet, which helped to make the Zapatistas the centre of global radical interest.

At a couple of meetings of trade unionists and students I spoke about the unfairness of capitalism, people fired off questions about what I thought would happen to the Zapatistas. Everyone nodded as if to say, 'Ah yes, the Zapatistas. We're fascinated to know how Mark feels they're likely to progress, as he must be far better informed than us, who haven't read their reports since half past four this afternoon. Come on, Mark, what's the latest?' And I had to waffle about the Zapatistas proving that people still had a brilliant spirit and could still be good but governments could be dreadful, then change the sub-ject on to something I knew about such as cricket.

I felt like a father who teaches his son how to play football, and when the boy displays skills he has learned from someone else, gets annoyed: 'You're not supposed to know that yet – now STOP it.'

Then came a march through London called 'Stop the City', in which protesters caused havoc in the City of London. And none of the activists I'd known for many years had any idea this was being planned, because it had been organised through the internet.*

*In truth I did know one person who was there that day, but he was one of the bankers who'd worked in the City. What did THAT do for my mid-life anti-establishment crisis? I had a nightmare that the day would come when someone would ask if I'd heard about the details of a huge demonstration and I'd say, 'Oh yes – because I was having

After that came a series of exuberant demonstrations, such as the one in which the statue of Winston Churchill had a piece of turf placed on his head to make it look as if he had a green Mohican haircut. It's hard to imagine a single act that could be better designed to infuriate the *Daily Mail*. Kidnap the Queen and force her to perform 'Young Black Male' by Tupac Shakur as if she was on *Stars in Their Eyes*? Spike Tim Henman's barley water with ecstasy just before the final set of a match on centre court at Wimbledon. And the expectation of these protests, from both supporters and those outraged by them, was that they would build to a grand finale in which the windows of McDonald's would be summarily destroyed. If that didn't happen it felt like going to see The Who in 1967 on a night they didn't smash up their instruments.

These protests weren't against anything in particular, they were just referred to as 'anti-capitalist'. Causes were taken up – such as the plight of the Ogoni people in Nigeria, whose villages were being destroyed by a Shell oil pipeline, or the imprisonment on Death Row of the Black Panther Mumia Abu-Jamal – that would once have been noticed by few people outside the Far Left. This was even more true about the sinister machinations of the World Trade Organization, the World Bank and the International Monetary Fund. Throughout my life the only people who knew about the International Monetary Fund were economists, bankers and socialists. Suddenly these bodies became the targets of mass international protest.

In 2000, Naomi Klein's *No Logo* sold over 100,000 copies in Britain, and among the best-selling books of the year were

lunch with the Chief Constable of Manchester.' To be fair, the banker, who was absurdly posh, had resigned a few months earlier and was now skint and living on a mate's settee, having been thrown out by his wife. He'd arranged to meet some old colleagues for a drink, and was then charged at by a crowd of spiky anarchists demanding to know how much he earned. In his words, 'So I suggested they might be somewhat surprised, and offered to swap their salary for mine. They were pretty scornful at first, but when I informed them of the paltry level of benefits I was existing on, they were flabbergasted I can tell you. They turned out to be jolly decent and one of them bought me a drink.'

Globalize this!, *Globalization and Resistance* and *Resist Globalization.* It seemed before long all the permutations would be used up and books would have titles like *Resisting Globalising Corporate Trans-corporate Globo Globalisingness.*

Not all of this could be down to the growth of the internet. Around the world there was a growing recognition that when vast corporations move into Africa or South America or India to set up business, they don't always have the population's interest at heart.

To take just one example: the government of Tanzania applied to the IMF for help to fund its debt. The IMF kindly agreed, with a few terms, one of which was that Tanzania should privatise its water supply. The water companies that won the contract (Biwater International, Gauff Ingenieure and Superdoll Trailers) tried to persuade the Tanzanians that the privatisation would help them. Through the Adam Smith Institute, a media campaign costing £430,000 (of public money) publicised the joys of private water, including a pop song with the lyrics 'Young plants need rain, businesses need investment. Our old industries are like dry crops and privatisation brings the rain.' Which is probably now a favourite at Tanzanian weddings, after 'Daydream Believer'.

Water became crucial to economic and political power. In South Africa 10 million people had their supply cut off following privatisation in 1994. In Argentina a water company became so despised that a referendum was held in Santa Fe as to whether it should be evicted from the area; 230,000 said it should go and 434 said it should stay. It stayed anyway.

This happens because in the world of finance water isn't water, it's business. Walter Lewin, head of investment bank Credit Suisse, told a conference in 2007, 'We believe investors will embrace this opportunity to invest in the companies that are involved in one of the world's most vital industries – the provision of fresh water. Water is the world's third largest industry after oil and electricity, and you also have the very positive price dynamic, a limited global supply and increasing global demand.' Or he could have said, more succinctly, 'There's less and less of it and the fuckers can't do without it, we can't lose.' Because there is another way of phrasing 'limited global supply and increasing global demand' which is that one billion people have no access to clean water, causing around 50,000 deaths per day. Still, we can't all be winners, can we?

The journal *Business Week* (and the title provides a clue as to whether it generally supports the aims of business) announced in a 'special report' in 2000: 'The plain truth is that market liberalisation has caused severe damage. What's more, there's no point in denying that multinationals have contributed to labour, environmental and human rights abuses.'

An example of this was the system of 'user fees', whereby the IMF and World Bank could force countries by law to charge for schools and hospitals. Which led to reports such as the one from UNICEF that told of a 14-year-old boy in Zambia with malaria who was turned away from a clinic because he hadn't the registration fee of thirty-three cents, and two hours later was brought back dead.

Fortunately the World Bank strategy didn't always lead to such stinginess. They did provide $60 million to Coca Cola as 'political risk insurance' to help it set up shop in the bits of Africa it still hadn't conquered.

Stories such as this weren't one-off flights of madness, but part of a strategy by the leaders of corporations and governments to mould the world into the free market model they desired. The World Trade Organization was set up in 1995 with the aim, they said, of 'liberalising trade'. For example, the WTO prevent 'errant' governments allowing goods to be sold at a lower price than the WTO had set. So the logic is that it's in everyone's interest to spread the rules of the free market, as that's the only way to ensure everyone gains access to the necessities of life. Which means that if people gain access to the necessities of life cheaper than the free market dictates, they must have them taken away, otherwise they'll disrupt the laws of the free market and won't be able to get hold of the necessities of life.

The writer Eamonn McCann, when we were discussing this one drunken December night, declared, 'Surely the WTO will have to take stringent measures against Santa. How dare he subvert the natural prices of the toy market by flooding the economy with free gifts?'

The chillingly rational irrationality of the WTO was only an extension of the way capitalism had behaved for centuries, but it was an unashamed drive to ratify the logic of profit on an unprecedented global scale. And now, through the internet, the details of the world elite's machinations can be spread round the world in an instant, as can details of those who were opposing them.

It may be the process was accelerated because, to the teenager of the year 2000, the rest of the world was closer than ever before. I'm still impressed with travel in a way today's generation finds baffling. If someone tells me they're going to Portugal the next day, I'll say, '*Are* you? To *Portugal*? Bloody hell, that's exciting.' And they'll look as if I've misheard them and imagine they've said they're riding across the Indian Ocean on the back of a whale. 'It's only to Portugal,' they'll say. 'The company I work for has an office there and I go twice a month.' And I must look how my granny did, when in the 1970s she still pointed every time she saw a plane.

When I was twenty and read about the victims of wickedness in Nicaragua or Bhopal, I thought 'oh those poor people'. I supported them, but they occupied a world that was mine only through a series of loose connections. Only the most adventurous actually visited such places, and you had to be acutely aware of their plight in the first place before attending a meeting at which someone from the region would speak. But now average British 20-year-olds feel Morocco or Mexico is part of their world. If they've not been there yet they expect to go sometime and they'll know people who have. It's much easier to identify with a landless Mexican peasant if you know you can e-mail them at any moment. One of the ironies of globalisation is that it created the possibility of a globalised anti-globalisation movement.

For a while, there were regular international demonstrations against the IMF, the WTO and the World Bank whose meetings had to be cordoned off behind armoured cars and water canon, lest they were besieged by protesters.

While on holiday in Athens in 2000 I was contacted by a group that was aware of articles I'd written, through the internet, and asked if I would speak at a meeting of 'anti-capitalist protest'. Based on experience, I expected to be in a room in the back of a bar, probably double-booked with a Greek weightlifting club. But I was taken to an open-air theatre, where around 700 people sat beneath bats fluttering above clicking crickets before a backdrop of lights flickering from the Acropolis. Huge speakers flanked the entrance, from which what I presume was radical Greek folk music rattled out in that crackly European sound that reminds you of football commentaries from abroad in the 1970s.

I spoke about Tony Blair and the free market and war, and a translator repeated what I'd said. When I told a joke, if it worked well I got a laugh from those who spoke English and then another one from those who didn't when the translator finished translating. And such is the ego of the comic that at the end of this wonderful experience, a symbol of a flourishing movement for humanity against profit and war, I sat on the steps beneath the bats grumpily thinking, 'That last joke should have got a bigger laugh than that the second time round – I bet the bloody translator fucked it up.'

As long as the anti-globalisation movement was meeting and marching and publishing books I was on steady ground with it all. But there were strands of this movement I couldn't help but feel uneasy about. For example, there was the emphasis on boycotting goods from companies that were deemed especially rotten.

Stickers popped up on railway stations asking you not to buy anything from Esso or Nike or Gap or Microsoft or Nestlé and other institutions exposed as globally misbehaving. The first problem with this, it seemed, is that a company as vast as Esso is hardly likely to notice the loss of profits caused by a few thousand activists buying petrol up the road instead. And there's the implication that, for example, Adidas trainers, because they're not the subject of a boycott, are made by a company that is perfectly decent. Most unsettling of all was the sense that this wasn't an attempt to curtail the practices of the multinationals, that its main aim was to make the person doing the boycotting feel better about themselves.

There's nothing wrong in behaving like that, which is why we all do it to some extent. I was so angered by a rude local newsagent that I didn't go in there for ten years, even though after four years it had changed hands and was now owned by entirely different people. I was so pathetically stubborn that even if it had been demolished and reopened as a go-kart shop and I desperately needed a go-kart, I'd have gone to the next one, somewhere in Coventry instead.

But this is hardly a strategy for reducing the misery these global brands can inflict on the planet. If the main threat to the likes of Nike and Esso is collective action, such as mass marches, rallies and strikes protesting against their inhumanity, the boycott seems to be the opposite, an individual act designed to satisfy yourself that child labour in the Philippines is nothing to do with you.

Similarly, I'd hear of stunts such as buying a handful of shares in order to attend a shareholders' meeting of a company to ask the board embarrassing questions the way Gertrude Baartman did at Tesco. My response would be to giggle politely. This may be fun, but that's all, as with the stunts of direct action groups, such as those that chained themselves to the Docklands Light Railway to prevent arms dealers getting from their hotels to an arms fair. I'd admire the audacity but doubt what could be gained, as the arms fair was sure to go ahead anyway.

There was also the growth of groups such as the International Solidarity Movement, a heroic bunch that went to Palestine and sat in hospitals and schools, the idea being that the Israelis were less likely to fire if these places were occupied by a handful of crusties from Surrey listening to Orbital on an Ipod.

It was all courageous and spirited, but none of it seemed designed to build a mass movement. This wasn't the sneer of a cynical disillusioned ex-activist, as I'd always been uncertain about the merits of these methods. In the 1980s I was extremely sceptical about the value of refusing to buy South African grapes and oranges as a tool for dismantling apartheid. That didn't mean I'd ever break the boycott, but it seemed an irrelevance compared to mass marches and an uprising within South Africa.

And now I carried this sentiment towards many of the anti-globalisation activists. For example, Helen Steel and Dave Morris distributed a pamphlet about McDonald's, pointing out that they were responsible for pollution, cruelty to animals and serving food that was full of chemicals. Had I bumped into them the day before, I'd have commended their spirit but suggested that to really get back at McDonald's they should take part in building a mass movement against all the polluting multinationals. Certainly no SWP branch would ever decide members should stand in a street distributing information about the levels of filth in a mass-produced apple pie. Where could such a protest go?

McDonald's weren't so blasé about the pamphlet, though. They took the authors to court and became embroiled in a celebrated legal battle that caused this apparently invincible symbol of a corporate planet immense international embarrassment. The marking of McDonald's as a particularly repugnant example of globalisation forced them on to the defensive, to the extent that they started to include in their menu a 'salad option', in an attempt to re-market themselves as purveyors of healthy wholesome meals.

If there's one branch of the corporate planet more ruthless than the burger business it's the arms trade, and in recent years they've also, as a result of this style of campaigning, been put on to the back foot. Partly this is because they have to, in Britain, maintain that they're *honourable* arms dealers and would never knowingly sell laser-guided missiles that incinerate their target on impact to anyone who might use them to do harm. When, for example,

Britain sold tanks to the Indonesian army, we assured anyone concerned that they were to be used for peaceful purposes. Maybe the army there spends most of its time making giant pies for hungry villagers and the tanks are the only things that can roll that amount of pastry.

The company EDO MBM make guidance systems for the F16 bombers used by the Israeli airforce to drop bombs on the occupied Palestinian territories. But in 2006 a campaign of weekly protests outside the factory making these things in Brighton caused the company sufficient embarrassment that they took out an injunction against the protesters. (This included banning anyone who'd been at the protest from walking near the home of anyone who worked at the factory, although they weren't to be told the addresses they couldn't walk near. Thus they sought the world's first transcendental injunction, in which hundreds of people would have to accept that 'The place I'm not allowed to go near is – somewhere.') But the protests intensified, the court case brought by the company collapsed, and the plant recorded a loss of £2 million which it blamed on 'legal costs', resulting in the managing director getting the sack.

Reed-Elsevier, the company that staged the annual London Arms Fair (it sounds so innocent), announced in June 2007 they were abandoning this line of business because 'It is becoming increasingly clear that a growing number of important customers have very real concerns about our involvement in the defence exhibitions business.'

What caused them to back down? Maybe it was the protests or the countless letters and complaints. It might have been the student at Loughborough University who won a £2,000 literary prize, but discovered the award was sponsored by BAE Systems, so denounced them in his acceptance speech and sent the money to Campaign Against the Arms Trade. Or it might have been my friend Jim's son, who worked for a company providing corporate hospitality and had never shown the faintest interest in political ideas, but when he was offered the job of organising hospitality at the London Arms Fair, told his employers he wanted nothing to do with such trading in death and refused to do it.

In Palestine, the Israeli army did refrain from firing indiscriminately in areas where the International Solidarity Movement members were stationed (though eventually they did kill Rachel Corrie with a bulldozer).

In all these cases the activists had been able to impose themselves only because there was a wider movement and an international groundswell of opinion in their favour. The mass of the confused, with their distaste for the values of our times, applauds the activists, the leafleteers, the splendidly eccentric peace protester covered in badges who's lived for years opposite the House of Commons, and that converts an individual protest into something more potent. Local communities write letters backing them, they're voted heroes in radio and television polls and juries refuse to convict them. But without their wonderfully eccentric and imaginative actions, the humiliations inflicted and the retreats forced on these powerful bodies wouldn't have happened. There was no disguising the fact that my initial scepticism was wrong, just as it had been wrong on the boycott of apartheid fruit. There were limitations to these victories. The arms dealers won't be decisively put out of business by a direct action stunt, or if they are it would have to be a bloody good one. But in a small way they've been forced, by people I would once have dismissed, to check back from the unbridled drive for profit to take account of the requirements of human beings.

The traditional animosity between left-wing groups seemed to thaw in the first years of the new century. Several of them got together to form the Socialist Alliance and stand in elections, and in Scotland the SWP joined the Scottish Socialist Party. To those not familiar with the habits of the Far Left this may not appear very special, but ten years earlier it didn't seem possible such groups could ever work together without the sort of process the ceasefire went through in Northern Ireland, with a panel of ex-

US senators and retired generals observing the gradual dismantling of all hostile leaflets.

The Scottish Socialist Party was a rare success. Tommy Sheridan, a well-known member of Militant, became prominent in Scotland as leader of the campaign against the poll tax, and was arrested on demonstrations against the nuclear base at Faslane. At that time Militant seemed to be at permanent war with the SWP. They would speak about us with such contempt, an outsider would have assumed the SWP was the ruling military junta. The SWP in return called publicly for unity and comradeship, then in private called them a bunch of wankers. I reckon I must have said on average once a day for twenty years, 'Oh for fuck's sake, have you seen what the Militant's done now?' But then Tommy Sheridan formed the Scottish Socialist Party, and was elected to the Scottish parliament, where he became one of the most popular and best known political figures in the country.

In the 2003 elections for the Scottish parliament, the SSP won 7 per cent of the total vote, getting six people elected, and this despite being marginalised in the media to the extent of being included in 'Other parties', along with the Fishing Party.

I spoke at several SSP events over the next year, each time inspired by the fact that a party based on socialist principles had attained a level of popularity that couldn't be contained round a pool table. Nor was their growth simply about elections, as they led a wide number of campaigns, including the movement against the war in Iraq. In general it seemed that other methods of campaigning and organising had succeeded, where those I identified with had not.

In my confusion at this realisation, I found myself listening to people from a variety of campaigns, movements and parties, and *really* listening, not just to argue with them, but saying 'Hmm, I think you're right'. This was a weird sensation, like your first joint or how I imagine you feel the day you become a Buddhist.

Not every aspect of the anti-globalisation movement made me so confused. Make Poverty History, for example, did a magnificent job of mobilising the people most appalled that poverty is not yet history, but its faultlines were clear to see. In every campaign you want to extend the breadth of support as wide as possible, and sometimes you may be uncertain as to where you should draw the line. But you should always know to draw the line before Mariah fucking Carey. Whatever else the poor are lacking, surely they retain their right to a smidgen of dignity, and you've been robbed of that once a concert to publicise your plight includes Mariah fucking Carey. She probably thinks if Africa isn't getting enough money it ought to sack its agent.

Somehow they managed to trump that, and as a guest speaker at the Make Poverty History concert there was Bill Gates, probably the richest man in the world. Surely, surely, this was a joke, like a comedy sketch in which the speaker at an anti-racist festival comes on in a white hood with a burning cross.

The hundreds of thousands who marched at the G8 summit in Edinburgh were clearly not of the Mariah Carey wing of the movement. The belief that world poverty is the result of uncaring Western business became so accepted that Western businessmen were forced to defend themselves publicly in ways they clearly weren't used to. Each evening on *Newsnight* a spokesman from an organisation with a name like the Inter-Galactic Forum for Fiscal Enrichment would appear before a backdrop of the White House to inform us that 'If we just give them money, the evidence is they'll fritter it away. But if we tie the aid closely to trade agreements, they'll spend it wisely, by paying us back the interest on the money we lent them *last* month.'

'We don't solve poverty by throwing money at it,' they'd say, which makes as much sense as saying, 'You can't stop something being dry just by pouring water over it.' The problem, they agreed, was that African leaders were corrupt – unlike Western businessmen, such as the board of Enron, Robert Maxwell, Conrad Black, Jonathan Aitken, etc. The argument was that giving money to destitute states benefited only the corrupt leaders, making things even worse. So if you really want to help a starving African, when you've got a bit of spare cash, keep it for yourself. *This* is how the rich get to sleep at night; they convince themselves that by paying as little tax as possible and spending their money on castles and boats, they're practically solving the problems in Uganda at a stroke.

During the Cold War, Western leaders had actually welcomed corruption in African countries, seeing it as a point scored for enterprising business spirit in defiance of the state control of the communist countries. One writer, Samuel Huntington, declared third-world corruption was 'an effort by enterprising strata to circumvent the stultifying deadweight of oppressive states'. And *that's* why I ran a protection racket and a series of brothels across Angola, your honour.

Make Poverty History, as a member of the anti-globalisation movement, played its part in countering these arguments. It worried the bankers sufficiently for James Wolfensohm, head of the World Bank, to thank the campaign 'for pointing out the problem'. Presumably up until then he hadn't noticed bits of Africa were poor. But the campaign was divided between two contrary ways of trying to change the world. There was the Bono method, which, leaving his personality out of it – it is hard I know so I'll give you a moment –

seeks personally to persuade the rich and powerful to be more benevolent. You meet Blair and Bush and Brown and Berlusconi, you praise them at their conferences, and you wince when demonstrators shout abuse at the leaders you imagine are your friends.

The other method is to try to force the issue on to the world leaders' agenda, against their will, by mobilising people and using stunts, the media and any imaginative protest you can create, to embarrass Blair and Bush and Brown and Berlusconi, and you wince when the spokesmen for your movement share biscuits and a joke with the leaders they imagine are their friends.

The problem you have if you try to befriend these leaders is it doesn't matter how much you impress on them the gravity of the human situation, they believe that profit is all that can drive the world. They will not, cannot act against the interests of the Rupert Murdochs, the drugs companies, the private water and electricity companies, the oil companies. They believe Africa, or anywhere else, cannot function without these multinationals enjoying the freedom to reap profits there, just as 250 years ago world leaders believed the slave couldn't survive without his master.

These politicians sit on black leather chairs opposite Bono and smile for CNN, and then, if they're like New Labour, they co-opt the movement and announce they love the demonstration and the concert with Mariah Carey and they'll do all they can to make poverty history. But a World Development Movement report suggested Britain's aid money was going to 'expensive advice on water restructuring with a massive bias towards privatisation' and 'public relations offensives designed to convince communities that privatisation is in their best interests'. And two years later, after the G8 summit in Heiligendaam, the world leaders even cancelled most of the aid programme they'd announced at Gleneagles during the week of Make Poverty History.

After each of these summits they publish complex documents. Bob Geldof described the one that followed the 2007 G8 summit as 'indecipherable and that of course is the point'. Sending aid is complicated you see. And it's easy to be dragged into this thought process, studying the figures and the speeches and wondering how indeed it can be achieved, this complex project to provide water and food to regions without any. And that's when you have to shake yourself and remember that between 2004 and 2006 military spending in the US and Britain went up by 18 per cent. And not once do I remember a minister of defence on television saying, 'Well, we've negotiated *some* extra funds for the year 2012, but obviously we can't just solve the increase in military spending by throwing money at it, so we're going to try and find ways to link the promise of extra tanks to a series of measures that will improve the behaviour of their armies and remember 0.3 per cent of the original 8 per cent of tanks have already been delivered to 4.7 per cent of the 9 per cent . . .'

The confrontational element to the movement not only worried the bankers, it forced them into retreats. In the Cochabamba region of Bolivia, a battle known as the gas wars, followed by the water wars, involving mass strikes and boycotts, forced the multinationals to abandon their plans to privatise gas and, obviously, water. In Turkey, the plan to build the Ilisu dam, which would have made millions for Balfour Beatty but flooded the Kurdish town of Hasankeyf displacing 78,000 people, was abandoned following an international campaign.

At the very least, the way in which these frighteningly powerful bankers have been rocked is illustrated by the venues they now choose for their summits. Where once it was Seattle or Prague, now they meet halfway up a Swiss mountain, or in Doha, in the Gulf state of Qatar, or somewhere very hard to get to with a truck full of banners, whistles and demonstrators.

Consider it from the World Bank's and IMF's point of view. You're aware of the Zapatistas, the campaign of the Ogoni people of Nigeria, the gas wars of Bolivia, and you're aware these movements now link up instantly with campaigns in the West. And you fear the impact of boycotts, demonstrations, stunts in which activists dress as clowns and sit in the lobby of your head office and end up as an item on regional news. And however ruthless you are, you don't like having your meetings behind thirty lines of armoured cars and water cannon. You probably wouldn't fear a press conference with Bono quite as much.

Alongside globalisation, another issue grew and grew in its ability to terrify: global warming became mainstream. Almost every scientist – except those funded by the oil giants – confirmed the link between carbon emissions and potential disaster.

The opponents of this widespread view fought their corner

with admirable ignorance. For example, a columnist in the *Sun* argued: 'Global warming is simply the new way of screwing more and more taxes out of us.' So the scientists and weather experts and botanists and people measuring glaciers made it all up so the government could propose a twelve quid airline tax for a return trip to Copenhagen? Maybe there's a secret group in Greenland hacking icebergs to bits with a shovel to make it look more convincing. I wondered if he'd continue: 'And what about these so-called "sound waves"? Have you ever seen one? Of course not, because they're simply another scam dreamed up by the BBC so they can charge us a licence fee.'

The details of the science *are* confusing and uncertain, but the Inter-governmental Panel on Climate Change report was produced by 600 scientists from forty countries, assessed by 600 reviewers who agreed global warming is happening, which suggests there must be a case.

On the other hand, one night I appeared on a TV panel show, on which the other member of my team was Johnny Ball, the 1970s children's TV presenter. He was amiable and bubbly, full of stories about appearing in Southport with Arthur Askey and sharing bed-and-breakfasts with Des O'Connor. Afterwards I made the mistake of telling him I was cycling home. 'Worried about your carbon footprint?' he asked.

'No such honourable reason,' I said. 'It's just the quickest way.'

And he was off. He grabbed my arm and told me there was no such thing as global warming and the scientists who say there is are paid to say that, citing examples that whizzed by, like 'Did you know Philip Tidmarsh who wrote *Meteorology and the Boiling Planet* was paid eight-thousand pounds by the University of Hull which gave a doctorate to Al Gore?'

'No, I didn't,' I said, but he was already on to the next one, and he wouldn't have noticed if I'd said, 'Yes, I did know that because Philip Tidmarsh is my dad.' Minute after minute rolled by, my arm still gripped, until I wondered if I could claim I was technically a hostage. Maybe this would go on for sixty days and would end with the SAS storming the building. At one point he said, 'Do you know what causes more global warming than anything else?' He left a gap, that wouldn't end until I said something – anything, so he could carry on, as when a computer screen orders you to 'Press any key to continue'.

'I don't know,' I said. He gripped me more tightly.

'The methane from spiders,' he said.

'The little buggers,' I thought, and wondered if he'd go on to explain that they use coal-powered webs, and instead of hanging from beams in sheds on a thread, they're flying round garages in Boeing 757s they've had built by bees.

For some reason this jolly soul has become one of the main media spokespeople for the creed that disputes man-made global warming, and this encounter *was* informative because it illustrated how the balance had tipped, and it was they who had to learn a list of dubious facts and recite them with desperation to anyone whose arm is grabbable. They look like the crazy ones. The trouble is what to do about it? And here the issue runs into the same dilemma as Make Poverty History.

Governments may want to reduce carbon emissions but they believe in the rule of profit, and the two ideas collide – with a predictable winner. For example, a serious attempt to lower emissions would try to reverse the growing obsession with cars, which are responsible for 26 per cent of them in Britain. Instead, even the AA calculates that in the ten years to 2007, the cost of public transport rose in real terms by 14 per cent, whereas the average cost of motoring fell by 8 per cent. The amount the government has spent on widening the M1 is seven times as much as its total budget for combating climate change.

To coax millions of people out of cars requires a massive investment in public transport, to make it cheaper, cleaner and more reliable. It would mean trains travelling through the night even if they ran at a loss. And new lines into rural areas even if they ran at a loss.

The growing Panzer divisions of carbon-puffing SUV Jeep

things that litter suburban Britain have to be challenged, which means confronting the obsession with wealth and status their owners share with the government. Because I imagine you could show these people evidence that their vehicles are contributing to entire islands sinking into the Pacific Ocean, and they'd say, 'Well, it's all right for them, now if they want fresh salmon they can just scoop them up from their living room, I have to go all the way to Waitrose.'

The anti-globalisation movement left many old campaigners behind. It wasn't just the use of the internet, or even the idea that a protest against an organisation called the World Bank could be led by a group of blokes dressed in purple skirts with yellow face-paint lying on the road in front of an armoured car. It felt distant from us. I'd hear things were happening – a conference in Brazil or a march in Florence – but it always seemed like something taking place far away, even if it was in Brighton.

The trade unions and the old left-wing groups were humbled by the flair of the activists, but the new movement could also learn from some of the stuff the old activists used to do. Despite the joys of the internet, it *is* true that a meeting or a rally draws local people to the ideas more thoroughly than a video clip. Boycotts have proved far more effective than I ever imagined, but to be at their most powerful they *do* require a level of organisation, with meetings and protests arranged to publicise them, and sanctions against those who break them, as happened with musicians and sportsmen who went to apartheid South Africa.

The courage of activists who've cycled to Palestine or cut the wires at US bases has had a much greater impact than I anticipated, but it would be greater still if the network was in place, as it was twenty years ago, to take these people round to trade union branches, to student unions and community groups to suggest what *everyone* can do to participate, even if they're not willing to dress up as a pink tank and dance into McDonald's on a demonstration in Helsinki. And there *do* need to be debates and discussions about how to confront the ruling powers, because otherwise the greatest enemy of any movement, the feeling that you're not making a difference, will surface.

The boycotts, direct action and flamboyant colourful protests have had an impact not just because of the wit and artwork of those involved, but because their ideas, that would once have seemed wacky and ridiculous, now connect with millions of people. When a company finds itself the subject of a boycott, it must fear this will catch on with enough people to dent its profit. When a spokesman appears on the news to defend his employers against the charges of demonstrators who have chained themselves to the gates of the head office, they're aware a wide section of the population will sympathise with the demonstrators, in ways that would once have been unimaginable.

It was the anti-capitalist forum in Florence that called for the global demonstration against the war in 2003, so it's fair to say one movement reconstituted itself, Doctor Who style, into a new one. But by 2007 that movement appeared to be dwindling, although there have emerged a number of new parties around the world as a result. If we could combine the invention and imagination of the anti-capitalist movement with the organisation and networks of a more humble Left . . . Well, surely it's worth a try.

LIKE JUDAS OF OLD, YOU
LIE AND DECEIVE

It's a remarkable aspect of human behaviour that we gradually get used to a new set of circumstances, no matter how ridiculous they are, until eventually we accept them as normal. The citizens of East Berlin may not have liked their monstrous wall, but most of them learned to cope with it, and probably imagined it would be there for ever. The Greeks must have felt the same way about being ruled by the Ottoman Empire, once the first 100 years had gone by. And I was getting like it about sleeping on the settee.

Sometimes I felt privileged, such as the night I was mesmerised by the night-time output of a racing channel. 'What,' I wondered, 'could a racing channel show at midnight?' The answer was it showed a table, in the middle of which there was a box, with six more boxes around the edge numbered one to six, each with a hole at the bottom. And that's all there was, for about a minute. This was magnificent, already destined to end up on a show listing the Top 100 TV moments, just ahead of Del Boy falling through the bar. After a few seconds a sign flashed up saying 'Place your bets now'. Then a hand came into shot and picked up the box in the middle, revealing a gerbil. The gerbil wandered in a circle for a moment, then strolled into one of the boxes, presumably to the delight of the one-sixth of the audience who had bet on the right box. And then the process started all over again.

If my family status were repaired I'd be denied treats like that. And there were plenty of other things in life to get on with, so the settee just fitted into the routine, an inconvenience but tolerable. Occasionally I'd mention this to an outsider and they'd screw their face up and say, 'You can't carry on like *that*,' much as you might reply to an East Berliner in 1975 if she said, 'There's snipers and barbed wire right round the perimeter but you soon get used to it.'

Something I did learn from my exile was precisely how warped your mind becomes if you go too long without sex. In *Down and Out in Paris and London*, George Orwell wrote that the worst part of being a tramp was the celibacy. I remember thinking as I read it that he must have got that wrong. Surely the grubbing around for food in bins is more horrible. But after the settee period I knew what he meant. After a few weeks there are days when it's simply impossible to concentrate on anything. It's surprising, given today's obsession with staff efficiency, that someone hasn't done a time-and-motion study on the effect of having a wank on levels of productivity. Obviously you lose a certain amount of time for the act itself, but that must be quickly made up by the fact that you can think straight for a while. I'm sure we'll read one day about a scheme in Japan whereby on hot days everyone pops into a special cubicle for ten minutes, and that since it started profits are up by 37 per cent.

Sometimes I'd worry these thoughts were taking me over completely, and without realising I'd write a newspaper column that was supposed to be about the council election results, but just went 'Oh for God's sake the woman off *Newsnight*'s doing the local round-up on *BBC London* in a short skirt, I'm going round the BEND here.' This obsession is even more all-encompassing in your forties than your twenties, because back then there's a stringent upper age limit on who you find attractive. But the 40-year-old libido stamps right across that barrier. I was almost on the point of seeking medical help when I lay on the settee watching *Question Time*, as a Conservative politician called Julie

Kirkbride twittered on about something or other, and I suddenly realised I hadn't been listening at all, just pondering her sexuality. *Aaaagh!* I did a horizontal jump of horror. It was like the moment in a film when someone realises they're turning into a werewolf. I had a vision of sitting in the doctor's office, shouting, 'NOTH-ING TO WORRY ABOUT? SHE'S A TORY FUCKING MP.'

How bad would this get? In another month would I start getting tingly at the thought of Melanie Phillips? Or the Queen? Would I get so demented a mere glance at a stamp would have me thinking, 'Well, if I ever *was* offered an OBE . . .'

And yet to leave altogether seemed an awful, unimaginable prospect at every level – from trying to calm inconsolable kids to having to set up a new broadband account. There's the stench of chaos: legal documents, financial agreements, access arrangements, finding somewhere to live, buying a new settee. And the dreadful finality and acceptance of failure. Despite the high number of families that break apart, each one is categorised as a 'failed marriage'. You can have fifteen glorious romantic years, involving treks across Mexico and setting up a snorkelling school in Crete, producing a bunch of charismatic compassionate children who are the first to be invited to every party, but if you eventually grow distant and part, you've failed. So the longer you've been together the more time you've wasted on this failed project. It would be like buying a camera, and when it packs up after ten years throwing it down in the street screaming, 'I WISH I'd never got it in the FIRST PLACE.'

Aligned to this sense of failure is the humiliation of giving up. You used to gaze at each other across a table splashed with takeaway curry and communicate with tiny twinkling facial expressions, affectionate puffs and grunts, and it's achingly mournful to accept it's gone. You feel it must still be there somewhere, if only you look hard enough, in the same way that you search through the house over and over again, refusing to accept you've lost your favourite jacket. To part in your forties with children in tow is so different from doing it in your twenties with nothing more to row about than who gets the blender. All continuity will be lost for ever, in twenty years' time there will still be awkward arrangements about who goes where at Christmas and there will be no time when everyone sits together joyfully recalling the years until now. So after a few months on that settee, it took only a half-decent week without a major cacophony to convince us to give it another go.

I left the settee, and everything was marvellous. We held hands on the way to the shop, and some people came for dinner, and we had the floors done up, and we saw Crystal Palace get promoted in the play-off final. But of course it wasn't really marvellous, because nothing had been repaired. We were like an old car that's packed up, but then suddenly one day for some reason when you turn the ignition splutters along again for a while.

The arguments resurfaced, rarely about the issue causing the friction, but instead attaching themselves to whatever subject was being discussed. From the angle of the bed I was reinstated in, there was a wonderful sight to greet us each morning, of a sparkling Venus, proudly displaying itself in the twilight before politely disappearing. 'That's Venus there, how brilliant,' I said. 'I haven't got time to look at bloody *Venus*' was the less than astronomical reply. And I maintained that she might enjoy looking at Venus, and it really wouldn't take long. Which is a stupid response because obviously neither the time nor Venus itself was the issue. She wasn't thinking, 'I can't be distracted for Venus, why can't you find me a *really* nice planet?'

When someone's reached that frame of mind, it can feel impossible to create a positive feeling about anything. You can give them a bouquet of flowers and say you've booked a weekend in Venice and they'll carry on fuming because they had to wait for a bus that morning. In a field of blooming daffodils they can see only the one thistle. If they became accountants they'd write down all the expenses on the debit side, nothing on the credit side and make everyone file for bankruptcy, bringing the economy to its knees in a fortnight.

Eventually every sentence has the potential to lead to mayhem. There could be a failing marriage *Mastermind*, in which the correct answer to 'Have we got any eggs?' is 'When have *I* had time to get eggs?' Some days we'd refrain from any comment at all, and I'd stop myself saying something like 'England are doing terrible in the cricket,' in case I got the reply, 'Well, what the bloody hell do you expect *me* to do about it?'

One night, after a particularly fraught five hours, I realised the front and back doors were both hidden behind a tower of chairs, planks of wood, buckets and assorted useless objects from under the stairs. 'We've barricaded you in,' said my son and daughter, 'because we were afraid you might leave.'

These are the issues that are weighed up before anyone takes the decision to finally part from their family. Around this time, the government and opposition were both suggesting financial incentives should be offered to families who stick together, to curb the blight of broken homes. Even that, they believe, comes down to money. They really haven't got a clue.

Sometimes, being proved right can be more painful than being proved wrong. One by one by one, as the carnage unleashed by the occupation of Iraq unfolded, the journalists and politicians who'd supported it made their apologies. 'It seems,' they would say, 'that I was possibly naive to accept the necessity of military action that has revealed itself as a misadventure . . .'

And a bit of me wanted to acknowledge that at least they'd owned up and done the decent thing. But another bit of me wanted to put them all in a giant classroom – while a teacher waved a stick and boomed, 'WHY haven't we learned this before – we've BEEN through it enough times already. WHAT happens when the Americans invade somewhere – YOU, BOY.'

A boy would mumble, 'Fawap and mathawasa' to which the teacher would yell, 'COME ON BOY – OUT WITH IT!'

'They fuck everything up and make things worse, sir.'

And the teacher, thwacking his stick on the boy's desk in time

with each syllable would bellow 'They FUCK-EVERYTHING-
UP-AND-MAKE-THINGS-WORSE,-SIR – now LEARN –
IT – FOR – NEXT – TIME!' – thwack thwack.

It wasn't just that the predictions of the anti-war movement
were chillingly accurate (except they underestimated the scale of
the disaster). It was that the blatant lying to justify it was so comprehensively exposed that it was a daily source of anguish that
those who'd told the lies weren't made to appear once an hour
naked on live television being sprayed with the oily deposit from
a tin of tuna.

To start with, as the world knows, there were no weapons of
mass destruction. In previous wars the incident allegedly justifying the initial invasion has been fabricated, such as the Vietnamese
firing on the US in the Gulf of Tonkin. But never before had the
entire reason for war been acknowledged as a complete fabrication.
It was as if, a year after the Falklands War, it turned out that the
Argentinians had never invaded the Falklands at all. Or, after the
Vietnam War, that the North Vietnamese had never even supported communism and Ho Chi Minh was a member of the
Conservative Party.

I expected them to find something. Before the war they'd
shown us pictures, grainy images they claimed were Saddam's
deadly weapons; now that they had the run of the place they were
sure to come up with a shed full of potentially deadly chemical
something or other. They couldn't possibly live with finding
nothing – then they'd *have* to be called to account. It would be
one of those moments when someone's proved utterly, comprehensively wrong with no qualifications, as when you can't find
your keys and shout, 'Of COURSE I've already looked in my
pocket, I can tell you they are DEFINITELY not in my pocket,'
and then you find them in your pocket.

At first they tried to maintain the lie that the weapons existed.
And the word is *lie*. For example, the Iraq Survey Group, sent by the
Americans to locate the weapons, issued a report in February 2004
stating that they had found no such weapons and were unlikely to

find any in the future. The head of that group, David Kay, resigned, making the statement 'I think we have found 85 per cent of what we're going to find.' John Reid, when asked to comment on this on *Newsnight*, said, 'What David Kay *actually* said was he admitted they've found 85 per cent of what they were looking for.'

No, he didn't. He didn't say that at all, because I checked it in three newspapers and in each one he was quoted as saying what the interviewer reported him as saying. And John Reid, on *Newsnight* to comment on precisely that report, must have known that. This wasn't a different interpretation or a mistake, it was a fucking lie. It was the lie of the cornered liar, whose web of lies is finally revealed for all to see and so comes up with something more preposterous than ever, as when Basil Fawlty tells a thousand lies to conceal the fact that there's a rat loose in the dining room. When he offers a customer a biscuit and there in the tin is a rat, he says calmly, 'Would you care for a rat?' As I watched John Reid it wasn't the war driving my fury, it was the lying. I wanted a character from *The Bill* to grab Reid by the collar, say, 'I think the game's up, Mister Reid' and handcuff the bastard.

How were they getting away with this? Then they changed strategy and said it didn't really matter that there were no weapons of mass destruction, as the main thing was they'd overthrown Saddam. *Didn't matter?* This was the whole reason for the war – for over a year, several times a day, ministers had repeated that military action would be in response to Saddam's refusal to give up his weapons of mass destruction. They'd said over and over again that if he *did* give them up there'd be no need for a war. Now they had their war and they were saying that it didn't *matter*? George Bush even said he 'wasn't that bothered' about finding them. It was as if the Wile E. Coyote finally caught the Road Runner and said, 'To be honest I'm not that hungry.'

Then came the revelations that American and British soldiers had been torturing Iraqis at Abu Ghraib prison, with the same inhumanity as Saddam was so proud of. I wondered whether the excuse for this would be that under Saddam the Iraqis had become addicted to being tortured and it would be dangerous to stop suddenly as they'd go cold turkey, so we were weening them off it bit by bit. Eventually though, the United Nations reported at the end of 2006 that there was more torture happening under the occupation than used to take place under Saddam. What an achievement! Supporters of the war used to ask opponents, 'Don't you care about the levels of torture Saddam inflicts on his people?' I never realised they meant he wasn't doing enough.

Around the same time, the medical magazine *The Lancet*, using the grisly methods it's employed to calculate such figures in other conflicts, estimated the number of deaths caused as a result of the invasion as over 650,000. Maybe they're way out – maybe it's only half that. But we do know, for example, that in November 2004 the US army laid siege to the city of Fallujah, in 'Operation Phantom Fury', and that countless thousands were slaughtered. Around the same time the contractor Ken Bigley was kidnapped and eventually murdered. Throughout this sickening business we learned about his frail mother, his gutsy anti-war brother and his young wife. When he was beheaded it felt like the demise of a human being we knew, who had laughed and loved and was one more victim of the slaughter. From Fallujah there was nothing. At best there were disputed numbers of those killed. Imagine if, every day, we had been bombarded on the news with details of a selection of the inhabitants, so they were no longer faceless statistics but individuals – so we knew which football team they supported, who they'd hoped to marry, what quirky nonsense they collected, the dreadful bands they'd been in, what made them cheer and cry and scream, and who they called out for when they were dying in a pool of blood.

There had been one other justification for the war, that it would reduce the threat of terrorism. But before the war there was no Al Q'aeda presence in Iraq, and now they were every-where. One morning, having arrived early at Television Centre in west London to write some jokes for a programme about Charlie Chaplin, the production manager answered her phone. 'Oh my

God, what's happened?' she said, in that chilling quiet way that suggests something genuinely alarming and makes anyone nearby look their way with foreboding. Over the next few seconds she turned a shiny red shade and shed a light-reflecting tear. She called to mind a face you sometimes glimpse on a train that makes you wonder whether you should lean across and ask, 'Are you all right, love?'

It was her boyfriend on the phone, clearly shaken, after being evacuated from the underground station at Edgware Road with hundreds of other commuters after an explosion. There'd been a power surge, it said on the news. But in fact there'd been four bombs, killing another random bunch of people in more futile destruction. London responded with calm panic, phone networks jammed as everyone rang relatives and mates and watched the reporters above the red strap that flashed 'BREAKING NEWS'. All day we heard the stories of those who'd been close to the bombs.

Once everyone had arrived and given their accounts of what an extraordinary morning they'd had, and laid out their theories and speculated about what would come out, and stood round the table stretching to watch the film of flashing fire engines on the tiny television, and rang their mum, and made their attempt at telling *the* joke that everyone would remember for its timely dark brilliance, most Londoners who'd made it to work faced a question of etiquette. Given that some people had suffered unbearably in the day's events, at what point was it all right to say, 'How the bloody hell am I going to get home?' It felt shameful, but I'm sure on the day Hiroshima was bombed someone must have been driving through Japan, heard the news and thought, 'Oh bollocks, who knows *where* I'll be diverted to because of this.'

Eventually I walked for two or three miles, the streets packed with people almost enjoying the challenge of dealing with disruption. I got on a train to Clapham Junction, where my partner had driven to pick me up with our kids, and the four of us went to a café for a meal. My daughter was four but aware that day was different and important and she'd always remember it. She asked if I'd seen the bomb go off, in the tone I must have used when I was four and asked my dad if he'd ever shot a German. For an evening we swapped stories and joked together, and the children were alarmed but excited, and not only was there no conflict but there was no *prospect* of conflict, given the relief and the drama, and everything was strangely content. So there you are – don't let anyone tell you *no* good came out of the war with Iraq.

Amid the general sadness and confusion of the day, however, there was a strange sensation in a freshly bombed city – of inevitability. For about a year, conversations on the war, or religion, had usually reached a point where someone said there was bound to be something go off bang one day soon. Among the people most certain this would happen must have been Tony Blair, because, we now know, parliament's own Joint Intelligence Committee had reported before the invasion that 'The threat from Al Q'aeda and associated groups would be heightened by military action against Iraq' and had personally informed Blair of this.

Eventually everything connected with the war got even worse, until it became beyond question that it was a débâcle. Even the head of the British Army, Sir Richard Dannatt, announced he was against it. This meant that if there was a military coup, the country would be moving to the left. Armies exist for wars. Traditionally the role of army chiefs is to cajole governments into supporting a war, and you can picture them in Downing Street poring over a map and snapping, 'Well, what about Finland, they must have done something.' But this war was too ridiculous even for him. Which must be like going out for a night with Pete Doherty that ends when he says to *you*, 'I'm going home, mate, you're just being ridiculous now.'

The statement by Richard Dannatt was hugely embarrassing for Tony Blair, but he responded by saying what the general had *actually* said was he agreed with the government's strategy. No, he hadn't. The head of the navy could have announced, 'I hope Tony Blair dies a lingering agonising death – the slimy warmongering cunt.' And Blair would have said, 'If you look at what he *actually* said, we're pretty much at one on this.'

A poll in the *Observer* in June 2007 showed 14 per cent of the population thought the decision to invade Iraq was right. Fourteen per cent! Even in the US when they were about to pull out of Vietnam nearly 30 per cent still backed the war. Fourteen per cent was low enough to warrant war supporters claiming minority status. If they had formed a society they could probably have won a court ruling banning people from being malicious about their beliefs, and got local councils to put a ramp in their house.

I'd been involved in campaigns where I'd been surprised at the unlikely people lining up to oppose the establishment, but I'd never seen anything like this. Dolly Parton made anti-war statements, Major James Hewitt said on a chat show we shouldn't be there. Flicking through my local paper one morning, I was casually reading an interview with Leo Sayer about his forthcoming appearance at the Fairfield Halls in Croydon, when suddenly there was a paragraph about how he thought George Bush was a war criminal. Leo Sayer! Would Roger Whittaker produce an album called *Whistle Against the War* with Des O'Connor singing extracts from Robin Cook's resignation speech?

The influential think-tank Chatham House issued a report describing the war as a 'terrible mistake' that had made the world 'more dangerous'. The language of these groups is usually incredibly measured. If they were publishing their findings about the Charge of the Light Brigade, they'd say 'Within certain quarters there existed a tendency towards erroneous calculations with regard to the outcome of the charge.' So when they say 'terrible mistake', that's official language for 'AAAAAAAAAAAGHH-HHH!!!!!'

Margaret Beckett, by then Foreign Secretary, was asked on the *Today* programme, the morning news show on Radio 4, whether she opposed this report. The answer was so wonderful I listened to it six times on the computer playback service to write it down exactly. Her precise words were: 'Well – yes – I might well um yes it's a very serious um discussion and it's not um er one for doing in two seconds early in the morning.' She must have a rule never to discuss atrocities until after *Cash in the Attic*.

But then she got worse. On two separate occasions she said that Tony Blair had never claimed Saddam was a threat to Britain. So she was reminded about the claims made by Blair that Saddam could launch his weapons at us in forty-five minutes and she said, 'That statement was only made once – and nobody thought it was relevant.' NOT RELEVANT! It was the argument that justified the whole escapade. The Nazis should have tried this at the Nuremberg trials. 'We only mentioned the Final Solution once and no one thought it was relevant.'

All this created a new sickening I'd not experienced before. I'd seen countless events in which governments and corporations defended injustice and been frustrated that anyone believed them, allowing them to get away with it. Occasionally I'd seen them unable to carry their arguments, such as with the poll tax, and have to retreat as a result. But here they'd lost all authority on the issue. Everyone knew they were talking shit, but they carried on anyway.

One morning in Glasgow I was due to speak at a conference of the Scottish Socialist Party after Rose Gentle, who became a spokeswoman for Military Families Against the War. She'd opposed the war from its beginning, but opposed it even more fiercely when her son, Gordon, was killed in Basra by a roadside bomb. Part of the process of moving through your forties is your reaction to hearing of a death like this. At one point I'd have felt it from the point of view of the soldier – imagine your life ending so early like that. Think of the experiences you'd miss, the relationships you'd never have, the sheer incompleteness of it all. Now I instinctively see it from the perspective of the parent. How would I react if it were my son? Catatonic trance? Drink? God?

Would I ever be able to tell a joke again? More immediately, how would I feel if I was making a speech about his death, and some bloody comedian was sitting next to me wondering how to follow this with his jokes?

I imagine a relentless heavy numbness that allows for no joy, the way nothing can break free from the gravitational pull of a black hole. And yet Rose Gentle did find a positive response, which was to campaign tirelessly against the continuation of the war. That's not to say drink, God or a catatonic trance wouldn't be perfectly reasonable and valid. But the drive of Rose, and others like her, must have been nurtured not just by the death of her son, but the contempt that followed it, in the form of justifications for the war that were sheer gobbledegook, as if they couldn't even be bothered to try.

And somehow they got away with it. They didn't get away with it because people fell in with patriotism as at the start of the First World War. They got away with it because most people thought it was a disgrace, or at least a mistake, but didn't know what mechanism we could use to stop them getting away with it.

How could they be not only guilty but understood by so many to be guilty, and still avoid the slightest retribution or censure? It was like watching a gangland boss on trial, see the judge pronounce him guilty but then let him off and sentence all his victims who were watching from the gallery.

The scale of destruction wrought because of the decision to support Bush's war has been so great that throughout the last four years of Blair's premiership every other complaint about him, such as his attitude towards pensions or education, seemed almost trivial. As if someone said, 'I don't like that Ian Huntley, you know – 'cos apparently he was a really useless caretaker.'

Feeling helpless can lead to the most futile acts of pointless rebellion. This may take the form of grotesque and hopeless guerilla actions, but in my case was to get so annoyed at the persistent hounding of the Arabic channel Al-Jazeera, which was said to be

'glorifying terrorism' for not adhering to the Bush/Blair version
of events (the US airforce even fired on their office, killing a
journalist), that after one of these outbursts I subscribed to the
channel for the minimum six-month contract. Despite the fact
that it was all in Arabic. So now I had even more channels to
accompany me on the settee.

Now I'd lie there watching a channel of reputed quality,
having no idea what was going on. I'd know when there was a
discussion programme, because the presenter would sit in the
middle, while on one side was a groomed businessman-type
politician and on the other was a man with a straggly grey beard
and a white robe, and they'd start rowing. They'd really go for it,
the smart man's fists thumping on the table while the robed man
boomed like an operatic baritone, every word seeming to contain
that gutteral 'hch' sound, the sort Scousers make at the end of
'work'. And both at the same time, with the occasional calm but
pointless protest from the presenter, presumably saying something
like, 'If we could just leave the matter of who will be repaid for
his infidel treachery with mighty regal vengeance and return to
the issue of the inflation figures, gentlemen?' But neither of them
was having it. By now they wouldn't even be addressing each
other, each making a simultaneous speech building up in a
crescendo, as if they were on horseback about to lead their battalions into an assault across the studio to capture the camera
crew.

Then some Arabic writing would roll across the bottom of the
screen, which was probably saying, 'We apologise for the late
showing of the snooker, which will follow immediately after the
end of this debate.' And in a way it was quite liberating, because
whose side I was on I had absolutely no idea.

In Britain, the growing acceptance that the war had proved disastrous didn't mean there was a visible mass movement to end the
occupation. This was partly because of the sense of helplessness,
but also because many of those who opposed the invasion
believed that for the American and British to leave too quickly

would make things even worse. We'd caused all that trouble, the argument went, it was up to us to sort it out.

This assumes things had gone wrong because of a lack of planning, or a series of mistakes had been carried out, the way a builder who wrecks your ceiling would be expected to come back to repair it. But the history of the occupation suggests the cause of the chaos was not just mistakes, but the fact that, in accordance with the Project for the American Century, there was no intention to ever 'give Iraq back to the Iraqis'. The moment the Americans arrived in Baghdad they set up a Coalition Provisional Authority, the head of which was a man called Jay Garner, who'd criticised the Bush regime for not showing enough support for Ariel Sharon, the ruthlessly anti-Palestinian Israeli. An Israeli pro-Sharon newspaper announced: 'Israel's friend to rule Iraq'. So this was like an army occupying England and saying, 'We're giving England back to the English, so your new leaders are the Hezbollah and Diego Maradona.'

Garner gave way to the joyously named Paul Bremer III, a former assistant to Henry Kissinger, who introduced 100 orders to reshape the country. The *Los Angeles Times* reported: 'They lock in sweeping advantages to American firms, ensuring long-term US economic advantage while guaranteeing few, if any, benefits to the Iraqi people. The Bremer orders control every aspect of Iraqi life, from the use of car horns to the privatization of state-owned enterprises. Order no. 39 alone does no less than "transition" Iraq from a centrally planned economy to a market economy virtually overnight.'

This was the strategy: to privatise the entire place and hand it to American big business. Bremer III wasn't acting on his own. There's no evidence the US government thought, 'Oh my God, what's he doing? We were hoping he was going to use the oil revenues to build Iraqi youth clubs and old people's homes; boosting our oil companies' profits is the *last* thing we wanted. Maybe we've picked the wrong bloke and it was Paul Bremer *IV* we meant to put in charge.'

As the reality of occupation became clear to Iraqis, even those who'd initially welcomed the invasion turned against it, so the troops could trust no one and fired on anyone. Newspapers that opposed the invasion were shut down, and a series of polls in 2007 indicated that between 61 per cent and 80 per cent of all Iraqis supported attacks on US troops. So if the Americans really wanted to back the wishes of the Iraqi people, they'd have sent forces out there to fire on themselves.

Throughout all this we were always told we were one step away from a solution. The handover to the Iraqi authority would bring stability, then the elections would introduce a new era of peace. When Saddam was captured, this would rapidly bring the insurgency to a halt.

But all these things passed and the Americans were forced to send another 27,000 troops in a 'surge' that still left them in control of one heavily fortified area in Baghdad called the 'Green Zone', which sounds like the backstage area of a rock festival you can only get into with a purple wristband. But with a catch that, although they were the only people allowed in, none of those in could safely get out.

The 'insurgents' are not a unified army, and certainly don't have a global outlook that would make it comfortable to support them, like the ANC or the Sandinistas. Iraq would not become peaceful as a result of the occupying forces leaving. All manner of religious sectarians and warring factions would no doubt continue on their missions. But it seemed perverse to declare that our troops must stay in a place when the overwhelming majority who have to put up with them want them to leave. That's to assume we know better than them, in a similar way to when Margaret Thatcher opposed sanctions against South Africa, arguing this would 'harm the blacks', although it was the black organisations who were demanding the sanctions.

Also, no matter how violent and inhuman a situation has become, when part of the biggest army the world has ever seen is plonked in the middle to ensure the entire place is sold off to the richest people in the empire that the army serves, and anyone who doesn't actively support that process is deemed the enemy, then that army is not part of the solution.

Your forties are a time when all your flaws seem to be laid out before you, and so is your decline. When I went running it didn't feel all that different from ten years earlier, but then I realised the reason I was no more puffed than before was because it was taking me twice as long. One night I was overtaken by a jogging couple who were casually talking to each other about kitchen units. Then you pull a muscle, just a bit, and it takes three months to heal. And if a doctor said, 'Well, that's inevitable now you're forty-five,' I'd want to scream, 'But that can't apply to me. You see, I listen to Lady Sovereign.'

People around you start getting ill. Words entered my vocabulary that I never knew existed; ones like aorta and prostate and colon. Paul Foot, the socialist journalist and full-time inspiration who had become a friend, had a burst aorta, which apparently is unhealthy, but against the odds survived. We continued to meet occasionally at his house, which was a maze through a ridiculous number of books, nearly all of them beautifully crumbling old hardbacks that you feel compelled to sniff before you open. Often we'd meet in the Star Cafe in Soho, with Linda Smith and Jeremy Hardy. Paul would gently lower himself into an oak chair, and thump the table declaring 'This is MARVELLOUS,' as if he were a medieval king in his castle declaring, 'Let the banquet begin.'

I first came across Paul Foot when I heard him speak about the revolt of the 1871 Paris Commune and the revolutionary nature of the poet Shelley. And while he would explain complex ideas and convey such passion for the downtrodden of history, mostly I loved him because he was funny. One of the first speeches I saw him make was for the Right to Work Campaign in Brixton around 1981. That day the closure of a carpet factory in Yorkshire had been announced, and Paul did a routine about the logic of this. 'Is this because no one in Yorkshire needs carpets any more? Everyone in Leeds and Sheffield is arriving home and saying, "For goodness' sake, I can't even get into the house, it's stuffed with carpets up to the ceiling, please please everyone stop making carpets.'"

All those speeches and articles and books and campaigns I'd been inspired by, and I could sit there and listen to it personally over shepherd's pie. It was like finding yourself once a month going round to Bob Dylan's house, where he'd play 'Just Like a Woman' between supping soup. Some months I couldn't make it, though, for whatever reason, and sometimes three months would drift by, but once I saw him and he was more enthusiastic about life than ever because Plymouth had been promoted. A couple of weeks later he died.

Amid the sadness of a friend or relative's death is always a selfish regret, that you didn't spend more time with them, which you would have if you'd been aware they were going to die. No one ever says, 'My dad died last week, and luckily we'd discussed everything I ever wanted to ask him, and over the last couple of years I'd spent exactly the right amount of time with him – plenty, but not *too* much because that can be stifling.' What forgettable reasons had there been for not having seen this remarkable person more often? But there we are – there must have been friends of Einstein who were invited out by him one night but rang back to say, 'Sorry, Albert, I'm creosoting my shed.'

There was another sadness to Paul's death. Those first times I'd seen him speak, at a socialist gathering in Skegness, at a miners' club in Wales, that Right to Work rally, there had been hundreds and hundreds each time, young, inquisitive and excitable. It all seemed a long time ago.

10

SELLING EVERY BRICK IN THE WALL

I still fear school. One night, I was watching an Open University programme around midnight, out of the same curiosity that would later lead to my study of Icelandic buggy-racing. The lecturer was stumbling through his lesson in front of some graphs as I drunkenly went into the kitchen to make a pot of tea, and I genuinely flinched because somewhere in my mind I was expecting the lecturer to say, 'And WHERE do you think YOU'RE going?'

I knew, therefore, that once my kids were going to school every day, I'd be tempted to continue the war of attrition against teachers I'd waged twenty-five years before. My instinct would be to give them prepared lines to wind up the supply teachers, so they could have 'all the opportunities I never had'.

So it was hard to know what to do when a letter informed me that my son had been sent to the headmaster because he'd announced to the class that he didn't think the teacher was listening to what the kids were actually saying, so from now on if he were asked to say anything he might as well say it to the flowers. When the teacher did ask him a question, he walked across to the vase and gave his answer to the lilies as promised. 'The trouble is,' a different teacher told me at parents' evening, 'he says things in class not in order to move the lesson on, but simply to get a laugh.' And he looked at me as if he was about to continue, 'And you can wipe that smirk off your face RIGHT away, Mr Steel.'

The route through this conundrum, I suppose, is to remember that the problem with schools and universities is not that they try to educate you, but that given the job of inspiring a new generation with the joys of history, culture and language, many of them manage to bore everyone senseless. Thus the problem is they're *failing* to educate you.

For example, the most frustrating result of making a series of lectures for radio and television is I regularly hear people tell me they've seen one of the programmes, before moving rapidly on to say they never had any interest in Chaucer, or Beethoven, or Isaac Newton, because they had to learn about them at school and it put them off for ever. The scale of this failure is astonishing. Given the task of enthusing children about a subject, the education system has managed instead to piss them off so completely that thirty years later they can't bear to think about it. Could anyone else be so thoroughly useless? For a salesman to be that bad, he'd have to annoy the potential customer to such an extent when trying to sell him a car that thirty years later he wouldn't even accept a lift in one and went everywhere on roller skates. Or I hear people say, 'I've always been useless at history and science or anything like that.' And within three minutes it's clear they are interested and aren't useless at all, but have been made to feel useless and become uninterested. School can't take all the blame for this, as even presentations of 'serious' subjects on television are usually treated with such pomposity they'd make almost anyone feel stupid.*

*One night, educating myself from the settee, I flicked on to a channel on which there was a discussion about classical music, from the Royal Festival Hall. A presenter was clasping her hands and almost wincing with joy as she explained the piece she'd just heard — 'examined the space between boundaries' and other such twaddle. I was just about to switch to Bravo or a Hindu channel when it became clear the piece she'd been talking about was 'Four minutes and twenty-two seconds of silence', which is just silence. Then it was back to the presenter, who, in all seriousness, said, 'And we were *particularly* lucky today because we also got to see the rehearsal.'

Most of the academic world seems dedicated to making as many people as possible feel stupid. While making the series of lectures, we were assigned an academic for each programme, who was asked to check the script for inaccuracies. A few were wonderful, especially the scientist who covered a table in a pizza restaurant with graphs, in an electrifying attempt to explain Einstein's theory of relativity. But more typical was the one with a huge beard who'd read the script about Charles Darwin. In his office, while my colleague James and I gazed nervously round the room, he sat grimacing, shook his head, grunted, all as slowly as it's possible to without going backwards, and I wondered whether he was about to tell us the script was *so* bad he could invoke an ancient bye-law of the university and have us executed.

Then he started. 'Page one, McCulloch,' he said, gazing directly at me while breathing out heavily through his nose. 'You've spelt McCulloch with one "c". It should have two "c"s. Everyone knows that.'

'Sorry,' I said. 'We'll correct that.'

Then, after a pause, 'And look here. Page two. McCulloch. You've done it again. What's the matter with you?'

'Right,' I said.

There followed a row about the significance of something or other and a disgusted groan about punctuation, and then, 'Page three – here we are again – McCulloch. With one "c". Tut tut, I don't know *what* you were thinking of.'

At this point James said, 'Well, it shouldn't matter too much as this is for television.'

He might as well have said he thought Darwin was a horse. 'SHOULDN'T MATTER? Harrrebbbrrrm brrrmmm – shouldn't matter indeed.'

He screwed up his face for a real stinker. '*This* quote here. Where on EARTH did that come from? Darwin wouldn't have said that. Pre*post*erous.'

By now my confidence was so low I wanted to look at my fingers and mumble, 'Don't know, sir.' I just about managed to say what I knew was true. 'That quote, er, that quote came from your book.'

And he went, 'Hrrrmmm. Now look at this – page four – McCulloch, you've gone and done it again.'

Another one sent scripts back with comments like 'NON-SENSE' scrawled all over in red felt pen, and on one page, right across everything, 'NO! NO! NO!' I expected to turn it over and see on the next page 'YOU THICK CUNT!'

Many people who found themselves dependent on these academics, I should imagine, spent the rest of their lives convinced they were useless. If I'd had the imagination, whenever I was in a room with one of them, I'd have gone and talked to the flowers.

Whatever else New Labour may have buggered up, they seem to have done well in education. There's evidently more money in schools than when they were first elected. When I saw the secondary school my son was going to, I was so impressed with the equipment that I almost wanted to complain. For example, in a corner of a landing was a line of cycling and rowing machines, for use at any time. And a bit of me felt like asking, 'What's wrong with a skipping rope and a medicine ball?'

The exam results are also definitely better, despite the people who grumble this can only be because the exams are too easy. Maybe they'd prefer it if people were employed to run round the exam room attacking the students with spongey sticks and tipping them off their chairs like in the old *Gladiators*.

However, when it comes to the philosophy of subjecting everything to the demands of business, no exception has been made for education: the five-year-strategy for education announced in 2005 told us the expansion of university degrees 'will be led by business'. In Tony Blair's speech to launch this initiative he included the word 'employer' thirty-six times. Almost every comment from the government concerning education insists on the necessity of education for business. The tuition fees that leave most students in thousands of pounds of debt are justified by the likelihood that someone with a degree will earn more as a result. Money business money business. City academies are encouraged, which depend on sponsors, so the Department of Education and Skills tries to attract those sponsors by promising that 'Sponsors will make decisions about the Academy's vision and ethos, and structures for governing and managing the school, and appoint a majority of the members of the governing body.'

This means the schools will be run according to the needs of business. Maybe one day, if your child falls behind in English, instead of being offered extra help he'll be voted out by angry shareholders. Maybe a few lucky parents will boast, 'We got Tamsine into a school run by a consortium of arms dealers which has a VERY good record in physics. And it's not at all elitist because they take a lot of deprived kids from the catchment area, and use them as guinea-pigs in the landmine experiments.'

Advertising hoardings now appear in schools, and big business sponsors school materials, with a healthy return. McDonald's produced packs for children that included a test, asking kids to compose a song called 'Old Macdonald had a store'. Hopefully somewhere a kid suggested: 'And in that store he had an anarchist e-i-e-i-o. With a smash smash here and a smash smash there' . . .

All this extra material and equipment directs children towards the goal of education – to pass exams. Because business needs to know who can pass exams. So there are tables telling you how many exams are passed in every school, and everything revolves round where in the table each school comes, so every kid is pressed and pressed, not to be as imaginative as possible but to do whatever it takes to pass the exams. I found myself, against every instinct, sitting opposite my son saying 'Next is "superstitious". You spelt "ambitious" so you should get this one.'

Everyone – children, parents and schools – is locked into this mentality that if the kids don't pass these exams, they will fail, not just the exams but all their life. It seems as if the moment you announce a baby's due, neighbours and relatives start placing an earnest hand on your shoulder and imploring you to think carefully about which school they'll be going to. By the time my son was seven, perfectly reasonable people would ask what plans we'd made for getting him into secondary school. And if I said I hadn't thought about it all that much, seeing as it was four years away, they'd grab my wrist and say, 'Oh, you *must start* looking round, you *must. Please.*' And I'd wonder if, by mistake, I'd said I'd been shitting blood but couldn't be bothered to go to the doctor.

For that reason half the country's planning on moving house, across the road, up a tree, into a sewage pipe, as long as it takes them into the catchment area for the school that's nine league places above the one their daughter might have to go to otherwise. And if that doesn't work they go to church, despite never having shown any interest in God, so they can get their kids into a nice church school.

They sing hymns to a God they're not bothered about, and pray to a deity they don't believe is taking any notice, which you'd think would make him livid if he's there. I'm sure I'll soon hear someone saying, 'We've been attending a Satanic coven lately because the Prince of Darkness High School has a very attractive prospectus. The biology lab has got plenty of dead goats, and the uniform's a lovely fetching black so there's no need to worry about stains.'

Maybe it's a scheme to get people back into religion, and next they'll try to take over other essential services, such as water supplies. Then you won't be able to get connected unless you turn up every week for a year to St Joseph's reservoir. Where everyone sings 'Thank you Lord, you walked on it, John baptised with it and now Reverend Bartholomew dispenses it at favourable rates compared to Thames Supplies Ltd.' While everyone else has to get three buses to a well in Hampshire.

One night I got in to find my partner fuming on the settee. 'Carol was round tonight,' she said. 'And we had such a row.'

'Oh no, what was that about?' I asked.

'She's been going to church so she can get Alfie into the church school,' she said. 'So I let her have it.'

Part of me thought, 'I don't think you should take out the tensions between us on your friends, whatever they've done.' But another part wanted to sit on the settee so we could give each other a rare hug.

You can't blame Carol, or the frantic hordes like her, because the future has become uncertain. Instead of offering the steady but unglamorous trades and professions of the past, the future beckons new generations to 'go go go' and be the one who clambers over the ordinary losers to get ahead. Success equals wealth times status. Even coffee and headache tablets are sold on their ability to give you that vital edge in the cut-throat business environment. The business of education reflects this world, just as the devotion to mass uniformed discipline in schools forty years ago reflected the black and white factories and shipyards of the day. Fall behind in the race and you'd better understand you're a loser, sunshine, and it's no excuse that you're seven. So please please *please* get a private tutor to squeeze your kid through the SATs, study the brochures and ensure they practise interview techniques so they'll get into the selective school because it's only four years away. Or you could start going to church.

For certain people there's another option. Two miles from where I live is the majestic tranquillity that is Dulwich College. Its grounds cover sixty acres and include twelve rugby pitches, ten football pitches and eight cricket squares, all of which are in constantly immaculate condition.

I did a few days' filming in the place, and almost every room I entered led me to exclaim 'Fucking Ada!'. The music room, which at my school was a cupboard containing a glockenspiel with three bars missing, is crammed with the sheen of immaculately varnished double basses, clarinets that glimmer, a Steinway grand piano that oozes grandeur, so you feel afraid to touch it as if it was an ancient parchment. 'What's in this room?' I wondered at one point, and when I peeked in, it was a theatre, better than the ones that serve most small towns. I began to wonder if I'd walk through another door and someone would say, 'Ah, in here is our desert. We find it helps with geography.'

They seem to own everything for miles. Every sports ground and building in the area is theirs. They even own a major road, and charge people a pound to go down it, through a tollgate. I suppose their next move will be to take control of the air space. Every plane passing overhead will have to throw a pound into a bucket, or be considered a legitimate target for the school anti-aircraft missile-launching team, who are practising for their quarter-final against the Kashmir Tribesmen Old Boys. Certainly if they expand any more they could apply to become a country, with their own entry in the Eurovision Song Contest.

Apart from the extraordinary facilities, what you mainly buy from these places is self-esteem. Your child will learn that they matter, that they're expected to 'do well', that they will mix with lawyers and TV executives and not drive a fork-lift truck for Somerfield because they went to a school that charges ordinary people a pound to drive past. That's why public school is, by nature, divisive. It's not just a means to ensure a good education, it's a mechanism for making those who attend it feel they're better than most before they even start.

That, however, wasn't the opinion of a new club that emerged in the New Labour years, the slightly uneasy fee-paying middle-class parents, who had their own motto: 'You can't put your principles before your children.' The first person from this club I came across was an actress with an effervescent 7-year-old who lived about 200 yards from a popular junior school. 'Ah,' I smiled naively. 'He must go to that lovely school at the end of your road.' And her face contorted into that awkward guilty expression, the one you see in sitcoms when someone's about to explain they've put the rent money on a horse. 'Oh, Mark,' she said. 'Oh goodness, I know you're going to hate me, but well, and he's our only son, and well, we both talked about it, and it caused us so much stress, honestly it did, but in the end we decided you can't put your principles before your children.'

My first reaction to this is to object on grounds of logic. The statement assumes there is a choice of priorities – principles or children. Surely one part of being a parent, possibly the most important part, is to convey a set of principles to your children: don't drop litter, share your sweets, that sort of thing. To put this another way, if poor people adopted the same attitude, they could say, 'I know you're going to hate me for this, but we both talked about it and well, in the end we decided to rob the old woman who lives next door for her pension so we could buy Jason a microscope, because you can't put your principles before your children.'

I'd become aware over the years of a term used by psychoanalysts – 'projection'. For example, someone might shout all day at you, then say you've been shouting at them. Something in their mind projects what they're doing on to you. Maybe that's what happens with this 'principles' argument, because what they argue, in effect, is that they're the principled ones, for not having principles. While you should be ashamed of yourself, for being so unprincipled as to still have principles.

Then they tell you their kid's a special case 'because the thing with Oscelot is he's exceptionally talented. We've already put him down for extra violin studies. He's not even born yet but you can tell from the way he kicks in the tummy he's going to be in the Royal Philharmonic.'*

The trouble is, they say, the local schools are *dreadful*. So they tell their stories of gangs and sword fights and protection money, and I expect them to explain how the cookery department has fallen under the control of Chechen rebels. It's as if their fear is that their children will come home crying, worrying that they'll

---

*Even the privately educated aren't escaping the scramble for exam results and status that dominates modern education and makes it so unnecessarily stressful. In fact, they suffer even more, and you can imagine their parents boasting how they're *delighted* to get Tarragon into St Dunstall's because they've had three students commit suicide this term before exams, which shows they're really committed to pushing the children to the best of their ability.

come out in a rash because they've bumped into kids from a council estate, spluttering, 'Mummy, Daddy, it was dreadful, they smelt of buses and fish fingers and ITV.'

I used to say they couldn't be *that* bad, but secretly I worried that by not taking part in a six-year process of investigations, bribery and private tutors, I was condemning my son to a stretch in an apocalyptic ghetto. When he was ten we had to visit the schools he was eligible to apply for. At the least selective of them, the place crackled with the urgency and impudence of young life. Boys called to their mates across crowded corridors, eager to recite their joke or their cuss or relay information about where to meet, because they couldn't wait until they were next to their friends to speak quietly, sensibly, like adults, because that would waste five seconds and mean *waiting*. Girls in groups shrieked with joy or astonishment or laughter, with a vivacity adults could never match without a bottle of tequila.

In the classrooms they were mostly gazing earnestly at whiteboards or a computer screen, some arrogantly assured, others baffled, it seemed, not just by the lesson but by the world; every dimension of life mattered to all of them. Even those who were bored were properly bored, not just with a 'pheeeew' but an 'I'm FUCKING BORED'. Wandering amid these fireworks of emotion, I considered the condemnations of these schools as so gripped by violence and urban squalor that no responsible parent dare let their offspring even go past the place in the back of their four-wheel drive Jeep Cherokee. Should such a family accidentally find itself in the vicinity of the school, the father would probably issue instructions to 'Look straight ahead, don't express fear because they can smell it, and if they obstruct our path I'll say we come in peace and offer them a trinket.'

Of course, behind the frenetic jollity there might well be knives and gangs and filming something horrible on a bus with a mobile phone, but that's not the daily experience – just as there are arsonists and jihadists in London, but you'd be peculiar if you moved to Norfolk to get away from them.

The enthusiasm, the will, the equipment and the potential are all in place to make education more productive than ever. But the philosophy is that of New Labour, of business and profit and the oil companies. In some universities it's *literally* that of oil companies, as Cambridge has a Shell chair in chemical engineering, and there are BP professorships in seven universities. Nowhere in the speeches, documents, promises and boasts about education that have poured from the government is the idea that learning is a fundamental motor of life just because it's a brilliant thing to participate in; that it's wonderful to learn Italian or how to paint or how sound works, not because it enables you to secure a job in IT or qualify for funding or earn 16 per cent above the average wage or pass an exam, but because it's enthralling. To suggest such a thing is to enter a world New Labour simply couldn't compute. With all we know about Tony Blair, did he ever exhibit any indication of having read a book or seen a film or heard a piece of music that moved him, that made him gasp and lose his mind in its beauty or poignancy, regardless of its effect on exports? When he became friendly with the Bee Gees, to the extent of staying in their holiday homes, was that because he genuinely admired them? Did 'How Deep Is Your Love' always make him weep with emotion? Or did he revere them because they were rich and famous, which in his world means successful?

He can be proud of his role in education by that measure of success. Because more kids are passing exams, more parents are moving to different catchment areas, more private tutors are being hired, more schools are selecting better-off children to improve their pass rates, more students are getting into unfathomable debt, more are delivering pizzas or becoming prostitutes, more are taking overdoses and more people are worrying more than ever about whether they and their kids can stay in the race by learning the stuff required of them by business.

Few people can have adopted the philosophy that everything is judged by how much money it's worth, more wholeheartedly than Dale's family. Dale was the cropped-haired lad in my son's class whose voice already sounded gravelly when he was eight. He lived in a block that was cordoned off by police tape twice in one week, which gave the residents a certain civic pride. Always the last to arrive at school, often in fights, no matter how mean he tried to look you wanted to ruffle his spiky hair and go 'All right mate' because his face was exactly the one you'd try to draw if someone asked you for a picture of an urchin.

'He's not in, Dale, sorry,' I'd say, when he knocked for my son, and he'd turn away, hands in pockets, without a word, and yet still seem so endearing, because he looked as if he'd turn the corner into a 1958 film about a bunch of scallywags from East London who found an unexploded Second World War bomb and tried to hide it from the authorities. And everything was judged by its price. 'New trainers, Dale?' I'd ask. 'Twenty-one ninety-nine,' he'd say. 'Have you seen my watch? Eighteen ninety-nine.'

One day, just after Christmas, Dale went out with my son to fly his remote-controlled helicopter. Half an hour later they both ran in, gasping that it was stuck in a tree. As I stood under the tree trying to dislodge the helicopter by chucking bits of branches and small rocks at it, he said, 'My dad'll kill me, it was thirty-four ninety-nine.' I wondered whether Dale assumed a ninety-nine was a form of currency.

One afternoon I asked my son not to disturb me for an hour as I was struggling to fathom out what Descartes was all about for a programme in the *Lectures* series. 'Don't worry, Dad,' he said, 'I'm having a water fight with Dale,' and he ran outside with his pink and green water pistol. Three minutes later the door flew open and my son ran in, utterly saturated, wetter than if he'd been swimming, as if he'd found a hitherto undiscovered level of wetness. I gave him some towels, mopped up the drips, threw his wet clothes in a basket and he went back out. Two minutes later, as I read the same sentence one syllable at a time, the door crashed open and my son ran in, even wetter than before. 'Bloody hell, I can't read Descartes in these conditions,' I yelled, and handed him some more towels and clothes. Then I went outside, where Dale stood at the end of the path, with a bright green, four-foot-long gun that he could only fire by resting it on his shoulder as if it was a rocket launcher aiming at helicopters in the hills of Afghanistan. If you wrote a comedy sketch about kids having a water fight and one of them was American, therefore brought round a water gun that was ridiculously huge, this would be the one the props department would make. 'Look at this,' he bellowed with delight, and a jet of water zoomed up and onto the roof of the house. From a certain angle it must have looked as if the fire brigade had popped round. 'Whooosh' – he aimed it into the road next, like a psychedelic water cannon, until there was such a flood the local radio was probably advising people to avoid the area because of a burst water main. 'What about that?' he said. 'Twenty-six ninety-nine.'

With such an attitude he'd be ideal to work on a Private Finance Initiative. Almost every major project in education or health is now undertaken through a Private Finance Initiative, and you can study the details if you like but there's a clue in the title as to whether its main purpose is to encourage a) education and health or b) private finance.

Another clue is that when Labour were elected in 1997, Harriet Harman, who was the Minister for Social Security, called it a 'Trojan horse for privatisation'. The way it works is that new hospitals and schools are built by private companies, who then charge the NHS or education authority for their trouble. This payment is made over thirty years, so defenders of the system describe it as like a mortgage. It's hard to see how this is cheaper. Buying a house with a mortgage is the only way most of us ever manage it, but it's hardly cheaper than buying it in one go.

The difference is that at the end of the payments, the private consortium still owns the building, and the Health Service or education authority will still have to buy it back, though they should get a cheap rate. The private companies charge fees for the consultations they go through before building the project, and for the lawyers and accountants they use to negotiate the deal, which all amounts to between £1 million and £4 million per project. And the companies get a representative at senior level in the hospital or school. Even with a mortgage you don't go home and find the bloke from the building society sitting on your settee, saying, 'Hello, mate, your bathroom could do with a lick of paint.'

The debate about how much this all costs is between those who say it makes a project twice as expensive as before or those, such as the health unions, who say it's five times as expensive. Businessmen are attracted to these projects because they're businessmen. If they'd wanted to put money into healthcare because of their love of healthcare, they'd have done it before PFI.

In some areas there's no doubt a business agenda has improved efficiency. For example, in 2006 hospital car parks made £95 million profit. What an example of modern spirit and enterprise compared to the old 'anti-business' ideology that allowed people to park at hospitals for free. These dinosaurs would never have had the imagination to say, 'Hmm, they HAVE to come by car as they're limping – we can charge the fuckers as much as we like.'

And they don't just charge, they charge more than anyone. In Edinburgh, for example, the car park at the hospital is more expensive than the one at the airport. Maybe this is the way to cut waiting lists. Because eventually it will be cheaper to park at the airport, fly to Canada and get it done there than pay to have it done free round the corner.

Every aspect of the system is poked at to see if it could be turned into a business. When they find something, they're like someone popping a sheet of bubble wrap who thinks they've squeezed it all, then goes, 'Oo marvellous, I've found a bit that's not been done yet.' For example, the contract to deliver items to hospitals was awarded to DHL, the parcel delivery firm. Making the announcement, Patricia Hewitt, the New Labour health woman, denied that DHL's main interest in this job was profit. Of course it isn't. After the first year I'm sure the chairman told the shareholders' meeting, 'The annual report gives us excellent news.

For in the year ending 31 March we delivered absolutely tons of stuff to sick people. We didn't make a single penny but you should have seen the look on their little faces.'

And this is trumpeted as the only way. A mental health trust in Manchester tried to cut costs by moving its patients out of the hospital altogether and into the voluntary sector. When one of the nurses, Karen Reissman, publicly objected to this practice she was sacked for 'bringing the trust into disrepute'. Because even to suggest there's an alternative upsets everything. There's probably a think-tank working out how to make the mentally ill profitable for business, perhaps by sponsoring the voices in their heads. So instead of spies and demons they'll hear, 'You can't get quicker than a Kwik-Fit fitter,' and explain that while they no longer feel the urge to burn anything down they have spent their life savings on exhaust pipes.

And yet there's something unsettling about the tradition of much of the British Left of constantly describing the NHS as on the 'point of collapse'. The other way to see it is that, despite nearly thirty years of being under governments committed to privatising everything they can, it's still there. It's still a source of wonder to Americans, who can barely imagine a health system not dependent on expensive private insurance.

There has clearly been an increase in funding under New Labour, which should be celebrated, but also recognised for what it is, a testament to the persistence of so many who depend on the NHS to preserve it as something owned collectively. Every proposed cut or closure in the service is met with protests, placards, petitions, and in the case of Kidderminster, the election of a local campaigning doctor as the town's MP. The principles of a free health service are so ingrained in our culture that the world of business seems to have accepted it can only burrow its way in by stealth, round the fringes.

Almost everyone who visits a hospital tells of a similar experience: the care was amazing and the staff wonderful, but the cleaning, catering and other peripheral services were dreadful. In other words, everything that's been contracted out to companies whose concern is profit is worse, not because they're inefficient but because they *are* efficient – at making profit. They scour every corner for opportunities to cut costs and raise charges, and employ agency staff who can develop little of the camaraderie and team spirit of those who work directly for the NHS.

The money clearly exists to fund healthcare without handing the NHS over to big business; companies can finance the construction of large hospital projects. But why is it not possible then to pay them back without them making profits that run into tens of millions of pounds? Because, it seems, it's simply naive to expect anyone to remove a tumour or deliver a baby unless someone's going to make a few bob out of it.

At least the National Health Service hasn't been sold off to the people who run the rail companies, or heart bypass patients would be told, 'We'll push you as far as the maternity ward. Then to get to cardio you'll need a Silverlink trolley but I haven't got a timetable for them, or you could go direct but that will mean going via Wolverhampton.'

Almost everyone thought it was a ridiculous idea to privatise the railways. For example, there was the speech in 1993: 'Any privatisation of the railway system that does take place will, on the arrival of a Labour government, be quickly and effectively dealt with, with the full support of the community, and returned to public ownership.' Which was boomed out by John Prescott, who then spent ten years as deputy leader of a Labour government that did all it could to ensure the railways remained private, in full opposition to the community.

It was certainly in opposition to the stern-looking man of about sixty who was studying the *Daily Telegraph* as if he was about to sit an exam on its contents and slammed it down in response to an announcement that we'd be stuck outside Falkirk for 'a few more minutes'. He snarled at me, 'They should *never have been bloody well privatised,*' as if it was me who had done it.

The real measure of disgust, however, is not the outbursts of anger, but the way during most delays few people react at all. So you all grab your bags and get out at Stoke where the train is being taken out of service because of a faulty engine, then play Snake on your mobile or queue twenty minutes for tea in the Lemon Tree Café, that resembles a lemon tree as much as a burned-out car resembles a rhododendron bush, and an hour later you suddenly have to run with your bags down the stairs and up to another platform as the next train's come in there for some unexplained reason, and clamber on to a now packed compartment where you stand in a huddle for the rest of the journey, except when a child needs the toilet and has to be passed overhead like an exhibitionist at a rock festival. And you do all this with barely any expression of fury, because it's what you expect. An unsuspecting foreigner must think it's all deliberate and part of a religious festival, just as if you were in an Argentinian village and saw a crowd running away from someone dressed as a bull you'd think, 'How colourful and quaint' and never imagine this wasn't supposed to happen and that now they'd have to ring up work and say they'd be an hour late because the bull person had disrupted their morning again.

One of the boasts of the private companies is that they must be doing things well because so many of their trains are so popular. What a magnificently rosy way of looking at it, to see 200 people squashed into a compartment at ten to eight every morning, in the sort of trance showmen have to achieve in order to endure squatting for three days in a barrel of ice, and interpret this as an expression of their product's popularity.

Mile for mile, a British train journey is double the cost of the more efficient trains in France, Germany or Italy and the most expensive anywhere in Europe. And the greatest achievement, especially on Virgin, is the attention to detail because *everything* is shit. Anyone can make trains late or crowded or expensive but they leave nothing to chance. As often as not there's an announcement that there's no tea or coffee because the boiler's busted, and on one crowded train from Liverpool no food was served because they couldn't find the key to the fridge. The automatic toilet door may or may not slide open and you daren't lock it in case you're stuck in there for two days and the bastards charge you 7,000 quid for all the journeys you've been on. Inside the toilet there's a soap squirter that coughs out one sticky globule, an automatic water sprinkler that responds to the pressing of a rubber knob by spurting out no water at all, so you're now worse off than before as you have to wipe the spunky stuff off your hands on the back of your trousers.

Then you see these charts declaring that 97 per cent of the trains are on time, making you think you must have been on every one of the 3 per cent that were late. But it turns out whole days can be declared void if there is 'substantial disruption on the network' and Virgin claimed this happened on 137 days in one year. Football teams ought to be able to do this. Then they could all declare the bad days void, only count the days they won and everyone would be promoted every year.

One Saturday morning I set off from Glasgow aiming for London. The timetable suggested I should arrive at Selhurst Park for a football match at two o'clock. But the train got stuck, and stuck again, and probably lost, and finally arrived eight hours late. The brilliant thing I learned was that once you pass two hours of lateness it stops being annoying and becomes funny. Because you become resigned to writing off the day, and the train becomes your new home. At Birmingham, already at around three hours late, the train sat obstinately still with no announcement until the driver got off, shouted, 'Fuck this' and left. Being English, we all stayed on a while despite there being no driver, maybe thinking, 'Well, you never know, one of the passengers might be a wizard.' But gradually we all got off and someone said we could get another line from a different station about a mile away, so hundreds of people with suitcases clambered round the Bull Ring like very lost refugees and we got the other train but that one broke down too and we had to get a bus. Then another train and then a coach and I wondered if next we'd be taken round a corner and put in a gondola. On the coach I noticed the person next to me was Martin Bell, the war correspondent who became an MP. He was wearing a white suit, just like he always did on the telly, and he was charming. And now I panicked that I was actually having a very vivid dream and at any moment Chris Tarrant would get on and accuse me of stealing his gooseberries. Eventually we all learned to enjoy it until, on the last leg from Reading, I was almost willing the train to conk out one more time for a brilliant reason, such as running over an elk. Instead of arriving home an hour before the match, I got in just after the start of *Match of the Day*.

We are told all this was designed to remove the cost of railways from the taxpayer, but the public subsidy to the private firms is £1.3 billion a year, more than it used to cost to fund British Rail. Railtrack were especially inventive: in 2001 they lobbied the government for an extra £1.5 billion subsidy in order to keep going, then, on the same day they were granted it, immediately passed on 10 per cent of that as a dividend to their shareholders.

On a global scale of human suffering, the waiting and sweating and jostling, screaming 'HOW MUCH?' and wandering around bemused in a car park in the countryside wondering whether this special bus will ever arrive, and being told aggressively to pay a fine for not having a ticket when you spent twenty minutes trying to slide a £10 note into a machine that delighted in shovelling it straight back out again, so you start wondering whether they employ dwarves to stand inside the machine and poke the notes back out just to annoy you, is not up there with events in Burma or Sudan. But it's possibly the most visible evidence of the disdain the mass of the population is treated with, in order to make a handful of rich people richer, and how we puff and sigh and know it's wrong but put up with it only because we know so much of it could be put right, but have no idea how to make it happen.

I met a couple of friends one evening in a gloomy local pub when there was one person in the public bar who spent the whole night on the fruit machine and chatting to his mate, the sole barman, about whether he should buy a new car.

In our bar there was a table with two Goth couples who must have been attracted by the darkness, and a table with two married couples, all of them big, in a way that suggested every one of them knew the perfect technique for applying a Nelson headlock. One of the men heard us talking about asylum-seekers and leaned across in an inquiring way. 'You like them asylum types then?' he asked, not threatening but genuinely interested. We all muttered a version of 'They're all right' and he said, 'Oh right. Thing is though, they're taking the piss, don't you think? Mugs we are, mugs.'

We exchanged our different opinions, fairly amicably, while the second big man glared into the gloom, occasionally supping his beer, every lift of the glass or turn of the head carried out in a jerky, abrupt way, as if he wanted even the inanimate objects he was touching to feel an element of threat. Suddenly he spoke, his solid frame perfectly still while his hand made a fist with one finger poking out, and from his growling, gravelly tone it seemed even his voice had been in a fight. Every syllable was enunciated clearly while he managed to look all three of us in the eye at once. Whatever he said would have been threatening, even if it was about his pets. It would be something along the lines of 'My fucking rabbit – it's got more fucking fur on it – than you lot have ever seen in your FUCKING life.'

Instead he said, 'Asylum-seekers, fucking slags. I'll TELL you what them fucking Kosovans do. They'll work for fucking nothing. On all the buildings. Put our boys out of a job.'

'I don't think that happens as much as people say,' I said.

'Oh yes, it FUCKING does,' he said. 'I know, 'cos I fucking employ the bastards.'

As I pondered this contradiction, the other man asked the Goths what they thought. When they all agreed that they really didn't mind asylum-seekers at all, the big man went back to glaring, while his wife sipped a Dubonnet and fidgeted slightly. The first man leaned across and said, 'He gets wound up. He's got a building firm and a couple of pubs and the Kosovans wind him up.'

'I don't fucking let them in,' he said through his glare.

Then the second man changed the subject. 'Basically I mean to say we're all just trying to earn a living at the end of the day. I've got three sons. The first one, he's twenty-seven, director of sales. Goes all over the South of England. He made sixty-four grand last year. Bought a house up Wimbledon way, hundred and eighty thousand, valued now at three twenty-eight. The second one, in the army. Bought somewhere up Bromley, one twenty-five, had loft conversion, extension, the lot, worth two sixty to two seventy, just had it valued. Last one, he's only twenty-two, develops what do you call it, software, for computers, all that. Two-bedroom flat, I give him a bit of help like, gone up in value fifty grand already. They're doing all right.'

By now the glaring man was revving up for another burst. 'They're fucking robbing us.'

'Come on, mate,' I said. 'You're getting angry with the wrong people. Rupert Murdoch, he's robbing us, he pays hardly any tax, he's short-changed the country by three hundred and fifty million over the last ten years.'

'Why SHOULDN'T he enjoy himself, he's fucking earned his money,' he said. Then he rolled up a sleeve over a worrying forearm. 'How much do you reckon that watch is worth?' he asked.

'Sorry, mate, I'm useless with watches,' I confessed.

'Two grand,' he said. 'Two grrrrrand.'

'If it was Dale he'd have said, "Two grand ninety-nine",' I thought.

'I've earned it,' he said. 'Brought up in Brixton, started with nothing, earned every fucking penny.'

At this point I remembered a scene in the film *True Romance*, and thought it might come in handy. 'Blimey, were you brought up in Brixton? Was your family from there then?'

'Right back we go,' he said.

'So you must know the history. Brixton was all swamp until it was built up by the Huguenots. You know, from France. They all came over here in the 1800s fleeing the mobs that were after them, so your ancestors were French. So, when you come to think about it, *you*'re French. Amazing, isn't it?'

He glared, possibly snorted, snatched his coat and his wife's hand with equal vigour and stomped out of the door with them both. And just as I was feeling very pleased with myself, the second man's wife patted me on the wrist. '*She'll* pay for that,' she said.

11

AND THE CLOCKS WERE
STRIKING THIRTEEN

So many people infuriated at the way big business pokes its tentacles into every orifice – and yet so hard to get many of them together in a room to do something about it. One way some of the old Left respond to this, is to put on events that couldn't possibly attract anyone who hasn't been part of the organised Left for at least thirty years. For example, I arrived at one anti-war meeting to find I was speaking after a socialist choir, whose big closing number involved the front row singing 'There's a rumble in the air tonight', while the back row sang 'Oh no it's an imperialist bomb'.

Or I find myself at fund-raising benefits, head in hands, as a Palestinian singer introduces a song by saying, 'This one is one I hope you will sing along with the chorus. It goes "Everyone in my village has been shot".'

One night I was performing at an evening for Palestinian rights, and was told I'd be on in the second half. The audience, bless them, appeared to be made up almost entirely of old CND marchers from the 1950s, some of whom couldn't be guaranteed to *make* it to the second half. During the interval I went backstage to get ready, where Tony Benn was waiting to make a speech, and the actress Susannah York was walking round in circles learning the lines of a piece of prose she was performing. Later there'd be

someone playing a lute, and while it was all very honourable it
seemed unlikely that the audience would be boosted by the arrival
of a coach party from Wigan.

Susannah York was doing breathing exercises, 'Meee miiii
moooo maaaa', while I chatted to Tony Benn about the formation of Israel in 1948. Then she started walking round in a circle
again, right round us, making me wonder if this was a religious
ritual and Tony Benn and I were about to be sacrificed. Just as she
was going to be introduced, Tony Benn said to her, 'Oh well,
break a leg.' And she pulled that face actresses pull to express great
anxiety, as when the girl in a silent movie realises she's about to be
tied to a railway line, and said, 'Oh my God, I wish you hadn't said
that. The last time someone said that I immediately crushed my
heel against the side of the stage.'

'Oh goodness, I'm so sorry,' said Tony Benn, and there was
something brilliant about watching the real Tony Benn, waving
his hands in that Tony Benn way, saying, 'I had no idea you see,
I just thought it was something you said, I do hope it doesn't
affect your performance.' It was like being in a kitchen with Mick
Jagger as he pursed his lips, clapped and screeched, 'I can't find the
marmalade.'

The route to the stage was through a wide door that opened
out directly on to the back of the stage, and when it was open the
audience could see through to the backstage area. Susannah went
through the door to perform, as we continued chatting. In the
background we could hear her soliloquy; then it stopped in mid-
flow. After a dramatic pause the door suddenly swung open in front
of us, and we both looked up to gaze directly at the bewildered
audience, as they peered back equally puzzled, at us. To one side
stood Susannah York, holding the door knob. She breathed in as
she raised one arm, as if she was about to say, 'A handbag?' Instead
she went, 'Could you please keep quiet – I can't possibly concentrate.'
Tony Benn and I looked at each other, at her and at the audience,
and then she slammed the door, before continuing, 'Oh indeed
thou that hath thither' or whatever it was. I shook, quietly, with

laughter, while Tony Benn stared at the wall and went bright red like a schoolboy caught looking at porn.

Afterwards you're left wondering quite what the point of the evening was, and being thankful that none of your neighbours, or anyone who knows you from outside the Left or anyone under forty was there.

Performers who aren't familiar with the rules of these events can end up feeling as if they're performing to a branch of the Mafia. One joke that could be interpreted as deviating slightly from the official line of the organisers, and the room chills into a jury of folded arms and judgemental glares. At a Cuba Solidarity event, I started with five minutes about Cuba, then went on to a joke about another subject, whereupon someone walked right in front of me and yelled, 'Denounce the American blockade.' As if he was worried that, since I'd gone a whole sentence without denouncing the American blockade, I must have suddenly decided to support it.

You develop an instinct for knowing how an event is likely to turn out just from the way you're asked to take part. I was once asked to perform, and get other comics to perform, at an outdoor gig for a campaign, at about three days' notice. 'To be honest,' I said, 'I'm a bit worried it could be a fiasco.' And the organiser came out with a sentence that I'm sure has never been said at any other time in the English language: 'Oh no, it *won't* be a fiasco – Pete Doherty's going to be there.'

Often you feel the real purpose of these occasions is to create an evening where the audience can be with people who agree with them, and keep the unpleasantness of the real world away. For example, I was asked to speak at a Stop the War rally organised by a diligent but eccentric woman called Beryl. The week before, I was besieged with messages: could I be sure to speak only for twelve minutes, then, 'We're letting a local poet say a few words so could you adjust your speech to eleven minutes,' then could I be there fifty minutes early as someone would like to take a photo for the newsletter but could I wear nothing blue because that might not show up against the blue walls in the hall. Then on the Monday of the week of the rally, at twelve minutes to nine in the morning the phone rang.

I knew it was twelve minutes to nine because I was taking the kids to school. To get there on time we had to leave at ten to nine, so twelve minutes to nine was always overflowing with panic, calls of 'Clean your teeth', 'Where's your shoes?' and 'You can't start a new game of Tumblin' Monkeys now' all at once. No level of organisation can avoid this. Even if your kids are dressed, washed, fed, with teeth cleaned by half past four in the morning, at twelve minutes to nine your daughter will announce, 'Oh I forgot – I have to make a model iguana.' And somehow it gets done. Perhaps this technique could get those projects that are years late built on time. If building Wembley Stadium had been a school project, a parent would have been hurriedly helping their son hammer in the goalposts at twelve minutes to nine, then dragged it up to the school and just got it and the boy into the door as the whistle went.

I gasped, 'Hello, I'll have to ring you back I'm just getting the kids out the door who are you?'

And a woman said, 'Ah, now, yes, well, ahem, hello, er, right, well, good morning, this is Beryl from the Stop the War rally . . .'

'Beryl I'll have to ring you back I'm off out the door,' I puffed.

'Oh yes, well, you see, what it is, yes, I'm from the Stop the War rally and . . .'

'I've got to go right now I'll ring you back.'

'Now,' she said, 'can you confirm you'll arrive at, oh, let's see what was it, hang on, I'll get my sheet.' And I went.

At the rally there were about sixty people in the audience, most of whom seemed to know each other, all white and all older than me. Beryl began with a ten-minute monologue that meandered in entirely unpredictable directions: 'Now what a MARVELLOUS turnout and if Mister Blair thinks this war will go away well he ought to be here to see this WONDERFUL crowd and then he'd realise but there's a wonderful article I read somewhere about that poor chap in that prison and apparently Starbucks have been supporting George Bush so it's very important we boycott it and anyway they do horrible coffee far too frothy and I recommend Luigi's by the station or there's Bar Piazza but it's up to you . . .'

One by one the speakers said there had to be loads of protest, and everyone clapped, and then the local imam claimed the state of the Middle East had upset God which you could tell from the number of earthquakes and tsunamis there'd been lately. Then it was my turn to be introduced. 'Well,' said Beryl, 'what can I say about our next speaker? Well, to be honest I'd never heard of him so I looked him up on the internet and here are some of the things it says.' She unfurled a wad of printed sheets and ran through a few random quotes, including a scathing review, adding, 'And apparently someone said he does comedy so who knows WHAT to expect and the only other thing I know about him is if you ring him up when he's taking the children to school he can be rather grumpy, so please welcome Mark Steel.'

The Beryls who organise these meetings, who turn up and distribute leaflets and tell their neighbours to stop using Starbucks are principled and dedicated; each one a stubborn little dam against the multinational tide. But these gatherings are also depressing because anyone from outside their social circle would be utterly lost there. Anyone young popping in feels completely out of place, like when you come home as a teenager at one in the morning and find your parents are still up with their friends.

The young aren't attracted to the Left primarily because socialism appears to them as an archaic belief, but the problem is compounded by these occasions that can appear as cliquey as a giant dinner party. Everyone at these events seems despairingly familiar with the etiquette of the group. Everyone knows who the speaker is talking about when they mention an obscure columnist from the *Guardian*, everyone knows at which points to clap (like an audience at a classical music concert), which minor government figures to jeer, and no one says 'cunt'. If the Left was attracting a layer of people from outside this group, this etiquette would come under threat. But instead there's a cosiness that makes anyone from outside feel what they are – an intruder.

In 2006, when Tony Blair revealed he'd definitely be resigning within a year, the socialist MP John McDonnell announced he'd be standing against Gordon Brown for the position of Prime Minister. As campaigns go you couldn't fault this for ambition. And to be fair, I doubt he ever thought he could win. But it wasn't that long ago that leading positions in the Labour Party *were* fought fairly evenly between left and right.

At this point, with Labour's standing so damaged by the war in Iraq and such unease about the domination of big business, you might expect the left challenge would be stronger than usual. And yet John McDonnell, who'd campaigned against the war, stood no chance against Gordon Brown, who'd helped to finance it. He couldn't even get enough support for there to be a vote at all. So he'd have done better if he'd stood to lead almost any organisation other than the one he was in; ornithology societies, the Scouts, Coventry City Supporters' Club, the Women's Institute, the army, any random group would probably accept that an amiable chap who's spent his life supporting the poorest and hard-done-by and opposed the war should be on a ballot paper as candidate for leader. But the party set up for hard-done-by people thought, 'Sod that, he'll be an embarrassment when he meets Rupert Murdoch and George Bush.'

Even worse, of the six candidates for deputy leader, all of them had backed the war. If that poll suggesting the number supporting the invasion was 14 per cent was accurate, the chances of finding six random people who all supported it were, by my calculations, 46,656 to 1. Never have so many people been in agreement with the left of the Labour Party against the right, and yet never has that left been so utterly frail that it couldn't even mount a worthwhile challenge. However, instead of acknowledging this reality, the organisers of the campaign told

audiences at their rallies that they should expect 'stunning victories'. I heard one of them say, 'Hundreds of young people have
joined the party through our website so they can take part in the
campaign.' It was as much as I could do not to shout, 'WHAT?
Right, go on then, name me five.' It felt like being told at
Agincourt to venture once more unto the breach with nostrils
flaring for King Harry and England, then wondering whether it
would spoil things to say, 'That's all very inspiring but there's
only you and me here, sir.'

One logical answer is to accept that the Labour Party, even
down to the bulk of local members, is now to the right of millions
of people who are not members of anything. You're now more
likely to find sympathy for strikes or the anti-war movement
from someone outside the Labour Party than inside it. It takes
a glance into history to grasp the significance of this, as the
party was established to give a voice to such people. It's as if
you were more likely to find someone who plays cricket among
a random selection of people in a shopping centre, than in a
cricket team.

It must therefore make more sense to campaign outside the
Labour Party than inside. But the groups outside have failed to
attract more than a handful of the disillusioned either, and in the
case of the SWP have declined to the extent that I often hear
someone who's been hostile to the SWP in the past, asking,
'What's *happened* to your lot? They always used to be in every
shopping centre but you rarely see them now' – said with genuine pity, like when a sportsman laments the decline of his nearest
rival.

And yet when I complained to SWP stalwarts that things
appeared to be in disarray, they'd look astonished. 'Really?' they
asked, and told me there had never been such fantastic opportunities. The trouble was if I bumped into them again a year later
there was every chance they'd have given up altogether. Defying
reality is a perfect strategy for dealing with difficulties for a while,
but hard to maintain in the long term.

To the majority of people who have never been entwined with a tiny political group that aspires to overthrow every government in the world, it might not seem surprising that its behaviour strays towards the over-optimistic. But one of the attractions for me had always been its almost charming realism. The founder of the SWP, Tony Cliff, would recount how in the 1950s there were only fifty members, and some were understandably downcast when they discovered a different group had 500 members. So he said, 'Look – let's say to make a revolution in Britain you need one million members. We need another 999,950, whereas they only need another 999,500. What is there to be depressed about?'

As a teenager I was heartened as much by the honesty as by the ideas and activities. We'd almost brag about the modest size of the organisation, and this would spur people on. The attitude was that twenty people in a whole town isn't many, but together with a few mates they can make quite a difference. This was the opposite of a cult, because everything the SWP attempted, such as launching a movement to stop the growth of fascist parties, was judged by its impact in the real world. When things went wrong they had to be explained, as there weren't the get-out clauses of religion. If we called for a mass demonstration but only nine people turned up and were all beaten up by the police, we couldn't just say, 'Never mind – it just goes to show socialism moves in mysterious ways.'

During the years of New Labour this honest accounting seemed to evaporate. Everything was proclaimed as an indication of booming opportunities. There'd be excited pronouncements revealing new strategies with names such as 'Action Programme'. Rallies were called, the urgency of the situation proclaimed, then everything would disappear with no explanation. It was like having a friend who announced he was getting married, held a huge stag party, then never mentioned the wedding or the woman again, but a few weeks later said, 'Guess what, I'm getting married,' and it started all over again.

The result was that many of those who were involved became

demoralised because, having heard all these grand pronouncements, they looked round the room at their own branch, saw ever shrinking numbers and thought this was their fault.

SWP leaders insisted that there were 10,000 members, which was obviously a huge exaggeration. One answer given, if you asked how the figures could possibly add up, was: 'We have to redefine the definition of member.' Perhaps we had to redefine the membership as including people who weren't members. There was a discussion among leading members of the SWP about one branch, which was having difficulties to the extent that it was down to three members. After a debate about the causes, it was decided the solution was to split the branch into two separate ones.

At one point the denial took the form of membership lists being sent out to every branch, with the insistence that each name should be followed up rigorously, no matter how long since they had been seen. Getting the central office to accept that someone on this list was no longer a member was a feat of endurance. You might say, 'There was no one at that address and it's boarded up' or 'The bloke shouted "I've told you before – fuck off"' out of the window while he was shaving.' You'd most probably be told that somewhere or other a similar thing happened, but the local branch had gone back again and the man had apologised and now was back in the branch as a leading member. I imagined that even if you said, 'We visited that address and the bloke's dead,' you'd be told, 'Well, don't give up. Someone in Halifax branch went to visit someone who turned out to be dead, but they went back again and he filled out a standing order for subs and now he sells nine papers a week to other corpses in the graveyard.'

When I did a show in London for two nights, I tried to get the SWP to set up a stall outside, to publicise the campaign against the war in Iraq. But no one came. So the following week I asked why it wasn't possible for two people from the whole of London to set up a stall and was told, 'This just goes to show there are so many things going on we can't cover them all.' What are you supposed to say to that? I felt like replying, 'Yes, isn't it fantastic? Soon you won't turn up to anything at all anywhere and that will prove you're on the verge of taking power.'

It was as if the aim was to maintain a steady amount of enthusiasm, but because there was around one-fifth of the number there used to be, everyone had to be five times as enthusiastic to keep things even. Some people, unable to bridge the gap between the rhetoric and the reality, would drift away. And then the enthusiasm demanded of the remainder would become even greater. I had a vision that at the end of this process there'd be one person left, standing at the top of a mountain yelling, 'IT'S MAGNIFICENT!!!'

One afternoon I spoke at a protest outside the American surveillance base at Menwith Hill in Yorkshire. This surreal compound appears across the Moors like a city in a science fiction film from the 1950s, about a dozen domes that look like giant golf balls imposing themselves on the hills and dales, and you can't help imagine each golf ball full of figures in boiler suits carrying shiny metal boxes under a huge digital clock showing how long to go before a giant explosion will enable a madman to rule the world. The camp is entirely under the command of the Americans, so this annual protest, on 4 July, is called 'Independence from America Day'. When I arrived, I was immediately photographed as I got out of the car, and in my arrogance assumed it was a local reporter keen to get the winning picture of the visiting comedian. Then came the deflation of seeing the same thing happen to a pair of crusties and I realised this was what the police did to everyone who turned up.

The scene of around 200 protesters with tatty banners and Thermos flasks, standing in the drizzle while a gazebo offered vegan bacon sandwiches could easily be lampooned, but none of this seemed as mad to me as it would once have done. Firstly, because Alan Bennett turned up to speak, and he was magnificently Alan Bennett. I remember his speech as being full of stuff like 'I have to say the base behind me here is not a view I particularly care for.'

And I was willing him to carry on, 'I rather take the stance of my Aunty Edith, who always maintained that a nation that's never learned to brew tea with a crocheted cosy shouldn't be trusted to place military camps on foreign territory.'

Second, because the protesters, like the protest, seemed not to be apart from the rest of society but an integral part of it. So much has changed since the days of CND in the 1980s, that a teenager with a blue Mohican and a jacket saying 'Fuck Bush' is almost mainstream. And the crowd *were* part of their community, they worked in local shops, offices and schools and even though some of them must have been over seventy everyone seemed young and lots of them had pierced eyebrows. The organiser of the event was Lindis Percy, who's been arrested over forty times outside the camp. In the evening she asked me a poignant question that is the most relevant one we face: 'Do you think we *achieved* anything today? Or are we wasting everyone's time?'

It was fairly easy to answer this. The military establishment clearly take the protests seriously and would be delighted if they stopped, while those who support the protests would feel deflated, instead of inspired by the fact that there is opposition to this sinister establishment.

But at least she asked the question. It struck me because the Left so rarely dares to ask the question, and that's essential if you're to maintain your numbers, let alone grow. 'Did we achieve anything today?' You've got to keep asking the question, otherwise, when the answer's 'no', not only can you not put matters right, you don't even realise matters need putting right.

The theoretical debates that radical groups engage in can seem ridiculous and obscure, and a disagreement might be given an inflated sense of importance, with someone grimacing earnestly that it could be fatal for the local branch if they don't change their attitude towards Robert the Bruce's tactics at the Battle of Bannockburn. But sometimes those debates do have obvious consequences, such as those on religion.

Most people might expect this is the simplest of matters for a socialist. The church is the enemy. It's used to justify wars and subservience, and it's opposed to rational thought, freedom of speech and masturbation. What good can possibly come of it?

In recent years, however, almost every month there's been a religious debate that's proved far more complicated. Some Christians urged laws to deal with unflattering depictions of God. There were bitter public rows about Sikhs in plays, and it felt as if every religion sought controversy on whether its followers could practise their faith at work. I expected to hear the Hare Krishnas were involved in a court case because one of their members was a snooker referee but the authorities didn't let him bang a gong all through the semi-final of the British Open championship.

Mostly, though, the heightened religious tension revolved around Islam. Muslims objected to blasphemous portrayals of the Prophet with a variety of protests, and in turn a powerful section of the government and media categorised Islam as a threat. For example, cabinet member Jack Straw announced his distaste for Muslim women wearing the veil. This was followed by a flurry of newspaper stories, such as the one in the *Sun* under the headline: 'A growing number use the veil to provoke us', adding that the veil is a 'threat'. Because some of these veils have got serrated edges you know. And there are a growing number of incidents involving Muslim women holding up banks with a sawn-off veil.

To anyone who associates with Muslims, the image of fiery fanatics is painfully ridiculous. The young Pakistanis I play cricket with are almost indistinguishable from white South London lads, to the extent that after a good shot they'll shout, 'Man, that's a *sick* cover drive, you get me.' Portraying them as a threat makes as much sense as claiming we're in danger from hordes of nutty Christians, all talking in tongues and threatening us with their Jesus car stickers. 'Onward Christian Soldiers, marching as to war' . . . it's obvious, they're planning to do us all in.

But many people who would consider themselves anti-establishment radicals are also adamant that Islam constitutes a major threat to a decent set of values. Some were reluctant to officially involve the Muslim community in the anti-war movement, as they disagree with traditional Islam about the treatment of women and gays. But any genuine mass movement depends on accepting anyone who agrees with its central issue, and given that the Muslim world would be the victim of the carnage, it seemed reasonable it should be entitled to oppose it. Just as, if someone asked you to help stop their brother being beaten in the street with a shovel, you wouldn't say, 'Well *maybe*. But first let me ask you a series of questions about your attitude to gay civil marriages.' Also, the involvement of Muslims in such numbers played a part in turning the most angry of them away from jihadist ideas. Because the argument that all non-Muslims are warmongering infidels carries little weight, if there are a million of them marching alongside you. In every mosque, those who preferred to isolate themselves from non-Muslims were forced into retreat by the scale of the anti-war movement.

The alliances formed in the anti-war movement made possible a new electoral effort involving the SWP, other groups on the left, George Galloway and radicalized Muslims known as Respect.

The sometimes complex arguments behind seeking allies within the Islamic faith became a fucking doddle compared to the conundrums unleashed by working with George Galloway.

Sometimes the task of defending George is simple, because the accusations made against him are so absurd. The *Daily Telegraph*, along with the *Christian Science Monitor*, claimed he was taking money from Saddam Hussein, which they claimed they could prove using documents discovered in an Iraqi building that had been burned to the ground – the Galloway-related papers the only things to survive intact – and in strangely pristine condition.

This is fairly standard for the ruling powers, who always seem to concoct stories about their egalitarian enemies being secretly on the make, as much as they are themselves. I'm sure when St Francis of Assisi was wandering about in self-imposed poverty, there was a story in the *Sun* that his brown smocks were actually made by Versace and sent by Genghis Khan, under a headline: 'Saint Francis of a-Sleazy.'

George always retaliated to these charges in a magnificently gladitorial tone, as if he was addressing the citizens of Rome before a battle with the Persians. Having been summoned by the US Senate to answer the charge of having taken money from Saddam's regime, the manner in which he humiliated his accusers made him an international hero. His reply to the charge of having met Saddam, that 'I met him the same number of times as your Defense Secretary [Donald Rumsfeld], the difference being I didn't meet him to sell him weapons,' broke every rule of polite deference that's expected towards such bodies. The trouble is he uses the same tone when he's in a kitchen arguing about where to find the biscuits.

Following Galloway's performance before the senators, I wrote a column in which I suggested he'd been so exhilarating that he might be approached to appear on a reality show, and end up in the *Big Brother* diary room growling, 'Let me tell you, Big Brother, you stated categorically that two packets of biscuits would be forthcoming for today's luncheon. Now your spineless lickspittle nonentity of a disembodied voice informs us that they are to be withheld, in an action that, were it to be categorised as stinginess, would insult the stingy. We may be the ones deprived of our confectionery treat, but rest assured, Big Brother, when the housemates let their feelings on this issue be known, yours is the cookie that is destined to crumble.' Oh dear Lord I want to know this didn't put ideas in anyone's head and make me partly responsible.

George presents a radio phone-in on the Talksport channel, which is addictively entertaining because he speaks as if he's addressing a mass rally in São Paulo. So you seem to hear such snippets as 'Your obfuscations and half-truths will succeed only in accelerating your descent into the snake-pit of oblivion you have brought about by your own reptilian actions – *that* is all I have to say to you, Dave from Basingstoke.'

But it is true, undeniably cringeingly true, that George not only met Saddam, he famously saluted his courage, truth and indefatigability.* At one level there's an easy reply to the accusations of grovelling, which is that Galloway took the decision to meet Saddam because he felt it could strengthen the chance for peace, and then had to follow the required degree of courtesy. Once in Saddam's palace, George couldn't very well refuse to shake his hand by taking his own hand away at the last moment, putting his thumb on his nose, wiggling his fingers and going 'wulawulawulawulawula'.

On its own, however, the explanation of due respect isn't enough, and there is a further reason why George may have saluted him so earnestly. The tradition of socialism and anti-war campaigning that George comes from owes a large part of its ideology to the Communist Party. For a variety of reasons the Communist parties around the world, as ordered by their leaders in Russia, took the view that when a nation was under attack from the West, its leaders should be supported almost uncritically, regardless of whether they were brutal to their own population. (The reason for this is that it suited the leaders of the Soviet Union. They wanted to deal with a strong diplomatic ally, not a rebellious mob.) No distinction was made between the leaders of a nation under fire and the rest of the people. For example, in the Vietnam War, most anti-war groups, following a similar line, made a hero of Ho Chi Minh, the leader of North Vietnam. This didn't seem so bad because his transgressions were much less obvious than Saddam's, but it flowed from a similar reluctance to make any criticism of those in opposition to the American army. In other cases, such as Saddam's, this approach is more obviously riddled with problems.

However repugnant it is to shake hands with a mass murderer,

---

*Seeing as this had to be conveyed to Saddam via a translator, using the word 'indefatigability' was a bit dangerous, wasn't it? I'd have thought when meeting Saddam it would be best to use phrases that couldn't be misunderstood or mistranslated, such as 'Good morning. The tree is near the post office.'

Galloway clearly wasn't a supporter of Saddam when there was an obvious conflict between the dictator and his population, and he'd supported many campaigns against Saddam's brutality. The problem arose because he felt that once Iraq was confronted by American rulers, Iraq would become a united nation, so to support the Iraqi people meant supporting Saddam. Even so, his opposition to the war, and dedication to that cause, is clearly principled, which is why he attracted an impressive following. And attracting any following at all is quite a feat when your most famous image is of you saluting Saddam Hussein. So when he was expelled from the Labour Party and helped to found Respect, it seemed the new group could attract some of the army of the confused and disillusioned.

To stand a chance of becoming credible enough to compete consistently in elections, Respect would need a network of supporters in each town, willing to campaign on local issues and prove Respect was more than just one politician. I was asked by the SWP to play a small part with a speaking tour. I was assured there'd be interviews and radio slots publicising the tour, there would be mentions in every local paper and student magazine and it would be *huge*. Two days before the first date, I got a call from one of these planning people, who asked, 'Where are you?' I told him where I was and he said, 'Can you get to Imperial College in the next five minutes?' I wondered if he was going to ask me to attend a presentation about buying a time-share apartment in the Canary Islands. 'Not really,' I said, bemused.

'Oh what a shame,' he said, with all the urgency of a dopehead telling you he can't find the teaspoon, 'Cos they're all here.'

'Who?' I asked. 'Who's all here?'

'All the people for the first meeting.'

'What meeting? The first one isn't for another two days.'

'Yeah, well we organised another one for today,' the last of his energy seeming to drain away.

'Oh,' I said. 'So you organised another one for me to speak at, but you didn't tell me you'd done it.'

'No, well, like, I was going to tell you about it, but the battery on my mobile went flat,' he said.

In most of the country there was a similarly stuttering opening to the Respect project, but in parts of East London and Birmingham, Respect became instantly popular, especially among Muslims. And at the General Election in 2005, Respect pulled off an extraordinary victory in getting Galloway elected as MP for Bethnal Green.

George's victory gave Respect credibility, but somehow it still couldn't take off as a national movement. Such a stunning success should have felt better than it did. Shouldn't there be a group set up now in every town, launched by eager activists inspired by this example, the way hundreds of people joined cricket clubs when England won the Ashes? In most areas Respect continued to be run by a handful of SWP members, and even many on the Left were reluctant to support it because they mistrusted its figurehead. Then came his performance at the US Senate in the summer of 2005, which impressed vast numbers – for the theatre as much as the statement – which created a new burst of hope. Of all the scenarios that might puncture that hope, no theorist or mystic could have predicted the one that actually took place.

Backwards and forwards I went from bed to settee, but then there was a definite serious attempt to really try one more time. We even went on holiday, and for a few weeks there was a creaking cordiality. One evening, I was in the kitchen when my partner produced a quick alarmed shriek, driven partly by pain but more by shock, as when someone becomes aware they've been stabbed. I ran into the living room, where she'd been half-watching the contestants arriving for the 2006 *Celebrity Big Brother*. And there on the screen in front of us, becoming acquainted with Jodie Marsh was George Galloway.

Oh no! Surely that monumental effort, the leaflets, the fundraising, the rallies, the knocking on doors, the daring to hope of hundreds, maybe thousands of people wasn't for this. Within

moments the phone rang, and all evening supporters of Respect
called each other to say, 'Have you seen – aaaagh, what on earth,
why, what do we do, whose idea, aaaaagh, what is he *thinking*?'

As with all major shocks, once the initial horror calmed down
came the realisation of what this would mean. The best you could
say is that in some twisted naivety he thought he could use it as a
platform for 'getting his message across to a wider audience'. (This
is what he later claimed.) But inanity and petty bickering is the
point of the programme and they ensure that's what comes out.
You could have Noam Chomsky in there with John Pilger, Joan
Bakewell and Richard Dawkins, and by day two Chomsky would
be yelling, 'I'll tell you something ELSE that faith doesn't explain,
Dawkins, SOMEONE'S been eating my CUSTARD FUCK-
ING CREAMS.'

There was no way this could turn out well. He wasn't going to
transform the Big Brother house into a cauldron of debate about
global politics. We weren't going to hear the announcer say, 'It's
3.46 p.m. and George is discussing the election prospects for
Hezbollah in the Lebanon with Chantelle and Maggot.'

There is no possible motive for going on this show other than
desperation to 'raise your profile', apparently unaware that
although many more people will know who you are, most of them
will be saying, 'Oh, he's that wanker off *Big Brother*.' You might
come out of it to be offered more jobs presenting vacuous television shows, but no one is going to put forward anything
meaningful on that show. They're not going to have on there a scientist who can be so persuasive with his theory about the food
chain in the North Sea that at last his paper on molluscs is published by the Royal Society of Marine Biologists. On the other
hand, a scientist might go on there and become known for his
crazy sticking-up hair and get offered an advert for conditioner. So
no one believes anyone who claims high ideals for appearing on it.
You might as well say, 'I wanted to publicise the appalling level of
human rights abuse in Burma. So that's why I entered the Miss
Wet T-shirt competition during "Tits 'n' Totty night" in Ibiza.'

Yet somehow it was so horrific it was compelling. I found myself at odd moments, waiting for the tea to brew or for the computer to get started, flicking on to see George in his dressing gown chopping carrots with Michael Barrymore. And not only was he on it when he really really really shouldn't have been, but having gone on it he was being as awful as it was possible to be, barking about an accusation that he'd broken the rules as if he was defending himself for leading a mutiny in the First World War. And then he pretended to be a cat. You would think that once you've put yourself in a position where you have to act being a cat licking Rula Lenska's cream on mainstream television, despite the fact you're an MP famous internationally for uncompromising anti-imperialist rhetoric, that you couldn't make things worse, but he did. Somehow he achieved the perfect blend of inanity and actorish Susannah 'don't-say-break-a-leg' York pomposity that made you literally shriek in a high-pitched voice you never knew you could achieve, '*Nooo, oh my God no-o-o-o-o-o*' and curl up shivering like a victim of shell-shock.

'Hmmm, prrrrr, prrrrr, miaow.'

'Oo you like that don't you, puss?' There probably was a way of doing this, with a twinkle of mischief or a look of 'What the fuck am I doing?' that could have minimised the damage, but it was acted so earnestly that it was truly shocking, like the sort of footage on a documentary about a rare condition that has people immediately sending in half their savings to try to find a cure for it. And if it was bad enough for most people watching, I'd campaigned and raised money for him. It felt like I was in school and my dad had suddenly wandered into the assembly stark naked and stood next to the headmaster with a banana up his arse. Then it got worse.

One night, my household had reached a state of such apparent conviviality that my partner and I actually sat on the settee together to watch the television. The tea was poured, the kids were in bed and we settled down for a cosy hour of George and his new friends. And we saw the most magnificent surreal volcanic explosion of words that can ever have taken place outside a crack-house. Without stumbling or hesitating once George eloquently but insanely gushed syllable after syllable of invective against every other living creature in his view, the barrage so relentless you wanted a moment of respite to take in the last insult before the next came tumbling out. Until Preston, the innocuous boyish singer with a boy band, started to yell, 'Wanker – WANKER' across the table. At which George, resplendent and poised, turned to shower Preston with a tirade that ended 'Preston – the nation will judge you for what you are – a *lying plutocrat.*'

'What's a plutocrat?' I thought, assuming that Stalin may well have been one, but doubtful that the same charge could be made against Preston from the fucking Ordinary Boys. For a full twenty minutes this carnage raged, and George couldn't have been more venomous if his housemates were Paul Bremner III and Robert Kilroy-Silk. At the end of it all, I realised I had never truly understood the expression 'open-mouthed' until then. My partner and I looked at each other, but for some time couldn't close our mouths. It was to be the last cosy night on a settee we'd ever have. Maybe George knew, and wanted to give us something special.

The next day anyone associated with Respect in whatever capacity was the butt of eager scorn and jollity. And you had to acknowledge there'd be something wrong if we hadn't been. I met a camera crew I'd worked with who were tripping over themselves with glee at my discomfort. My partner arrived at work to a cacophony of colleagues demanding, 'How can you be *associated* with him?' as if she herself was a politician involved in a scandal arriving at a press conference. One woman I know, who'd persuaded four women from her housing estate to give out leaflets for Respect at the election, was rung by all four who said they would no longer be connected with it. Then it got worse.

I assumed there would be meetings called by the Respect committee to deal with this peculiar crisis. Or a discussion on how to respond. Or a circular or a phone call or something. Instead the National Secretary of Respect, who was also a leading SWP member, appeared on *Newsnight* and defended the whole thing, saying it had been worth it because it had given Respect publicity. 'For example,' he said, 'I've been on Radio 4 today, and now I'm on here.' Maybe Fred West comforted himself in the same way during his trial.

In the weeks afterwards the official SWP response to this bewilderment was to tell people to stop going on about *Big Brother*, as surely there were more important issues than that. And that would have been adequate if the people complaining were all war-supporting hypocrites. But the greatest bewilderment came from those who were sympathetic to the anti-war movement.

Around this time we took our children to a pantomime, in which Ian McKellen played Widow Twanky. At one point, while sifting through a laundry basket, Twanky found a pair of long johns with a map of the USA on the rear, and a hole in the middle. 'These are George Bush's long johns,' she said. 'And the hole is somewhere for Tony Blair to put his tongue.' And the audience didn't just laugh, they yelped and lots of people emitted a deep gutterul 'YES', as if they'd hit the right double at the end of a game of darts. A few moments later another character said, 'Puss in Boots will be appearing here next year – played by George Galloway, just you see.' And the same people who'd cheered at the notion of Tony Blair being an arse-licking warmonger, clapped and sneered with derision at the mention of George's name.

Of course he'd done nothing remotely as awful as lying to participate in a barbaric war. And in an abstract way it made him even more fascinating. The most gripping characters in history are those who surprise you, doing something like inventing central heating and then working in Bangkok as a ladyboy. But if you're going to set out with the aim of winning elections, and then your icon, whose name is on the ballot paper and whose picture is on every publication, makes himself a national pantomime joke, shouldn't someone try to do something to explain how this happened and how to repair it?

Then it all got explosively, tragically, hilariously, disastrously so so so much worse.

The camaraderie between George and the SWP had reached such a point by 2006 that at an SWP rally George and the national secretary of Respect had been introduced as 'not just national but *inter*national leaders of our movement', before striding on from the wings to an orchestrated standing ovation, as if this was someone like Kirk Douglas collecting a lifetime achievement award at the Oscars. (Although many people declined the opportunity and stayed seated.) You had to wonder where this was leading. The following year, would it be staged like the MTV awards, so they'd each take turns to scream 'yo yo yo' through clouds of dry ice while everyone had to yell back 'he the man he the man he the *inter*national man'?

In any case, while George Galloway is known internationally, that's not a claim that stands up with regard to the national secretary of Respect. If you took him to a bus drivers' union meeting in Istanbul and said, 'Here's a special treat – it's one of your international leaders,' I expect you'd get some very funny looks.

But then in the autumn of 2007, George Galloway wrote an internal document for Respect that quickly flashed around the internet. In it he lamented that the local groups were tiny, which he blamed partly on the national secretary, and suggested someone else should work alongside him. The SWP leaders, in their own words, 'went nuclear'.

The suggestion that someone should work alongside the national secretary, they said, was a 'vicious witch-hunt'. SWP members who were working full-time in Galloway's office were instructed to resign immediately, and when they objected were expelled. Special meetings were called to denounce him in magnificently flowery language. It was as if they were saying about Galloway, 'When he saluted the courage of a murdering dictator, well we all do that from time to time. And impersonating household pets on *Big Brother* can happen to anyone. But *criticising an*

SWP member, even suggesting he needs someone to work alongside him!
WELL, THAT'S IT!!!'

A few days later an article in the *Socialist Worker* informed readers: 'Last year Galloway earned £300,000. Some tribune of the
people!' Had they only just discovered this? Two weeks earlier, if
anyone had pointed that out they'd have been roundly denounced
for criticising the *inter*national leader. I wondered if they'd put out
another article that began: 'EXCLUSIVE. We reveal how so-
called socialist George Galloway once went on television and
MADE CAT NOISES!'

At one SWP meeting, called to make this new war official, a
typical speech went: 'Although historic analogies are never completely accurate, this witch-hunt by Galloway is similar to what
happened in the coup in Chile in 1973.' This was a coup in which
the elected government was overthrown and thousands of people
were murdered. This speech might have been justified if, instead
of 'historic analogies are never completely accurate', he'd said,
'historic analogies can be utterly mental, and this one, even if you
dreamed it after accidentally swallowing a flagon of hallucinogenic
mushrooms, would mean you should probably seek an urgent
check-up with your GP.' But a room full of people nodded, and
the speaker was commended, above all, by the national secretary
of Respect, who was presumably shitting himself at the prospect
of Galloway bursting into the room at any minute with an army
and shooting the lot of them.

Maybe it was a game, in which people drew a historical period
out of a hat and had to crowbar it into their speech. So someone
else would say Galloway's document reminded them of the warning to Julius Caesar to beware the ides of March, then someone
would reply with 'Galloway's appearance on *Question Time* was
very much like the volcanic eruption at Krakatoa.'

Crazier and crazier it went. One SWP leaflet began: 'There is an
old saying in the West Indies, "The higher the monkey climbs the
more he exposes himself." George Galloway and his supporters
have climbed very high in the past few weeks.' Was this some sort

of code, I wondered. I stared at this statement several times, left it for a while, then returned to see if its meaning suddenly clicked. If I was Galloway I'd have been tempted to counter with the reply: 'Aah, but as they say in Senegal, "The cheetah's nostril will reach the river before the hind legs of a stupid goose."'

Within Respect there was chaos, especially as the organisation was due to have a conference. The pro- and anti-SWP wings issued fiercer and fiercer vitriol against each other, each pledging to defeat the other at the conference, so they sounded like boxers at a weigh-in. Maybe they should have had one, so Galloway and the national secretary could stand face to face in towels, eyeballing each other and growling, 'You're going down, punk, it gonna be JUDGEMENT day.'

At local Respect meetings there were allegations that people were joining just so they could cast a vote for which delegates to send to the conference. At one meeting the SWP stormed out, so Galloway shouted after them, 'Go on then, fuck off.' An SWP leaflet announced further evidence of the witch-hunt was that 'Galloway told our members to fuck off.' Then the other side had a T-shirt printed with Galloway and a speech bubble saying, 'Go on then, fuck off.' And by then I was wondering whether it might be more realistic to try to form a socialist group within the Conservative Party.

By November the acrimony was so great that two Respect conferences were scheduled for the same day, one involving the SWP wing and the other backed by most others. But neither faction wanted to appear inferior to the other, so each time one lot confirmed a guest speaker, the other side would book the same person to speak at their one as well. It ended up with two conferences, about two miles apart, with almost exactly the same speakers, full of people declaring the necessity of organising a new party against war and big business, but mostly hating each other. And to confirm this nuttiness a member of the Green Party, who spoke at the Galloway Respect conference, then scooted across town in a taxi to speak at the SWP one. Arriving at his second venue, he sat down just in time to hear the speech of a prominent anti-Galloway speaker, who declared, 'That Galloway conference up the road claims to be socialist, but do you know who they've got speaking there? A member of the *Green Party*. So much for socialism when they give over their platform to a middle-class bourgeois liberal from the *Green* Party.' And he was clearly unaware that the speaker following him was that very same person from the Green Party. My admiration for the Green Party grew when I saw this speaker's account of the episode, in which he said, 'The audience applauded, so I thought it only polite to join in.'

At one point the SWP spread a false rumour that a prominent trade unionist, who'd been a leading name in Respect but opposed the SWP in this war, had rigged a ballot in her union. Ken Loach, the creator of so many extraordinary films depicting working-class life, who was also a member of Respect, was categorised by a leading spokesperson for the SWP as a 'bourgeois individualist stooge', because he wouldn't join the anti-Galloway mania. I wished I could put my head in my hands and groan, 'Someone make them stop,' in the hope that social services might come round and take me away to be fostered by another party. Luckily, Ken Loach didn't respond to this comment, otherwise it would have ended up like teenage girls who've fallen out, with him screaming, 'Yeah, well, that's better than being a centralist despot's lackey' and the SWP replying, 'Shut up you anarcho-liberal kestrel-idolising bandit.'

My personal moment of surrender to despair with the SWP came on a night that oozed optimism. The Campaign Against the Arms Trade organised a comedy benefit at the Hammersmith Apollo. The 3,500 tickets had been sold out a week in advance, on every seat was an engagingly accessible pamphlet about the arms industry, and the vast room crackled with a beat of indignation and determination. The biggest cheer of the night, bigger than for any of the comics, went to the campaigner who initiated this legal challenge. Everyone there seemed to skip away from the place, like supporters whose football team has won for the first time in a year. It was an event that, even just five years earlier, would have swarmed with a presence from the SWP. There'd have been SWP papers, leaflets, maybe a stall, and groups from various branches using the night as a social event. But on this occasion there was a different approach. Nothing. They decided to ignore it altogether.

Yet the previous week 250 SWP members had attended the first of the crisis meetings to debate George Galloway's sudden new status as an enemy.

I decided to write a piece outlining my dismay for an internal publication open only to SWP members. I received a reply that almost made me clap with admiration. The article couldn't be printed, I was told, because according to their records I hadn't been a member for the past six years. You had to acknowledge its effective crude simplicity. Maybe when Robin Cook started his speech against the war, Blair should have yelled, 'Hang on. Before all this about the illegality of pre-emptive attacks on sovereign nations, my secretary has just discovered you've not paid your subs, so you're not allowed to speak.' This became a common problem, as long-standing members who queried the frenzied new tactics discovered they were somehow missing from the records.

The road to this madness involves a thousand incremental steps. You accept that the most important issue of the day is to win this localised feud, so you justify making outlandish accusations, no matter that they're starkly opposite to everything you said six months earlier. Then if some people wonder what on earth you're doing, they have to be denounced in glorious prose, possibly involving monkeys, and anyone who objects must be unmasked as a stooge. Until eventually you're like these warring next-door neighbours on television who insist it's obviously utterly reasonable for them to poison the other one's fish.

Eventually, having discovered they'd made an administrative error and I was a member after all, they agreed to print my article in a later edition, which they followed with their own reply. It seemed quite flattering to have been granted my own personal page of abuse, like having your own portrait drawn by one of the street artists you find at tourist spots. Maybe this could be an imaginative source of revenue for left-wing parties, in which they offer personal denunciations in Trotskyist language as a special gift. So you could request one for your dad for his sixtieth birthday, give a few details and back would come a closely typed page of vitriol beginning: 'Stan's continued forays into Southport Bowls Club display the extent of his decline into petit-bourgeois wood-rolling. His claim that, "It keeps me active and stops me getting under your mother's feet" is the frankly laughable bourgeois individualist justification we would expect from this stooge of Bill and Eileen who openly admits he organises the teas for the home matches!'

To most people this must simply confirm what they already thought, that the organised Left are as depicted in *The Life of Brian* – though even Monty Python's imagination would have struggled to conjure up the story of the Green Party speaker. But it *hadn't* always been like this.

For me it was like one of those harrowing accounts of visiting an old friend, a mentor and inspiration, but finding, instead of their usual lucidity, that the friend is going confidently crazy and insists that they're Christopher Columbus, about to sail round the world. Except in the SWP there were dozens of people going along with this. So it was like visiting dozens of friends, mentors and inspirations in the same week, and all of them telling you they're Christopher Columbus and about to sail round the world.

They'd never been like this before. Or had they? Was I like someone in the Conservative Party suddenly screaming, 'Oh my God, my own party has decided to support businesses making huge profits and some of them want to slow down immigration! What's become of them?' Had I been behaving like this all these years, and only just realised?

One of the advantages of being part of a political organisation is that when you're uncertain about an issue, you have a circle of people you trust whom you can consult and discuss things with. But that wasn't much help to me here. Because I couldn't very well ring them up and say, 'There's a question I'm confused about, and I'd like to talk it through with you – have we just gone mad recently or were we like it in the first place?'

Throughout this mayhem it should have been possible to continue drawing some comfort from the success of the Scottish Socialist Party, but they managed to find an equally creative way to self-destruct. The *News of the World* printed reams of salacious allegations that Tommy Sheridan had frequented a swingers' club in Manchester. So Tommy sued the paper, but the SSP split about whether he should do this, and although Tommy won his initial case, the party tore itself to pieces with all the usual wrath and bile, resulting in two separate parties standing against each other, and predictably every Scottish MP from either side in this split lost their seat at the next election. The fucking British Left. Around the world, when radical parties gain some degree of popular support, traditionally they come to grief because they're shot, imprisoned or exiled. Here they fall apart because of a row about a swingers' club or the leader goes on *Celebrity Big Brother*. On the other hand, as I surveyed another group with which I'd been associated hacking itself to pulp over fuck-all, I couldn't help wondering, 'Or is it me?'

12

US AND THEM

By now I was confused enough to feel I should make a list of the few things I *could* be certain of, starting with my own name, assuming I could be certain of that. I had to be certain that society was still divided by class, because I was invited to argue that case on the Radio 4 show *The Moral Maze*. Appearing on that programme is something that, ideally, everyone should do once as an exercise in coping mentally with extreme situations, along with being lost in a foreign city and building a bivouac in the snow. The show is an 'investigation' into moral issues, in which unfeasibly pompous presenters, led by the laconic Michael Buerk, argue their case and call 'witnesses' to prove their point. So I sat one evening, waiting to be called, in the stark gloomy basement of Broadcasting House, where it seems quite possible that a couple of blokes in face masks and carrying swords might turn up and make a video for Al-Jazeera. On an opposite seat was Andrew Roberts, a Conservative historian who enthuses with joy about the British Empire and the invasion of Iraq. He read the *Telegraph*, I read the *Independent*, and if the outside world had been wiped out by a poisonous gas and we were the last people left alive, we'd still have sat there ignoring each other for several years until we perished because we'd run out of biscuits.

We could hear the programme being recorded. Professor David

Starkey, one of the moral presenters, began a tirade in which he insisted the poor were less intelligent than the rich, as proved in a notorious book called *The Bell Curve*. Andrew Roberts looked up from his *Telegraph*, we caught each other's eye, and he said, 'Did he just quote *The Bell Curve?*'

'Yes,' I said. 'He did.'

'Goodness me,' he said. 'I've come out with some right-wing nonsense in my time but I've never quoted THAT.'

And I sort of admired him for that.

Eventually I was summoned to give evidence, and participated in one of the oddest conversations I've ever had. The professor fulminated that there's clearly no longer a working class, because no one thinks of themselves that way any more. I said I didn't think that was true, but in any case you don't cease to be working class just because you don't think you are. Then it went on . . .

Me: 'For example, skilled engineers before the First World War saw themselves as so superior, that they'd turn up to work in top hats, then change into their overalls. But you wouldn't now claim those engineers weren't working class.'

The professor: 'That's ridiculous. My father was an engineer and he didn't go to work in a top hat.'

Me: 'What? Your father was an engineer before the First World War? When was he born then?'

The professor: 'He was born in 1912.'

Me: 'So he was a skilled engineer at the age of two?'

The professor: 'We don't need lectures on being working class from comedians like you who earn hundreds of thousands of pounds a year.'

Me: 'I don't earn hundreds of thousands of pounds a year.'

The professor: 'Well, you're not much of a comedian then, are you?'

Michael Buerk: 'Thank you, Mark Steel, now for our next witness.'

Despite my glittering performance, to enter an official discussion about the state of the modern world you must accept that life is no longer determined by these antiquated notions of class. There's a boom industry in 'political commentators', the sort who write articles that begin: 'As a senior colleague close to the Liberal Democrat Treasury spokesman put it to me yesterday' and pop up on BBC *News 24* at ten past midnight to review the next day's papers. And they all agree that these days no one behaves or votes or succeeds or fails because of class, which was finally abolished around 1993.

One of Conservative Prime Minister John Major's few memorable comments was his statement that we were arriving at this new 'classless society'. Shortly after he said that, he shut down almost every remaining coalfield as 'uneconomical'. Presumably, with everything being classless, it would have been just as possible for the miners to decide the City of London was 'uneconomical' and shut down the stock market.

The most powerful exposition in Britain for class society's funeral came from New Labour. Their whole project was created and sold on the insistence that the class divisions of old have evaporated. Working-class jobs such as mining and shipbuilding had almost disappeared, and, though some people might still be poorer than others, there were few barriers left preventing them from becoming wealthy if they really tried. And anyway, there can't be a working class now, because most people have eaten taramasalata.

All of this seemed to lead to Professor Starkey's point that it's not worth trying to appeal to the working class if hardly anyone feels they're part of it. But one point here, even if it isn't the main one, is that it's not necessarily true that most people feel like that. According to the Social Attitudes Survey carried out every year, and reported in the *Economist* in February 2007, 'Class identity is as important to people in Britain today as it was in the 1960s' and 57 per cent of the population identified themselves as working class.

A consensus around the disappearance of class divisions could be hard to dispute if the gap between rich and poor was shrinking. Instead, the trouble with listing the evidence for a growing gap between rich and poor is knowing where to start. For example, in 2005 the average pay for directors of companies in the Financial Times Index was £2.5 million. The average pay for company executives doubled between 2000 and 2004, making their pay 113 times the average wage, whereas in 1984 it had been twenty-five times the average wage.

Perhaps we should mention Jean-Pierre Garnier, chief executive of GlaxoSmithKline, hired in 2003 on a salary of £3.6 million a year, but with a clause stating if he was sacked he'd receive another £22 million.★

Was there a point in the negotiations, I wonder, when they offered £18 million if he was sacked, and he said, 'Well, you can't expect me to take the job on those conditions'? Presumably, ever since getting this job he's spent his time setting off fire extinguishers and turning up drunk in the hope of getting sacked, while the board say to themselves, 'We didn't really think this contract through properly, did we?'

Best of all, when he was asked to justify this figure at a shareholders' meeting, he replied, 'I'm not Mother Teresa.' If only the greedy through history had been so honest! 'And Jesus turned unto Judas and said "Why hast thou betrayed me?" And Judas did wave his thirty pieces of silver and say, "Oh come on, I'm not Mother Teresa."'

Sometimes these people claim they're worth these sums due to their ability to make companies 'succeed'. Maybe this is why in 2005, bonuses of £807,000 were paid to executives of the Jarvis group, for their success in steering the company's share price from 566 pence to 9.5 pence. Jarvis also succeeded in being officially to blame for the faulty tracks that led to a fatal train crash at Hatfield. They also won the contract to finance new school buildings, including the one my son goes to. So now, if a local sports club wants to hire the sports hall, instead of booking it through the school, they have to contact a call centre run by

★That's right. It's not a misprint – 22 MILLION FUCKING POUNDS.

Jarvis. My experience of this was to be one among dozens of bewildered amateur sportsmen wielding a variety of bats and rackets in a hall that had been quadruple-booked. You can't buy that sort of genius cheap, it costs at least £807,000.

In 2006 the average pension for retired directors was £167,000 a year. This figure should be of particular interest because another area on which there's agreed consensus is that we can't go on expecting to have pensions paid by the state like we used to, now that we're living longer than we used to.

So when the trade union UNISON, which represents low-paid council and school employees, organised a one-day strike to demand a decent state pension, the *Daily Mail* said they were displaying 'the stench of crude self-interest' by not understanding that pensions can't stay at the old levels because we're living longer than we used to. That's typical of the unions, isn't it? Why can't they put their narrow-minded attitudes to one side and instruct their members that when they get to sixty-seven they should kill themselves? Instead it's just 'me me me' as usual.

No one disputes that the wealth is there to maintain decent pensions, the argument is about how we collect it and distribute it. We could do it the old-fashioned way, by taxing those with a pension of £167,000 a year, then sharing the proceeds; this would ensure everyone knows what they'll get and feels secure. Or there's the modern method, where everyone fends for themselves, so those with the least to spare have to somehow find the most to take out a private pension, which will pay out an amount no one can predict because it's gambled on the stock market.

However you measure it, the gap between rich and poor, which grew under Margaret Thatcher's rule, has accelerated under New Labour. And New Labour wouldn't see this as a failure but as part of their strategy. Asked by Jeremy Paxman whether it was acceptable that this gulf was widening, Tony Blair said, 'If you end up going after those people who are the most wealthy in society, what you actually end up doing is in fact not even helping those at the bottom end.'

All this must have been a relief to typical members of this new classless society, such as Philip Green, whose group owns Top Shop, Burtons and Dorothy Perkins. He pays himself £3 million a day, and spent £4 million on his son's bar mitzvah, which included a private show from Beyoncè. It would serve him right if, just as she was about to start, the boy said, 'I've changed my mind, I want Britney Spears.'

In 2005 Green's group declared a dividend of £1.299 billion. But £1.2 billion of this he kindly gave to his wife who, as luck would have it, was resident in Monaco and therefore didn't have to pay UK tax. Or maybe this is being cynical, and she was living there anyway because it's handy for the shops. It's estimated this saves the Greens £300 million, but that would still leave £1 billion – can't they get by on that? Or would Mrs Green scream, 'What am I supposed to tell the kids now? This week I won't even be able to buy them an island. They'll have to make do with a lake.'

According to a study by Prem Sikka, a professor of accounting, in 2006 the richest fifty-four people in Britain had an estimated income of £126 billion. And the tax paid on this was 0.14 per cent. The best part is the government BOASTS about Britain's tax system, citing it as the reason the world's super-rich come here. Maybe Brown's hoping that eventually he'll extend this attitude to other areas, and tell us excitedly, 'Such is our reputation as a low-tax, low-regulation vibrant economy that we have attracted no fewer than 20,000 pimps. The busy brothels, bright wide ties and lively jive banter of our inner cities are testament to our success in seizing market opportunities.'

David Harvey, head of a global association of tax lawyers for the wealthy, said Britain has become the billionaires' natural home, rather than America, because 'The IRS is perceived to be a much more burdensome tax regulator than the UK Revenue.' Eleven years of Labour government, and we were kinder to the super-rich than George Bush's America.

To put this another way, the government admits tax avoidance in 2006 was somewhere between £97 billion and £150 billion, whereas benefit fraud amounted to less than £1 billion. So their obsession with benefit fraud makes as much sense as if, after the Great Train Robbery, the police had said, 'We have excellent news. The robbers have got away and are a vital part of the economy. But we DID catch three passengers who didn't have a valid ticket.'

When there's an outcry about a particular example of gluttony, the figures will be defended on the grounds that the executive in question is worth it because elsewhere they could be paid even more. So we're lucky to have them slumming it by kindly agreeing to give up so much of their time so cheaply when they could be off to Japan to make REAL money. It's argued that such figures are incentives to entice the finest minds into management, as if no one can be expected to try that extra bit harder for only £21 million. And yet, as a five-year study of 1,500 corporations in the US put it: 'We looked at seventy-five years of company data and never found the slightest correlation between executive compensation and company performance.'

New Labour is proud of this contribution to a culture that celebrates absurd wealth. It's as if there was a new wing of the Catholic Church that insisted it should no longer be coy about its past connections with paedophilia, and from now on should give tax breaks to weird blokes in parks, make Gary Glitter a priest, and send the Pope on an annual holiday with Jonathan King.

How smoothly Tony Blair eased into this world, with his £4 million house and his wife charging thirty grand an appearance. The architects of New Labour not only rewrote their party's aims to embrace the wealthy, they *became* the wealthy. You can't accuse them of not sticking to their principles. And those who struggled, like Mandelson or David Blunkett, to live a lifestyle that matched their new friends, risked their entire careers to climb the greedy ladder, so they could feel on a par with their new buddies, the Berlusconis, the Hindujas and the Murdochs.

Then, and you have to admire this, having created an atmosphere in which the wealth and greed of a handful of rich people

dominate to an even greater degree than under Margaret
Thatcher, they insist they had to do this because otherwise no one
would vote for them, now we no longer live in a society divided
by class.

It could be argued that despite the growing inequality, Britain has
nonetheless become more 'classless' because promotion and success no longer depend on your family background. But it's still
true that two-thirds of land in Britain is owned by 189,000 families. And that half our company directors went to public school,
the most common being Eton, followed by Rugby, Winchester,
Marlborough and Harrow. In 2007, fifteen members of the
shadow cabinet had been to Eton. I suppose that's just coinci-
dence. They must have all sat round the table on the first day,
going, 'Oh my goodness, and YOU went to Eton, how extraordinary.'

And that 77 per cent of high court judges went to Oxbridge,
as did 81 per cent of permanent secretaries and 83 per cent of
senior ambassadors. Aha, but hasn't the background of Oxbridge
students changed over the last forty years? Well it has – in 1969 38
per cent of them came from public schools, now it's 45 per cent.

You can check whether class has vanished by flicking through
the pages of the London *A to Z*. You'll find plenty of roads in
Mayfair with Grosvenor in the title, because they're part of the
100-acre Grosvenor Estate, worth £10 billion. The effort
required by the current Duke of Grosvenor to acquire all this
was to be born into the Grosvenor family, which has owned the
estate since 1622. Or there's Portman Square, owned by the
Portman Estate since the time of Henry VIII and worth over £1
billion. Jermyn Street is part of the Jermyn Estate, Burlington
Place is owned by the Earl of Burlington, Bedford Square in
Bloomsbury has been owned by the Bedford Estate since the
Reformation and so on. You can only hope that when these
roads were originally named after these aristocrats, someone
wrote an article saying, 'Why do we have to call everything

these days after a bloody earl or duke? Honestly, it's political correctness gone mad.'

In a way all of this is secondary, however, because if you're one of the vast majority that doesn't come from this background you KNOW 'breeding' still carries enormous privilege. For example, take the army. How likely is it, when there's an interview on the news with a soldier in Iraq or Afghanistan, that the lad at the roadside will speak in a clipped Etonian accent? Equally, when they interview a commander or chief of staff in the studio, how likely is it they'll answer in coarse Glaswegian, or say, 'Given the parameters of our mission, it's essential we remain clear about the overriding objectives' in broad Scouse? If anyone is unsure about whether class division still dominates the army, they should listen to the interview given by Colonel Bob Stewart on the issue of troops being withdrawn from Bosnia. 'Will this give a free hand for the Serb militia to return to their old brutal methods?' he was asked. And Bob replied, 'Not at all, you can rest assured if they try any of that shenanigans, we'll come down on them like a ton of bricks.' Shenanigans? Mass graves, burning down villages – that sort of shenanigans, I suppose. Nearly as bad as Hitler and his dashed tomfoolery.

There's a layer of society brought up with the expectation that it will rule. At their schools, when they do subjects like the First World War, instead of being asked to write about what life must have been like shivering in a trench, they're asked to construct a battle plan for capturing Verdun. They consider, like Tony Blair, that to end up as a headmaster would be a failure. Instead of being taught to respect authority they're taught to BE authority. They ooze confidence that it's hard not to be intimidated by. For example, I was contacted by an Eton student who wanted me to speak at his debating society. I was doing a national tour at the time, so I called him to say it would have to be after that finished. He rang me back and left a message that went, 'Right. Now I've looked on your website and seen the dates of your shows, and you've got two days off one week so I'm booking you in to come down on the

Tuesday. It's quite simple.' And the words 'quite simple' were imbued with a slight exasperation, as if he was having to take time out from an important meeting with an admiral to explain to the servants how to serve the pâté.

On the other hand, whenever someone starts a request, as most of us do, with 'Oh er hello, um sorry to bother you but I was just wondering' you know they didn't go to Eton.

The media hierarchy is dominated by Oxbridge graduates. They can be wonderfully charming people, laugh about the *hilarious* sketch by Rory Bremner that really stuck it to Gordon Brown, and they might whisper, in their best Oxbridge accent, 'The truth is Blair's a fucking liar.' If they found a tramp on their doorstep at Christmas, maybe they'd welcome him in and ask what he wanted to drink. They'd probably even apologise, 'I'm afraid I don't think we have any Tennent's Extra – will five-star cognac do? Sorry.' But their points of reference, their outlook, the standpoint from which they see society is shaped by the fact they're from a different class. They know businessmen and politicians, people who have inquiries named after them, people who, if they were at a social function and Bill Clinton came in the room, wouldn't think, 'Fucking hell, it's Bill Clinton.' These are people who ask if you've seen the latest production of *La Traviata*, and honestly think there's a chance you have.

I once made the mistake of agreeing to appear in a feature for *Newsnight* in which they tried to 're-create a typical dinner party argument about the war in Iraq'. I went to this house in North London and was shown into a vast kitchen, to be one of six 'guests', three for the war and three against. Then the chefs arrived. Two African lads in full uniform – big white hats and everything – began chopping chives on a huge pine surface, as if this was the way normal people carry on, discussing carnage over the appropriate wine as the servants stir the sauce. It wouldn't have seemed out of place if someone had said, 'Ah, the Rioja '65, excellent choice for invasions.' Presumably for those who run current affairs departments, this represents a typical dinner party.

Incidentally, over dessert, Anne McElvoy, a fervent supporter of the war in Iraq and political editor of the London *Evening Standard* who regularly pops up as an 'expert' on politics, ended a sentence with the words 'once the weapons of mass destruction are found'.

I said, 'Well, hang on, there's no guarantee they'll be found,' and she glared back, waved a finger inches from my nose like an irate member of the mob in a Mafia film, and said, 'THEY'LL find them, Mark Steel, THEY'LL find them, oh THEY'LL find them' with such frothing manic certainty I wondered whether she had them herself.

There was something in that rage more pronounced than the misjudgement about the existence of Saddam's weapons. There was a contempt, almost a disgust that she had to answer such a yob at all. If a journalist of suitable pedigree had said, 'Oh come come, such certainty would appear premature, I venture,' she would probably have politely restated her case. If you live inside their world, even if they despise your argument, they consider you worthy of debate. They'd politely let you put the case for supporting Al Q'aeda, as long as you were from Charterhouse, wrote for *The Times* and said, 'But don't you feel, given the preponderance of largely false notions of individual choice that in reality act as oppressive signals, that sharia law offers one a degree of liberation in such circumstances, especially if enforced at gunpoint by a man in a black hood.'

Then John Lloyd, former editor of the *New Statesman*, supporter of the war in Iraq, owner of a very posh Edinburgh accent and becoming very drunk, slurred at some length about opponents of the war being defenders of Saddam. I waited until he finished to reply, 'It's really unfair . . .' and that's as far as I got before he interrupted by saying almost exactly the same thing all over again. I waited, said, 'It's really unfair . . .' and he interrupted by saying it a third time. So I said, 'Look, if you do that again I'm not going to bother answering. Now, it's really unfair . . .' whereupon he started the same speech a fourth time. And I said, 'Oh for fuck's sake, haven't you ANY fucking manners' – which of course was the bit shown on *Newsnight*. He got up, knocked over a whole bottle of wine, muttered 'eh, what', the chefs rushed across to mop it up, and he stood there watching them, mumbling, 'Who did that?'

They would all deny, these privately educated pundits who control the growing empire of news, that they have any class-based agenda, and they probably mean it. But their world, their references, their language, the milieu in which they're most comfortable, all serve to exclude the outsider, whether this is their aim or not.

Around the end of 2005 I was part of a panel, to judge a 'Best new comedian of the year' award. This was the grand final, at London's Comedy Store, and the other judges were three ex-Oxbridge senior executives in radio and television and Don Ward, founder of the Comedy Store, who's booked acts for thirty years. One by one the contestants did their eight minutes of jokes to moderate applause, until a Geordie woman came on, with an air of vulnerability but spitting vicious lines about school and life and men and sex in Newcastle that would make a hen night shriek. The audience roared and cheered, and it was obvious she'd win. The judges retired to a back room, where Don and I said, 'That's a simple choice then.'

'Well yes,' said the other three, 'I'd certainly give it to Jeffrey.' Jeffrey had played the character of a slightly camp fop embarrassing himself before his upper-class family.

The judgement seemed so warped, as if the judges at a boxing match insisted on awarding the match to the one who was in a coma, that it was hard to know how to conduct an argument against it.

'She'd storm this place any night,' said Don. 'But I can guarantee your lad would be crucified.'

To which the answer was, 'Yes, but we can't judge it on who'd go down best, because what else could she do?'

And I wanted to say, 'Ah, because the most important criterion for judging a stand-up comedy competition is to decide who'd be best at navigating a punt through Cambridge.'

But of course there *was* a logic. The character actor spoke of a world they recognised and the Geordie woman didn't. It was my job to announce the winner, and the audience gasped. Before that I'd had to go backstage and tell the contestants the result. I went up to the cheated Geordie and said embarrassed, 'Well, you're second.'

'Aah,' she shrieked. 'That's fanTASTIC pet, CHAMPION. I canna believe it – SECOND – ME!'

The winner took it in his stride that he'd won, almost as if it was his right.

The power of class can cut across political ideas, so there's a left-wing version of liberal snobbery. For example, here's Joan Smith, feminist columnist, on the enthusiasm for English flags during the World Cup: 'This epidemic of men driving around with the cross of Saint George is a pathetic gesture. I have enthusiasms but don't wave them in people's faces . . . I read Tacitus and Juvenal as well as Dickens'. She went on, 'But the flag represents the misogyny of thousands of England fans who will pay for sex with trafficked foreign women during the World Cup.'

And the eight-year-old in my road had one in his window – the misogynist little shit. Smith went on to blame 'the insecurity and frustrations felt on council estates and among blue-collar workers. True, they now have unprecedented quantities of consumer goods including cars and foreign holidays . . . but it's not just the *Daily Mail* that identifies asylum-seekers and East European immigrants as the source of everything wrong in this country.'

I've never flown a flag of St George but after reading that I felt I wanted to. It's not so much that her argument is wonky, but that it contains a deep smug contempt for working-class people. Smith sees them as a dirty threat, with their uncouth unenlightened ways. Some of those waving flags were indeed racist, but most weren't, but you couldn't possibly have any discussion with any of them, or with any council tenant or blue-collar worker, if you saw them as this vile block of bigotry who hadn't the good sense to stop watching football and read Tacitus instead.

Anyway, wasn't Juvenal a poet of the Roman Empire who hated foreigners? He probably drove around in a chariot waving a Roman flag and singing: 'Can you hear the Persians sing? I can't hear a fucking thing.'

Elements of this attitude are now widely accepted. For example, I was asked to perform at a north London Anti-racist Festival, a splendid event which included a series of bands and DJs playing in tents in the high street. In the working men's club, which you entered through a door on the second floor of a multistorey car park, there was a comedy show. Soon after I arrived, the organiser came across wearing an anguished sincere grimace, and put her hand on my forearm, in the way an official at an airport might approach someone waiting for the arrival of a plane to tell them it's crashed into the sea.

'I'm SO sorry,' she almost wept. 'There are racists here and there's nothing we can do about it. They're members of the club, you see.' I asked her where they were and what they'd done. 'Well,' she said, almost unable to splutter the words, 'they've – heckled the magician.'

The room was packed. An anti-racist banner was draped over the back of the stage, and a stall at the front was covered in anti-racist leaflets. But whereas each of the music tents outside was crammed with a mix of black, white and Asian youth, everyone here was white and forty and probably enduring their first ever venture into a working men's club. The dartboard, jackpot fruit machines, the glittery streamers hanging by the side of the stage, on which duets with names like Peaches and Cream had sung 'Quando Quando Quando', were alien to them. As was the group sitting round a table, frequently returning from the bar with a metal tray straining under Dubonnet and lemonades and pints of frothy bitter.

'Oy, can you make yourself disappear,' one called out to the magician. 'Oh my goodness, they've done it again,' squeaked the organiser. 'I just wish there was SOMETHING we could do.' The audience muttered and looked in their direction. Then someone came across. 'Look. I don't know why you're here but SOME of us are trying to enjoy the show and support this very important cause, thank you.'

After the gig those at the offending table called me over. Phil, a builder told me, 'We come here every Sunday afternoon, but this Sunday it's been booked out for this anti-racist thing, so some of our mates have gone down the Wetherspoons. But we thought it's important to support things like this. But, mate, that magician WAS shit.' And they were the only people all day who offered to buy me a pint.

It's a common suggestion that racism is a problem flowing from the uneducated, the poor, the council estates and blue-collar workers with unprecedented consumer goods. But on a council estate you're more likely to live among a variety of ethnic groups, to borrow sugar from them, share a spliff, complain about the busted lift and sit in the launderette together than if you live in a road where you meet the neighbours to discuss the relative merits of local landscape gardeners. A working-class white woman is twelve times more likely to have a child with a black man than a middle-class woman.

One of the most vindictive racist campaigns in recent times was in the Hampshire village of Lee-on-Solent, where the community worked tirelessly to prevent an old army barracks being converted into a centre for asylum-seekers. The leader of this campaign, from his million-pound house, said, 'Some of these chaps will be Muslims, and used to seeing women all covered up. Well, once they see our daughters in bikinis they won't be able to contain themselves.' When they forced the government to back down they had a champagne barbecue to celebrate, a joy not shared by one man scheduled to be billeted there, a Congolese student who'd fled his country after his father and brother were shot dead in the war.

The image of the BNP voter as a skinhead thug bears only an element of truth. There was astonishment in Burnley, where the BNP has ambitions of winning control of the local council, when the area where they won the highest vote was Cliviger with Worsthorne, a suburban ward that usually votes Tory.

No one who's even flirted with working-class life would pretend it's all liberal and cosy. From my perspective in the upper tier of the Holmesdale Stand at Selhurst Park I can witness how fans from Lancashire are always greeted with 'in your Northern slums'. (Except for when Manchester City were the visitors a week after Harold Shipman was convicted and around 10,000 people sang 'Did a doctor kill your gran?') Charlton always get 'You're all a bunch of pikeys' and a man who sits four seats away, at random intervals yells 'CUNT!' in a throaty South London baritone at no one in particular.

But contrary to the stereotype, it's the poor who are more likely to recycle their bottles and papers. It was in working-class areas that 10 per cent of traditional Labour voters switched to the Liberal Democrats in protest at the war in Iraq. Every study of charities suggests the working class contribute a higher proportion of their income to charity than the wealthy. It's unlikely any of this is due to a reverse of the Bell Curve, meaning that working-class people are genetically more likely to be caring and anti-war, if strangely more disposed to randomly shouting 'CUNT!' It's because their circumstances encourage them to think collectively. Working in Sainsbury's or living on a council estate makes it more likely that you'll develop the attitude that 'We're all in it together' than if you're the sort of person who books Beyoncè for their son's party.

13

THEY BURN SO BRIGHT AND YOU CAN ONLY WONDER WHY

One of the frustrating sides to any debate about class is when it gets stuck in those daft discussions about whether Steven Gerrard is working class or what class Bugs Bunny belongs to. Then someone will say their dad still gets a pint of cockles every Sunday from the stall outside the Fisherman's Arms, so he's definitely working class, even though he's managing director of Unilever and has just bought the Ivory Coast.

Even the proudest defenders of the view that a working class still exists can end up inadvertently agreeing with the New Labour view that it's disappeared, because they'll argue that proof of an enduring working class is that no one round their way eats *tapas*. But the cultural aspects of 'traditional' British working-class behaviour *are* in decline. It was always flawed to judge a socio-economic layer of society by its relationship to scotch eggs and dripping.

For the term 'class' to have any meaning, it must refer to the position you hold in society, and that position is determined above all by the work you do, in particular whether your job gives you any control over the way society produces things. What matters is not whether you work in construction or insurance but whether you own Wimpey or sit at a desk all day for Sun Alliance.

The old jobs of the working class haven't vanished to the extent that is often claimed; in 2006 there were still 3.2 million people in Britain employed in manufacturing. It's also true that the most effective British union leader in recent times has been the rail-workers' General Secretary Bob Crow, who even in the old sense is magnificently working class, to the extent that I heard him say one evening on a regional news programme discussing a strike over cancelled tea-breaks, 'It has got to the point where some of my members have not been allowed out for a urination.'

But even in the old industries with established trade unions, the working class looks different from its stereotype. My postman's a 40-year-old white man with dreads who answered my question 'How was your day on strike?' with 'Wicked, I went to Brighton for an all-day rave on the beach.' A bus driver is as likely to be a lesbian with a nose stud as a chirpy white *On The Buses*-type bloke saying 'All right, darling' and 'whoooar' all day. Builders have Mohicans, strawberry-pickers are Polish, car mechanics are likely to be young Pakistanis with a green bandana over their hair. Even union leaders have begun to reflect this. I saw Jeremy Dear, General Secretary of the National Union of Journalists, at Glastonbury the day after his tent had been washed away in the rain while he was asleep in it.

Also, while traditional industries have shrunk, the jobs that have replaced them give people no more control over their working day than was enjoyed by dockers or sheet metal workers. There are now 850,000 people in Britain working in call centres, who are not only working class but also have immense potential working-class power. A call centre strike, even for an hour, would cause panic in a variety of circles, and the management couldn't stock-pile answers in advance.* Tesco employs 250,000 people, more than the number of miners at the time of the 1984 strike.

---

*Nor could they draft in the army: 'Hello, you're speaking to Lance-Corporal Whittington – how may I help you? . . . Certainly, there are tickets available for Rihanna, have you booked with us before – WAIT FOR IT.'

Every morning, the earliest buses to the centre of every major city are crammed with cleaners, a nocturnal army that vanishes at daylight like vampires, leaving the nation's office workers to send each other e-mails to a vague smell of lemon as if by magic. Shopping centres are barely navigable sometimes, due to the obstacles of people waving clipboards at you to get you to sign up for something or other. Unless it can be shown that these people are minor royals, getting in practice for when they have to ask common people 'So what do you do?', they are utterly, thoroughly working class. And on and on this could go, to include the 450,000 care assistants, 50,000 social workers, the almost uncountable numbers of childminders and so on.

Staff employed by small shops would once have been almost impossible to organise into unions. The economic clout of young Granville in *Open All Hours* was somewhat limited. But the chains may have transformed that. Now if a teenage girl works in Costa Coffee there's an opportunity for her to identify with the 3,000 others who work for the company, in similar conditions. A bar worker is likely to be not just working for the local pub but be one of 11,000 employed by Mitchells and Butlers, who own chains such as O'Neills and All Bar One.

The nature of people using hotels has changed. Every town the size of Kidderminster now includes a Holiday Inn and similar establishments, to cater for the seminars and conferences, training sessions and stupid bonding weekends that the human resources manager assures everyone will be *such* a hoot and that the staff of publishers, law firms and insurance companies are obliged to attend. They generally make the best of it and might sit in the bar till one in the morning but many of them would rather be at home. The point is it doesn't matter whether they want to be there or not, they *have* to be there. And they're almost certainly on short-term contracts, budgeting from month to month and fretting about mortgage payments on a modest town house. If they all decided to stick together and not sell or solicit or publish until the managers agreed to improve their conditions their companies

would be fucked, and by any meaningful definition they're working class. (Meanwhile, tens of thousands of workers now staff
hotels, cleaning, serving and directing guests to their tedious seminars.)

Similarly I was invited to present the awards at the annual
Quantity Surveyors' Dinner, a ceremony that sounds as if it
should have been opened by the secretary-general of the United
Nations and conducted mostly in Latin. To start with, the quantity surveyors sat politely, clapping at the winners, but after
twenty minutes they began to shuffle until each award was
greeted with playful derision, as if they were mates at a wedding.* Afterwards, when we all went round to the pub, their ties
undone or scrumpled in their pockets, they queued up to tell
me about the most incompetent managers, the most unscrupulous companies and the most elaborate skives. Which, if they'd
been the subjects of the awards, would have made for a much
more fascinating afternoon. ('The skiver of the year trophy goes
to Gerry from TWN Construction, for surfing in Newquay
while claiming to be stuck up a crane at the redevelopment of
Wembley Stadium.')

The media now comprises a vast layer of production companies
and editing suites desperately ensuring there's sufficient film to fill
so many channels so that people in failed marriages can flick from
one to the other all night long from their settee without ever running out. Often a programme will be arranged, filmed, recorded
and edited in a basement by two or three people in a hurry.

Maybe the least prestigious I ever felt when taking part in a
TV programme was when I was asked to be a guest on a chan-
nel set up by a businessman called Raj, who humbly named it
Raj TV. Prime time every weekday evening on this channel was

---

*Incidentally, the main thing I learned about quantity surveying that day was that their
trade magazine has a 'Guess the building site' competition with a picture of a building
site, which readers presumably stare at before exclaiming 'Of COURSE – that's the
cement mixer at the Arndale Centre in Gloucester.'

a chat show recorded in a corner of a disused office which oozed emptiness, hosted by George Galloway, so I agreed to make an appearance. The only objects filling any space were huge empty cardboard boxes, the sort a washing machine would be delivered in, and apart from George there was one technician and a possibly unnecessary make-up woman; to one side was the lonely table you sat behind during the show. I wandered round the basement waiting for filming to start. In one corner, about ten yards from where George was sitting, was a bright red settee and another camera set up to point at it. Just as I puzzled why this was there, a woman brushed past me wearing only underwear and a tiny fluffy waistcoat, and leapt on to the settee with a microphone. Then a voice came from somewhere saying, 'Ready to go?' And she said, 'Hi, welcome to the show, who have we got on the line?' She was making a cable phone-in soft porn show, I realised. 'Ooooo hello Peter (she stroked the microphone), *that's* a hot name. Tell me, Peter, have you eaten anything hot tonight, I *like* hot things, don't you?' she went on. Then I noticed a sign by this alcove, written in felt pen: 'NOTES TO PRESENTERS. Number one – Remember, girls, NO HANDS IN KNICKERS.'

There was a time when if you worked in television, you were seen as part of a superior world, envied by the majority and boasted about by your family. Now, such is the prestige of the modern media, that if someone owns a disused room in an office, it's perfectly natural to rent it out to two entirely different television channels, one that expresses the views of anti-imperialism and socialism, the other specialising in phone-in porn.

There are countless people in jobs that would once have represented an escape from the working class, that now fulfil every criteria of being part of it. The 2007 Ministry of Defence report on potential future threats to national security, declared that the 'growing gap between the middle class and the super-rich' could lead to 'the middle classes becoming a revolutionary class, taking the role envisaged for the proletariat by Marx'.

Maybe cabin crew captains fall into that category. Because as I was about to board a plane for America with my children, the captain fiddled with his computer, which was slightly unnerving, then said he'd changed our seats so there was extra leg room for the children. Then he whispered into my ear, 'We need people like you who tell the truth, Mister Steel.' And I confess to feeling a smug sense of civic pride that's been largely absent from my life. This was my equivalent of the mayor saying in his speech after the village fête, 'Special thanks are due to Mrs Wilberforce, who has once again surpassed herself with her magnificent gooseberry crumble.' And just after the seatbelt sign was switched off, a stewardess came along to tell us they'd been asked to look after us specially, so would I accept a glass of champagne and a box of chocolates for the children. I don't even like champagne but I wasn't turning that down. All I needed to make this perfect was to overhear one passenger whisper to another, 'Why's he been given champagne?'

'Because he's always ranting like a maniac about our obsession with status and material wealth.'

There are vast barriers to the modern working class exercising their potential to act collectively. The trade union movement seems unable to relate to young working-class people. The modern working class no longer lives in communities where everyone works at one place, such as a pit or shipyard. It no longer pays mass allegiance to a Labour Party that it identifies with. But it's as true as ever that, of all the fears that plague those in charge, few concern them more than the possibility of workers uniting across their industries with their own demands. Because when working-class people stick together they tend not to demand that shareholders be paid an extra dividend or that the bonuses to top executives be tripled, but that society should act for the many and not the greedy few.

There is something especially grubby about the theory that nothing can be generated without a profit motive, in that it

writes off the entire human race as driven by greed. And yet one
of the ironies is that, the more profit-driven society becomes,
the more it depends on the generosity of its individuals. A typical recruiting advert for care workers shows a member of staff
helping a frail old man on crutches – and they seem to have
picked the frailest they could find, as if from a modelling agency
where they only take you on if you're ninety-six and gasping for
breath. But that's because the only appeal of the job is that
you're making a vast contribution to these people's lives. They'd
recruit far fewer if they tried a different campaign approach: 'See
this old man – make him a few pots of tea and you can keep his
crutches when he pegs it – just one of the perks that makes care
work.'

There was a section of the documentary *49 Up*, the seventh in
the series of interviews carried out every seven years with the
same people which began when they were kids in 1963, in
which Lynn from East London described her job. All her skint
life she's worked with children in libraries. She ran a mobile
library until it was axed to save money, then set up a club for
severely disabled kids, explaining, 'Teaching children the beauty
of books and watching their faces as that beauty unfolds is fantastic.' From the firm, confident dedication she poured on to this
scheme she was obviously someone who had only ever given to
society, and simply wouldn't know how to take. Now this
scheme was being cut too, and she'd no longer be able to pursue
the reading that was so central to these kids' lives. As she
described the latest cut, this compellingly tough, magnetically
soft woman told us, 'All my life I've had to fight this sort of
thing, but I've never known a time when no one was listening.'
And then she asked for the camera to be turned off because she
didn't want to be seen crying.

One of the most compelling political acts I've taken part in
during my forties was jury service. The trial involved a foreign lad
arrested for apparently trying to sell dope to a crowd on a sunny
day in London. But the three police witnesses contradicted each

other, one of them saying, 'He went up to a Spanish couple and spoke to them in Portuguese, except for the words "Do you want some dope?" which he said in English.' What would he follow this up with, I wondered. Perhaps he'd add, 'Then he said through a megaphone, "I'm banged to rights" in Argentinian.'*

I made pages of notes pointing out the discrepancies, as the judge told us to – 'Make your judgement, using your life experiences' – and we retired to make our decision. The dope he'd been found with was placed on the table as Exhibit A and an advertising executive was elected as foreman. 'As foreman, to start with,' he said, 'I'm having this,' and he picked up Exhibit A and went to put it in his pocket. This was disastrous – twelve random people and already one of the others has got the first big laugh.

The foreman asked me to start with my thoughts on the police evidence. I mentioned a couple of flaws but decided to leave the main ones for later. An engineer spoke next, pointing out a series of mistakes I hadn't noticed. Then a stern-looking woman, crisp *Daily Mail* in her Thatcher-esque handbag, said, 'Well, as far as I'm concerned the police were telling a huge pack of lies.' The foreman asked, 'Does *anyone* believe any of the police evidence?'

Everyone shook their heads. 'Well, let's dismiss that completely then,' he said, and I wanted to shout 'HANG ON. I've got loads more notes yet – look, two pages, with arrows and everything. Please let me read them out.'

The next issue was why, if the dope was for the lad's personal use as he claimed, he had a pocketful of the stuff. The advertising man said, 'Well, I sometimes buy a case of wine in one go, he was just doing the same with dope – stocking up.' And I wondered if he'd come out with a little jingle like 'The evidence mounts that he's not sold an ounce.'

---

*It's staggering just how useless the police can be, even in their own terms. Of all the people you've come across who've had their house or car broken into, how many have ever got anything back or been told that the burglars were caught? Imagine if any other service had a record that hopeless, so that for example the fire service never ever put out a fire – but occasionally did hose down the wrong house.

'It's no different from when I get paid and go straight out to buy a pair of shoes,' said a teenage girl.

Very slowly, with the authority of an elder speaking in a meeting of native American Cherokees, a Jamaican pensioner said, 'I've seen people in the music business smoke that much in one afternoon. There – the judge told us to use our life experience and that's what I've done.' So it was a unanimous not guilty.

The most gratifying aspect was how diligently everyone had exercised their duties. They all took notes, observed the mannerisms of witnesses and analysed their own instincts, in a thorough pursuit of their responsibility as citizens. It's the opposite of a modern general election, in which your choice between a collection of equally distant figures representing similar values makes it an effort to bother at all. The low turnouts in these elections are often described as evidence of 'apathy', but this apathy has boomed in a time of the largest demonstrations in British history. Millions engaged with the issue of Iraq, the younger section of the population more than others, yet these were the people least likely to vote. For some this wasn't apathy, just as I wouldn't go to watch Cliff Richard perform even if it was next door to where I lived – and that wouldn't be apathy, it would be wilful non-participation. I certainly wouldn't be lying on the settee thinking 'Hmm, he'll be doing "Bachelor Boy" in a minute, but as soulful and spiritual as I'd find it, I just can't be bothered.'

Most people may not think it through that way, but they're not enthused because voting appears to make no difference. Whereas nobody on jury service would say to the foreman, 'I can't be bothered to vote – guilty, not guilty, all these verdicts are the bloody same if you ask me.'

One of the most awkward questions for socialists is whether the mass of the population could collectively run society. But every weekend morning the parks are packed with kids playing sport that's been arranged by enthusiastic amateurs. In these days in which nothing can be expected to function without a push from business, Scouts and Guides, cycling clubs and cricket teams, pool tournaments and amateur dramatics shows, gigs and fêtes, battle re-enactment societies and nights with local MCs advertised on cardboard signs round lamp-posts operate with an efficiency that would secure a post with senior management in most companies. In most workplaces it's the imagination, experience and decisions of the clerks, the engineers, the nurses and builders that ensure the tasks of the enterprise are completed. In some ways we're already running the world, it's just that no one's got round to realising it yet.

If it's true that the working class still has the potential to transform society, the harder part is establishing how to help that change come about. One man with a useful contribution to that discussion is Peter Hain, who I interviewed in the Northern Ireland office where he was a minister, for a radio programme about the Rock Against Racism organisation of the 1970s, of which Hain had been, in fact, a founder member. In his youth he'd been an activist on various fronts, most famously leading the campaign against the visit of an apartheid-backed rugby team from South Africa, but in recent years had turned into a loyal supporter of Tony Blair.

After chatting with his amiable armed guards, who sat on a table with their machine guns rocking as they swung their legs, we were shown into Peter's office overlooking the Thames by Lambeth Bridge, with it's *two* leather three-piece suites and a mahogany table on which rested every daily newspaper, perfectly folded in the middle. I wondered whether, if you browsed nonchalantly through the papers, you'd perish amid a flurry of bullets, and the last thing you'd hear would be, 'No one gets away with creasing your *Financial Times*, Mr Hain.'

We set up the microphones and he started. Rock Against Racism and the Anti-Nazi League that spawned it, he said, gave him some of the proudest moments of his life. It was exhilarating to organise the demonstrations, including those denounced by the press of the time as violent. And he was immensely grateful to the

SWP for taking the initiative in setting it up, because sometimes it's only the mass action of the people that can bring progress. Then his phone rang. 'Sorry,' he said, 'I must take this,' and proceeded to try to persuade an MP to join with the government later that day and vote for 30 billion quid to be spent on Trident nuclear weapons. He put the phone down, asked if I still saw a couple of SWP members he'd known since the days he'd described and said, 'Well, if you see them you *must* give them my regards.'

Among the battalions of New Labour figures who have been crucial in handing society over to big business, there must be only a few that set out with that intent. Most of them must at some point have been driven by a committment to the unions, or CND or the anti-Vietnam War movement; not many will have joined the Labour Party thinking this was the best way to fulfil their ambitions of privatising the Underground and meeting Prince Philip. And those who have ended up like that haven't done so because they've been paid off or brainwashed in a dungeon. They've dribbled into it one drip of saliva at a time. It's the treacherous route that has snared so many who've set out with a passion to turn the world back in favour of the underdog.

The trade unionist, the activist, the spokesperson for a radical cause comes to the attention of local government or a police authority or some official body that meets at the House of Commons, and is invited to take part in a committee or working party that will influence their cause. And they innocently accept, proudly believing they're getting somewhere. They may even feel a sense of mischief as they're invited into a grand establishment building with lots of pillars, where they may meet an MP or someone who pops up as an expert on the news. And their host will be charming, not as a creepy strategy but because they're charming.

I arrived at a television studio one morning to find I was on a programme with Douglas Hurd, the old Etonian who was Home

Secretary under Thatcher, and he was charming. I could have told him I was dedicated to the violent overthrow of him, his family and everything he stood for, and he'd have said something like 'Well, I do hope you can wait a few moments because I was about to offer you one of these rather delicious-looking cream buns.'

They might be cheeky too. They'll tell you an inside story about how the chair of the bank is always drunk, or how two members of the cabinet can't stand each other. Inevitably, when you meet people in high places who talk freely with you in that way, you feel important. If you're given an official post you believe you're achieving something, and then you go to functions where a waiter hands you champagne as you enter, and you're introduced to someone you saw last week on *Newsnight* and someone who's over specially from Canada for the event and it all seems to matter.

The process is gradual and subtle; if you don't achieve much on the committee you've been appointed to, you assume it's because you need to get further inside the system. And then in order to retain your position you might denounce the campaigners, the demonstrators, the people you were once inspired by and whom you once inspired, because they're making it more difficult for you to reach inside the system and *really* change their lives for the better.

The British establishment has devised a remarkably sophisticated method for absorbing dissent within its ranks. I went to a party laid on to celebrate the twentieth anniversary of the *Independent*, naively thinking I'd meet a few people I hadn't seen for a while for a couple of pints. Which was a stupid approach because obviously this is not how posh parties work. To start with it was at Lancaster House, a prestigious Mayfair palace, where you'd look very odd if you arrived with four tins of Stella and said to the doorman, 'Can my mate Barry come in as well?'

Inside, I climbed the regally wide staircase that looked as if it had been bought from the set of *Gone with the Wind*, and arrived at this vast hall adorned with chandeliers like glittery UFOs, the sort of room that makes you feel you should speak to everyone in the language of Victorian melodrama, greeting people with 'Ah pray, 'tis Kevin who compiles the crosswords, I trust your journey here was not *too* arduous, sir.'

As I walked in there was a loud 'tap tap' noise, followed by the dying of the hubbub, and a master of ceremonies with a baritone delivery boomed, 'Pray silence for our speaker this evening, the Chancellor of the Exchequer Mister GORDON BROWN.' To which I thought, 'Fucking hell, I only popped out for a beer.' It was as odd as nipping round to your mum's to take her a birthday present, to be greeted with, 'Keep your voice down, dear, President Nicolas Sarkozy of France is delivering a keynote speech on Anglo-French relations in the kitchen.'

Even stranger was the fact that Gordon Brown was shortly to become Prime Minister of a government that had led the country into a war that the *Independent* had stridently opposed. And in the banqueting suite Gordon praised that very newspaper as an example of free speech and excellence. Such an approach probably isn't even conscious, it's just the way the system works. They don't have you hung, drawn and quartered. Instead they put their arms round you gently in corridors. They giggle with you over the trifles you might disagree about, such as attitudes to war. How easy it is to think they're all right really, that if you could just get in there and say your well-thought-out bit, you could gently persuade them to bend towards your point of view. Because you forget that the next afternoon they'll be speaking at a dinner for Exxon or British Aerospace and be praising them in the same way. And oil companies and arms dealers are probably better at gentle persuasion of governments than you are.

Maybe this is the answer to one of the questions raised by so many of the angry confused – *why* has the Labour Party become so shockingly craven to the rich and powerful? And it is a vital question, because if the problem is simply that it was taken over by

unscrupulous careerists, then all we have to do is replace the
dreadful people with decent people.

The truth is more complex. The bankers, supermarket barons
and associated corporate voices control the planet *whoever* is
elected. They meet governments, set up bodies with governments, undermine governments and occasionally overthrow
governments. Elected politicians quickly learn they have to work
'alongside' these people, which means befriending them and not
upsetting their interests. Any politician who retains a radical
objective either abandons any ambition to reach a senior level, or
crumbles and accepts their subservient role.

Peter Hain was decent, and so were many of his colleagues, but
his route has transformed him from anti-war campaigner to someone who enthusiastically backed the most unjustifiable war of all
so that he could stay on the inside, where he imagined he could
do more good than on the outside. I bet that, in the Spanish
Inquisition, there were torturers who said to their old Jewish
mates, 'But the thing is at least I'm in there arguing my point.
And if it wasn't me gouging people's eyes out it would be the
really vicious priests, and they're even *worse.*'

History shows that great injustices aren't reversed by those who
subtly burrow into the system that's delivering the injustice but by
those who stand outside and shake it until it falls. For example,
was apartheid brought down by wily members of the South
African government who went along with the pass laws and the
arrests of opponents because it cleverly got them to a position
where they could write papers suggesting a mild reform in some
aspect of the system? Or was it destroyed by the millions around
the world who screamed for its destruction?

When you're in a confused state of mind, something that does-
n't help clarify the world is to receive a series of increasingly
peculiar requests to appear on television. One evening, at my
scruffiest, I went round to the local Costcutter for a pork pie and
got home to find a message asking if I was available for *I'm a*

Celebrity, Get Me Out of Here. That's the sort of thing that could make you seriously mentally ill. In fact, if I'd gone back outside, still carrying my plastic carrier bag, and told the nearest person about the message, they'd have replied, 'Of course you did – and no doubt you've also been asked to appear as Madam Butterfly at the Royal Opera House and to partner Tiger Woods in the US Open golf championship, you mad smelly tramp.'

I was asked to do a programme in which I'd have to be taught how to conduct an orchestra and then display my new skill at the proms in the Albert Hall. I wondered if there'd be a follow-up called 'Heart of the Matter' in which six personalities would be trained in cardiovascular surgery and each week one of them would have to carry out a heart bypass operation.

There was an invitation to a filmed dinner with Michael Portillo to celebrate his fiftieth birthday. There was something that involved learning about beauty treatments from a woman in *Emmerdale*. And a request to appear on a programme called *Underdog*, which I naively thought would be about people who'd reacted against being 'underdogs' in life. Instead the message explained that a series of 'celebrities' would be matched with an untrained dog, and then try to teach the dog how to do tricks in front of an audience, with criticism from a panel and an audience vote to kick off the most useless celebrity/dog team each week.*

To each of these offers I'd react with 'Oh for fuck's sake, how ridiculous', and an hour later think, 'Well, hang on, consider it for just a moment.' That's the lethal point in any decision-making; there must have been people in history who've gone through a similar thought process and as a result ended up running a regional branch of the Saudi military police.

---

*How about one called 'Paedoph-idol', in which celebrities have to learn the skills required to lure under-age sexual partners. Each week we see them displaying their new talent, then a panel of experts criticises them, a harsh one sneering, 'There was *no* attempt to disguise the age, the internet chatroom session was frankly *clumsy*.' (The audience jeers.) – 'Yes, I'll say it again – CLUMSY.' (The audience boos and the celebrity stands limply and fights back tears.)

The lure of such enticements is that we live in an age where your value on earth is determined by your 'celebrity' status. You could be the world's leading physicist and it would count for nothing, unless you were a *celebrity* physicist, popping up on *Comic Relief* and doing a waltz with Natasha Kaplinsky dressed as a black hole. Mostly a celebrity is just someone whose job is to be famous; to read off an autocue or get photographed on a beach. Every poll taken among teenagers reveals that one of their most popular ambitions is to be famous. Not to be a famous footballer or singer but just famous. Until recently the notion of fame not attached to a reason for that fame would have made no sense. It would have been like saying, 'Yesterday I saw a beautiful.'

One of the most depressing road safety adverts ever made must be the series in which they showed someone enjoying a celebrity lifestyle, posing on red carpets or walking amid a sunglassed entourage. The film would suddenly stop and the slogan 'Don't die before you've lived' warned that if you're killed in a car accident you've no chance to lead this life. As if the only reason to live is that you might be famous, implying that if you know in advance you'll only be a shitty little librarian you might as well go ahead and drive the wrong way up the M6.

A party at the Beckhams' house was shown on television, just because it was full of celebrities. So to maintain your celebrity status you can't have friends who aren't celebrities, because ITV wouldn't want to film you chatting with your old mate Nigel the plumber. Presumably when the Beckhams have a central heating problem they get it fixed by Robbie Williams or the Black Eyed Peas. I imagine ITV must have told Beckham, 'We've got great news. Your mum can come to the party, but your old mum was a bit D-list so from now on your mum's going to be Diana Ross.'

And the show for those most desperate to be famous for nothing becomes more absurd each year, so it would be no surprise to hear someone gasp, 'The new series of *Big Brother* is *amazing*, one of them's incontinent, there's Siamese twins, a woman who thinks she's a zebra and a bloke who's dead but the other housemates don't know yet.'

Yet, while this vacuous army marches across televisions and magazines, it may be the situation isn't as alarming as it can seem. *Big Brother* may appear to provide a rapid route to prolonged unearned stardom, but even the winners are usually quickly forgotten, maybe popping up on Bravo or urging viewers to ring up and guess the missing word at ten past midnight, watched mostly from the nation's settees by those in crumbling marriages. Anthea Turner, the pointless celebrity's pointless celebrity, at the height of a publicity drive, published a biography that sold 451 copies. Les Dennis launched a theatre tour at a time when he was in every newspaper and in most venues sold only a few dozen tickets. Jodie Marsh managed to be voted out of *Celebrity Big Brother* as more unpopular than George Galloway. There seems to be a healthy contempt for people who demand attention on the basis that we must know who they are, which contradicts the obsession with celebrity that makes their stardom possible.

Even in a class at school in which most of the pupils may have declared celebrity to be the highest plane anyone could aspire to, the kids who'd be most admired would be those who were best at sport, or the funniest, or most engaging and generous, or best at fighting, but not the one who arrived every day in a specially designed backless dress to pose outside assembly waving and screamed at her publicity agent about the lack of photographers.

It's as if the population isn't really as superficial as it pretends to be. The books and films, the songs and performances that create the most enduring impact are still mostly those that inspire, that make an audience gasp or weep or reappraise their opinions, rather than go, 'WOW, it's actually Paris Hilton.'

In which case, how did I end up in a studio looking into a camera and talking about the most memorable aspects of 1998 for a show called *I Love 1998*? At one point I was asked about the popularity that year of Sunny Delight orange drink. 'Go on, just say a few words about how sugary and horrible it is,' said the director.

'But I've never drunk the stuff,' I said.

He told me, 'There was a story that year about a boy who drank so much of it he actually turned orange.'

I said, 'Was there? Blimey.'

'So just say that.'

'What, you want me to say, "Here, wasn't there a boy who drank so much of it he actually turned orange"?'

'Yes, that would be perfect,' he said.

Luckily I managed to persuade him that it would be better coming from someone else.

In the murky world of entertainment, when you're engaged in a project you feel driven to make, it's easy to reject the requests to participate in celebrity-based television (assuming you're not desperately skint). It's when you can't get your ideas accepted by TV executives, publishers or newspapers, when you're feeling worthless, that's when you're vulnerable. That's when it seems an appearance on a show, even if it's nonsense, would keep you on TV, recognised by the public, validated. I used to get annoyed with people I knew as comics or actors when I saw them abandoning their talent to be funny or moving in return for appearing on instantly forgettable television. I once spent an evening talking to a black comic who seemed to almost explode with earnest determination, because he was going to use his position to say what mattered, to be like Richard Pryor, to unravel the distortions of racism. And the very next night I saw him as a guest performer on a quiz show, dressed as a giant bee.

To feel let down by those who take the giant bee option, however, is to misdirect the disappointment. Most people in the entertainment industry have been driven at some point by a desire to tell a story or convey an idea, have sat up through the night puzzling how to make the ending more powerful or the dialogue more realistic. It's when that vision appears to have no outlet, when you can't see any way of achieving what you set out to accomplish, when the barriers set up by those who control the system seem too powerful, that the temptation grows to be 'realistic', to at least get inside the system and do something, be someone who's at least noticed. Until the temptation becomes irresistible, to the point where it seems a betrayal *not* to accept it. But you have to be careful because none of us are saints. One bad moment and it's, 'Here boy, here boy, come on, Rambo, over the see-saw, THAT's it, goooood boy, ha-ha-ha.'

14

PARTIES MAKE ME FEEL AS BAD

The final moments of a failing relationship are usually pathetically ordinary. Unlike in films, where there's a last brave embrace amid the hubbub of an Italian railway station, or a drunk but eloquent liberating speech delivered to a stunned family gathering, the last words are more likely to be 'I think this is your mug.' Just as the last innings of a great batsman will probably be 12 not out in front of 150 people when rain stops play, and I bet the last act of the 100 Years War was a regiment looking for a lost box of muskets, the end will almost certainly be miserably mundane.

There was a minor grumble, something to do with shopping, one sunny Saturday afternoon, that I think involved cat food, delivered with the intonation Al Pacino would have used if there'd been a cat food issue in *Scarface*.

And immediately I knew that was the end. I had no idea a few minutes earlier that we were one small-to-medium-sized snarl from termination, but when it happened I just knew. I'd run out of tolerance, and it seemed as definite and beyond my control as if I'd gone to make a cake but discovered I'd run out of flour. 'That's it,' I said, surprised. Just as there must be a definite point when someone knows, absolutely knows, 'I *am* going to try to swim the Channel' or 'I *am* going to explode myself in a public building' and they become mentally prepared for all that their decision entails. I knew right then that I'd soon be packing records and reassuring children, contacting the gas board and telling people they couldn't get me on that number any more.

Even then, every time I rang a letting agency or scrolled through the details of flats that MUST BE SEEN on estate agent websites, I felt myself thinking, 'What am I *doing*? We've only just got the garden done and the newspapers are delivered here. These are the stairs I chase my daughter down while pretending to be a shark, that game won't work with other stairs.' But the first real test of whether you've left, really left in your head, comes when someone says, 'How are you and your partner?' or 'You two must come round next week' and you reply, 'We're not together any more,' as if it makes an emotion official.

After I'd done this a couple of times, though, I became wary of saying it, not because I was having doubts but because I might get a response that went, 'Oh – oh dear, oh I'm SO sorry. Oh I had no idea. Oh that's such a shame. Oh you poor things. Oh I must give her a ring. And how are you? Are you managing? Oh Katherine will be ever so upset because she had a lovely time when we all came over that Boxing Day. Oh what a pity. And is she coping? It must be very hard with her job. Oh that's *such* a shame.' Although they're only trying to be sympathetic, they sometimes get quite personal: 'Was it the pressure of work? And I suppose you being away that time must have made things difficult.' It makes you wonder if they'll continue, 'Were you having disagreements about anal sex? Were you? Because that can be very stressful – for *both* of you. Oh what a pity.'

Or someone would say, 'Do you want to talk about it? How are *you* feeling, because you have to stay strong.' To which I'd mumble, 'I'll be all right' and they'd insist, 'It does help to talk, you know. Talking is the best thing.' So I'd say, 'Well, maybe' and they'd look me directly in the eye and say, 'Just call me – OK – I'm here to listen.' And I'd think, 'I've only ever met you twice, because my daughter's in the same swimming class as yours.'

Or they'd grab your wrist and say, 'Oh please *try* and get back together – think of the kids,' as if I might say, 'Oh yes, them. Do you know they'd gone clean out of my mind.' Explaining to anyone that you've split up is a nuisance, so sometimes I'd answer the question 'How's the family?' by saying, 'Fine. Everyone's fine,' although ten minutes earlier I'd been looking in an estate agent's window for a flat. I'm sure there must be people who've maintained this for years, saying, 'Yeah, she's fine,' when asked about their wife, although they're now divorced and have remarried with four kids and do a double act with their new wife as a knife-throwing team in a circus.

But then there's explaining the situation to the children, which involves a different style of deception. 'It will be exciting, because it means you'll have *two* homes' and 'Now whenever you see Daddy it will be special time so you'll have *more* fun.' And as you're saying all this, they gaze into the middle distance with an expression that says, 'You don't expect us to believe that twaddle, do you?' And you know you might as well say, 'Maybe all this will make Daddy bankrupt and homeless, which will be lots of fun because you can help him yell at strangers from a park bench. And you can stay with him in all the doorways of the area so you'll have *hundreds* of homes.'

I was given a pamphlet called 'Divorce and separation – helping children and parents to cope', handed out by doctors and social workers, which seemed to have been created in some fairyland. It advised, for example: 'Financial insecurity may lead to short tempers and anxiety that is hard to conceal from children – but do try.' Ah, I see, you have to try. Another little bullet point tells us: 'Try to put the children first.' Which was so helpful because I'd been putting them ninth. And it tells you to be patient and explain things calmly and maintain routines, but doesn't really cover what to do when they're pleading, 'Please don't go, Daddy, please, please, pleeeease,' while their mother sits on the settee in a ball.

Next comes the problem of where to go. You find friends insisting it really would make financial sense to buy a house rather than rent. Which is true, but you might as well suggest it makes financial sense to buy a 3,000-acre cattle ranch in Virginia or a region of the Antarctic rumoured to be an oilfield. The problem is that leaving makes you an instant financial disaster. Right when you need money more than ever in order to get somewhere to live, for a multitude of reasons you have less than ever. If one of those financial columns that answer readers' money problems in the *Daily Mail* was advising someone who could no longer tolerate their domestic turmoil, it would no doubt say, 'A sensible investor will secure their equity by secretly planning to leave over a two-year period. The shrewd move would therefore be to ensure a replacement partner before closing down the old one, by investing in a secret affair. With a little planning, this could be timed to mature just as you withdraw from your original partner, then you can purchase a new property jointly, which halves your outlay, or if your replacement is already attached to their own property you'll achieve instant security. And remember, secret affairs can provide considerable short-term dividends as well!'

Moving out is exhausting as well. It takes so much time and energy the outside world seems to disappear, and I found myself reading reports about Darfur while thinking, 'Hmm, the Janjaweed militia are an unpleasant bunch, but I wonder why that landlord hasn't rung back about the two-bedroom place by the kebab shop?' I even took a conscious decision not to take an interest in the state of the nation, forgetting issues such as how the country had been handed to City speculators, until I'd got somewhere to move into. I went along to an estate agent and asked how much houses cost, and the amiable woman, who would have been better suited to running a 'tea shoppe' in Dartmouth said, 'Oh it's disgraceful round here, dear. These blooming speculators come in, point to one of the pictures on the wall and say, "If I buy that one how much will I make in two years?" It's because they get these big bonuses from the City, you see. They don't have any intention of living there but they've driven the prices up by another 50,000, the arrogant so-and-sos.'

So I had to subject myself to the cheaper, if financially not sensible, option of renting somewhere. I was met outside the flat by a lad in his twenties with a very shiny ear-ring who shook my hand with far too much confidence. 'Have you come far?' he said, which must be his stock opening line, followed by 'Right, let's take a look' with the false enthusiasm of a game-show host. I felt he might lean against me in his speckly grey suit, put a hand on my shoulder and say, 'OK, Mark, fingers crossed, let's hope this is the flat you're looking for. You were asked to name a jungle animal and said "hyena" – computer, tell us is "hyena" one of your answers?'

His key, however, wouldn't open the door. He wriggled it and twisted it, then barged the door with his shoulder and eventually it rattled open, revealing a damp corridor that smelt like the room at London Zoo where the bats fly around. We crept through the gloom, looking for the door to one of the flats. You half expected a documentary team to sneak up, eventually bursting in through a door to reveal a surgeon illegally selling kidneys. Inside, the tiny dank rooms oozed with depression, and if the Archbishop of Canterbury moved in I'd give him a week before he'd turn into a junkie. 'The bath,' I said to him as I peered into the bathroom, 'it's full of rubble.'

'Oh yeah, we'll have to sort that out,' he said. I felt like replying, 'No, don't trouble yourself, my granddad only ever had baths of rubble, swore by them.'

Throughout this visit I had one overriding thought: 'I shouldn't be even looking at places like this – a) I've already got a house, and b) I'm forty-fucking-six.'

There followed a series of slightly less miserable visits, but each of them made me think I could have rented out my settee as a one-bedroom flat, until an optimistic agent rang about a lovely property, exactly what I was looking for, with a well-kept garden, but I must be available to see it very quickly because properties like this are so rare and it was sure to be snapped up, etc. I rushed off to meet the beaming, jolly and huge estate agent and together we knocked at the door. A cautious Irish lady of about sixty with an inquisitive and slightly confused face answered. 'You can't look at the downstairs flat, not now,' she said, 'because my son runs a bar and he got back late and he's in the flat and fast asleep and I shan't want to wake him, he works so hard, he always has done.'

Although we couldn't see the downstairs flat, the upstairs flat was also available, so we filed up three flights of stairs that creaked and wobbled like the rotting steps that heroes of action movies creep along when they're trying to escape, before one of the steps gives way and the woman falls through but is caught by her fingertips by the bloke she's falling in love with. The walls were bare brick but she was going to get it plastered and although there was no sink, her son was going to get one put in soon. There was also a tiny balcony with nothing to stop you falling off so that if you let a child out there it would have a life expectancy of forty seconds. 'I'd rather wait and see the downstairs flat,' I said. 'Could I come back tomorrow?'

She said, 'Ah, you can't really look at it tomorrow, as we've got someone coming round to deal with the rats.'

Eventually, when I found somewhere that, if it were visited by the council wouldn't have been immediately evacuated and surrounded by yellow tape warning DO NOT ENTER, it was tenser than when I'd looked at the worst places. Because there was no reason not to take this place. The contract was on the table and if I signed, this would be permanent, more permanent than anything that happens at the start of a relationship, more permanent than asking someone out or sleeping with someone for the first time, more permanent than moving in together. I signed the form and went to tell my children, aware that, seeing as they'd been through an array of hysterics at the thought of me leaving, the real thing would leave them in an inconsolable heap.

I told them where it was and how we'd work things out and my son said, 'Daddy, I have got one question.' I prepared myself for a sickeningly poignant moment, aware I'd have to be honest about the finality of all this, no matter what reaction it caused. 'In your new place,' he began, 'will you have Sky Plus? It's on special offer at the moment.'

Moving house in these circumstances can feel eerie, especially when three-quarters of television output is advising you that the reason for moving is to secure property with a potential for development in an up-and-coming location, like 'Mark and Janet' who we simply *must* persuade to take the plunge with this irresistible converted fort in Aylesbury. In a life free of setbacks, moving is exciting because it represents new opportunities: you leave your parents, or buy your first place or a bigger house to accommodate a growing family. But sometimes you have to move because everything's fallen to bits. There could be a 'moving house' programme called 'No option No option No option', where an expert looks at a flat with someone who has to move and says, 'I tell you what, mate, there's no rubble in the bath, no rats, you can't stay where you are, you'll have to take it, you've no bloody option' and it's all over in two minutes.

One morning I played 'Don't Think Twice, It's All Right' on the record player, then left the house as a resident for the last time and took the children to show them my new empty place, certain they'd be puzzled at how small it was and how empty it was. Instead, in the emptiness they clambered under the stairs, discovering you could hang from them, and yelped, '*This* place is *fantastic*, you can be a *gorilla* on the *stairs*.' Because they weren't old enough to have learned that everything revolves around wealth and status. If I'd had to leave even more urgently, they'd have ended up running into the bathroom and shrieking, '*This* place is *fantastic*, the *bath* is full of *rubble*, we can play *builders and site engineers* and get *wet at the same time*.'

One of the weirdest moments after moving out was the first morning I woke up in the new place. Not only was it chillingly still and quiet, this was what the place was always like. Before, there had been moments of quiet when everyone else was out, but it was always a slightly anxious quiet, a brief calm to be

inhaled before doors crashed open and the natural beat of child-
hood urgency ricocheted once more round the building. It was
the quiet of a stadium before the starting gun for a sprint final.
Now there was a different quiet, a permanent quiet. I could make
some artificial noise by putting on the Wu-Tang-Clan, but there
was no organic thud-thud – 'Aaagh' – 'Get OFF' – 'Dad can I
have a Twix' – 'pewaaa waaa kachakach COOL I've shot a
ZOMBIE on level 2'.

For the first few days I kept thinking, 'Hang on, what am I
doing HERE?' like a character in a science fiction programme that
suddenly lands in 1953. And I'd forgotten that unless you take
something with you there won't be anything there when you
move in. I wasn't used to this. I'd look for the potato masher and
think, 'Where's it gone?' before remembering I hadn't got one.
Then there's shopping, which is the saddest endeavour for someone suddenly buying for one. At first I'd get all I needed, look at
it barely filling one small wire basket, remember the carload of
boxes and bags that used to represent shopping and think, 'Surely
I can't live on that.' It's hard to adjust to the fact that on your own
you need so little. You need only one tomato. But you can't buy
one tomato, that's stupid. There's even things you need only one of
that don't come in ones, like eggs. Tesco will probably spot a gap
in the market here and start building shops called 'Tesco singles' for
people who've just split up, where you can buy 'single-person
quantities' such as an egg cup of olive oil or thirty-five peas.

Another thing that is odd is not having to tell anyone where
you're going. You just leave the house, and don't have to call out,
'Just nipping out for some Sellotape.' To start with I'd wander up
the road slightly disconcerted, as if there was some procedure I
hadn't been through, perhaps a form to complete when I left the
house, to send to the Town Hall.

Quite simply, finding yourself on your own for the first time in
thirteen years is lonely. And the irony with loneliness is it can
make you feel that all you want to do is be alone. Then, disaster –
I couldn't get cable. It wasn't available in the road for some reason.

Surely there was a law somewhere that said if someone is lonely cable has to be provided as a basic human right.

One night I forced myself to go to a party, where I was approached by an excitable woman who told me she was *such* a fan and was *so* pleased to meet me, and she'd had a splendid evening the previous night because she'd been to a reception at the American embassy and there were *such* important people there who worked for George Bush and there were lovely canapés. 'I don't think I'd have liked that much,' I said, and she countered, 'Yes, but surely we should talk to these people because otherwise we can't influence them.' So I asked what she'd said in order to try to influence the Bush administration, and she said she mostly just ate the canapés, but in any case the most important thing we could do to improve the world was to educate our children, and that's why she was making the sacrifice and sending her son to a private school because 'we can't put our principles before our children'. Oh for fuck's sake. The exact words. And at this point all the angst of moving out and rubble and rats and screaming and buying one tomato and no cable crystallised into a combustible reaction and I went into an unstoppable tirade, all the stuff about robbing old-age pensioners to buy Jason a microscope and the cookery class being taken over by Chechen rebels – it all came flying out. Her husband rushed over and boomed in an operatic voice, 'So – you believe we should sacrifice our children at the altar of political correctness, do you?'

As it was, none of this was what I'd intended when I popped out, but the situation was exacerbated by the fact that the husband was dressed from head to toe in a pink fluorescent dress. For some reason that made me feel lonelier than if I'd stayed in.

With some effort you can come to terms with a personal crisis, but what can completely knock you out are the supplementary dollops of annoyance that land on top. You would probably find that most of the businessmen who jumped off high buildings following the Wall Street crash had grudgingly accepted their financial ruin, but then had a day when they paid the bus fare but the bus broke down and the driver of the following bus wouldn't accept the original ticket, so they had to carry two heavy boxes which fell apart and papers flew down the street. And to top it all they bit their lip.

One afternoon the phone rang around the time my children were coming over for the weekend and a television executive told me the programme we all thought we'd be making had been cancelled. I can understand why someone might think, 'Oh poor you – I'm sure if the starving of Sudan heard about it they'd accept that put their meagre problems in perspective.' But if you ever propose an idea for a television programme, you ought to be sufficiently excited about the prospect of making it so that when it's rejected you shout 'Oh for fuck's sake, *surely* at its *worst* it would have been better than [insert your own lengthy list].'

While I was on the phone the children arrived with my ex-partner, and in my sparse new place they all began yelling at each other. As all three howled I could still hear in the background the TV executive: 'We do not feel this project is suitable . . .' Then over the top of all this came a hideous rattle, squeak and crash, the noise I imagine a train makes when it's derailed, and the washing machine shuddered to a violent halt, water flooding across the floor the way it does on those projected images of what it will be like if global warming continues unchecked.

So the start of the children's fun weekend with Daddy was to be driven around South London in search of an open launderette that could dry my sheets, otherwise I'd have to sleep on the settee, with no cable. After almost an hour I found one, its 'open' sign lit up and winking like a prostitute. 'Come in here, big boy, I'll dry your sheets,' it teased. I ran across and noticed it was due to stay open for another hour. 'No – no more – shut,' said the Polish man who ran the place. I smiled and pleaded and pointed to the 'Open until 8.30' sign, and then I offered a £5 bribe to be able to use his drier up to the time they were supposed to stay open anyway, and by now I was choking back tears and I must have looked so desperate that any witness would have assumed I'd promised to dry these sheets for the Mafia and they were coming round any minute. But he just kept saying, 'No – no – shut now – go home' and in that moment I discovered a depth of misery I'd never really known. It wasn't anything to do with sheets or rejected television programmes, it was just a plea swirling from head to stomach and back again – 'Can things please stop going fucking wrong?'

The intriguing part when everything's gone wrong is the uncertainty. According to the rules, at my age you're supposed to be settled and looking forward to paying off the mortgage, knowing where you're living and who with for the rest of your life, the only contentious points being whether to get new carpets or go for laminated parquet floorboards. Now, though, anything was possible. I could go to a showbiz party and meet Keira Knightley, who turns out to have adored my programme on Aristotle, declaring it transformed her attitude to Plato's forms and we end up living together in Mauritius. Or I could still be at this flat when I was seventy, spending most days in my underpants eating white sliced bread straight from the packet and going out only to get food for my twenty-five cats.

How on earth do you go about being single at this age? You can't become one of those creepy blokes who tries to lure women twenty-five years younger than him by telling them he can get them a job in the Foreign Office, or promising to serenade them with his flute. And of course at this age you're plagued by caution. Whereas at twenty-three you can meet someone and immediately think, 'Hey, she seems wonderful, what could ever possibly go wrong?', now I could be with someone for a year in which everything went perfectly and still worry that at any moment she'd howl to the stars and set fire to a hedgehog.

Contrary to the perceived image, it's more likely that as we get older the people we're attracted to are older as well. I couldn't go out with someone who's twenty-two, they've not been through nearly enough disappointments. To the 45-year-old a 45-year-old face etched with stories and travel and surprises can appear much more alluring than one twenty years younger.

One day when I was performing at a festival I met a record company executive and we were intrigued enough by each other to spend the day watching bands and meandering through the park, and she looked about thirty-six but it became clear she was forty-four, which made me more interested, and later on I thought, 'I remember this procedure. Isn't this the bit where I'm supposed to ask her out?' So we arranged a date and it was all so exciting, not just because of the attraction but because it was so unpredictable. I wasn't sure I could remember what you're supposed to do on dates. We saw a band, then went into Soho for a coffee and for a moment I had that 'What am I doing HERE?' feeling again. It all seemed to be making progress, until she told me about her son, casually mentioning that of course he went to public school. I didn't say anything for a moment but she must have been able to tell I questioned this because she said, 'Well, we can't put our principles before our children.'

I pondered for a moment that it was best to proceed with caution, especially given all I've had to consider about the dangers of being too belligerent. And then I burst into a rant, and to her credit she burst back with equal vigour, and because I was older and wiser than I'd ever been before I *thought* the words, 'Oh send him there if you like, he'll only get buggered and die of a drugs overdose,' but I didn't actually say them.

Still, because we were in our forties and mature instead of chaotically twenty-three, we politely agreed to disagree and to ring each other soon for another date, then left – both knowing we'd never see each other again.

This didn't make life depressing as much as confusing. There's another complication in your forties that didn't exist twenty years earlier. The break-up of a relationship is no longer final. Not when you've got children. You have to carry on meeting, to decide on child-related issues, and no matter how acrimonious the encounter, those issues have to be decided. So you

find yourself in dialogues such as 'How DARE you, how fucking DARE you blame that night in Bristol on ME . . . So I'll
pick them up from Sarah's party and you're going to get his new
school shirt on Wednesday, are you?'

The regular exchange of children between parted parents can
even be a source of developing creativity. One afternoon, as I took
them back to their mum, she asked what they'd been doing. My
son, who adores watching classic films, said excitedly, 'Mum, I
watched *The Wicker Man*.'

She asked, 'What were you thinking of, showing him a film
like that, he's only eleven, are you mad?'

To which I started grumbling back in a grumpy pathetic
whine.

And my son called out, 'Don't worry, Mum, Eloise didn't
watch it. She went to bed straight after *The Exorcist*.'

If we'd not broken up, that joke would never have been made.

Once you're no longer surrounded by the everyday torment of a
fractious relationship, it becomes possible to view the squabbles
and conflicts from a distance.

Even in the midst of wrath and fury, you realize it isn't aimed
at you, it's aimed into the air somewhere, at the universe, for
being a *bastard* of a universe. But somehow there seemed to be no
way of preventing the frustration from booming and crackling us
into court.

As I walked towards the court on the day, I saw her through the
window of Starbucks, reading the clinical legal documents of the
case. And in that image lay the potential for total despair, the triumph of cynicism. What was the point of hope or love or the
tingle of expectation if it could end sitting in Starbucks amending
'related' to 'pertaining' with a pink marker pen? Can there really
be people who stride into court for a case against their ex-partners
pumped up with the craving for victory, like American wrestlers?

If so you have to wonder whether they ever were in love in the
first place. My own overwhelming emotion in the courtroom was

bewilderment at how this happened. How do you end up dread-
ing a visit from the person you used to drive all night to see briefly
in the morning? You don't want to spend the rest of your life
looking back with disgust at every picnic and curry you shared,
regretting the times of ringing in sick to spend the day in bed
together, recalling festivals, boat trips, backstage passes, crazy
French bars, trips to the all-night beigel shop at five in the morning, the night the Tories were kicked out, the bewildered
newspaper man in the snow, as merely part of a marathon mistake.

If cynicism is right, the acrimony that can accompany the end
of a relationship doesn't just ruin now, it ruins then. Back then
when the most joyous times – the constant tingle of the early
months, the birth of your children, the serene moments that
bobble up, usually unexpectedly, maybe while just sitting in the
park or a café – made you both slightly breathless, neither of you
able to articulate your thoughts but both aware this is something
you'll always remember. They were driven not just by a sense of
instant joy but by hope, and if that hope ends by a Starbucks
window it's made a forgery out of the original joy.

Of course those moments were as strikingly real and electrifying as you remember them. Which is why the only true victory
in a family court would be one in which both of you were sen-
tenced to stay locked in the room until you could remember, for
the last time, the thrill of the first glance, the gulp at the first eye
contact, the smell of the hopeful decaying function room where
you first met. However vindictive either side may appear, what
most shattered couples really want, I suspect, is to smile at each
other one last time and mean it, and in that moment salvage all
the memories of hope.

If only I'd thought to say all that to the judge. When he was
about to sum up, he said in a *very* judgey voice, 'Well, we have
arrived at the point in the proceedings where traditionally the
judge has to make some patronising and meaningless remarks. I
hope you'll forgive me if I waive that privilege.' Oh no, a judge
was making me laugh. All the old certainties were in tatters.

15

TO DREAM THE POSSIBLE DREAM,
TO FIGHT THE BEATABLE FOE

To work out what's gone wrong between you and a political party can be more complicated than analysing the breakdown of a marriage. I first came across the Socialist Workers Party in 1978, in a field at an Anti-Nazi League carnival. It winked at me, I asked it out, and when it said 'I think the Soviet Union and Eastern Europe aren't socialist, but dictatorships governed by profit just like the West,' it was one of the most romantic things I'd ever heard.

So for twenty-five years I suggested to people who wondered how they could contribute to the campaign for a fairer society, that they should listen to or attend some wing of that party. But, eventually, it seemed unlikely that anyone could attend for the first time one of the depleted meetings, with its bewildering proclamations, and vitriol for people who were glorified a few weeks earlier, and come away feeling inspired and encouraged.

The hardest part to come to terms with was that their number still included some of the most capable speakers, writers and organisers, and were mostly defiant and principled agitators. What was making them behave in such a baffling way? Maybe it was a consequence of the confusion at the heart of our times, in which the widespread distaste for big business arrogance combines with a frail organised opposition, and a situation in which for most people socialism has become a peculiarity.

Partly this is due to the tarnished image socialism was given by the regimes in the Soviet Union, Eastern Europe and China, which ruled so barbarically in its name, so that if Stalin were still alive today, he'd be taken to court by genuine socialists for defamation of character.

But socialism also depends on working-class people being aware that they're bound together. As I've suggested, there are still strong ties, but the organisations and culture that makes people *feel* part of a common group have mostly been dismantled. There are few towns left dominated by one or two industries alone, and few replacements for centres such as welfare clubs that brought together hundreds of people from one workplace. Most importantly, the trade unions have made little impact on the new industries, and even where people have become members, trade unionism hasn't become embedded in the culture as it did in the old days. That can, and probably will change. But for now it's another possible reason why the socialist of today meets widespread sympathy but few active supporters.

This can make life awkward and frustrating, a bit like being one of those lads at school that all the girls like but none of them want to go out with. The response of the SWP has been to take the first half of this equation and declare we're in a time of huge opportunity for organising a socialist movement. So organisations such as Respect are set up with vast expectations. At this point all questioning is frowned upon and all on board are revered. But eventually, it becomes clear this movement isn't attracting activists in the numbers that had been anticipated, and that amongst those activists who *are* attracted, few of them join the SWP. Then there's a lashing out at the most unlikely people, blaming them for a colourful array of crimes. Veering between these two extremes the hierarchy deny all problems with their allies on the way up, then exaggerate them wildly on the way down.

Another problem with talking up the positive side, while shuffling the negative part away, is once you've gone down that path it's difficult to turn back. If you've said the turnout at a rally was massive, it's hard to say a year later, 'To be honest there were only twenty-three people there.'

This is a spiral it's hard to escape from. As you become more isolated, and organisations such as the Campaign Against Arms Trade appear capable of attracting impressive audiences, but few are inclined to join your particular group, there's a temptation to sneer at them.

Such an organisation, I concluded, was no longer helping. Those who remain members find themselves in an awkward situation, perhaps partly because there's nothing tougher than defying your peers. Telling a fat racist to shut his face is relatively simple, because even if he clobbers you, you retain your pride and friends. It's much harder to defy your long-term colleagues, who've inspired you and who you've got drunk with, who've explained how Marx's theory of profit works and babysat for you, who you've celebrated with after organising successful campaigns and commiserated with when three people have turned up, and who you've sat up all night with drinking bottles of whisky while discussing the American Civil War, and with whom you've encouraged and argued and hoped together.

To leave the group you've identified with can be an emotional wrench. The 'party' can become more than the means to an end, it becomes a routine, something you can't imagine being without. There is a strong temptation to accept the explanations given by those in charge, no matter how implausible, just as some women, when it's pointed out to them that their husband's shirt is covered in lipstick, will accept any explanation and maintain, 'Well I asked him about that, and it seems the lipstick was dropped by a passing crow. I *knew* it would be something obvious.'

There are also those who don't accept the explanations but carry on as if they do, for an easy life. Several long-standing members I know berated the dottiness while sitting in a pub or their living room, then went to the meetings and meekly sat there without saying a word, even voting for measures they'd privately declared to be ridiculous.

The problem isn't necessarily one of size or even isolation. Most successful movements have at one point been laughably tiny. But to stand any chance of progressing from that tinyness requires a recognition of your position, and a strategy for engaging with people who you hope to win to your point of view, rather than ignoring or insulting them.

It had been a brilliant journey. So many campaigns and debates, the satisfied smiles at small victories and jokes at comical failures, the books, the friends, the chaos and fun. We had a set of ideas that made sense of the world, not in order to pass an exam but as a means of changing it. I *hadn't* been crazy, and the people struggling to uphold this organisation now aren't crazy. It's one thing to take part in a party or movement, but running the thing must be a constant eruption of stress, especially once the momentum ebbs away from you. If they went haywire it's because they tried, and it's so much easier to avoid going wrong by not trying at all.

A party, like any other body made up of human beings and their ideas, isn't a static object – it can become something different from what it was. To leave a party after however long is not necessarily to leave what you once joined, it's to leave what it's become. Like a marriage that goes sour after ten years, to part company doesn't mean the ten marvellous years were wasted – the waste is the years you carry on after you know, deep down, that it's fallen apart.

I rang the bank, and after pressing a series of buttons and waiting a very long time to get through to a human being, I cancelled my subs while playing 'I No Longer Hear The Music' by The Libertines. 'All the nights and the fights and the blue lights and the kites we flew together, I thought they'd last forever. But I no longer hear the music.'

'That's cancelled for you, Mister Steel, is there anything else I can help you with?' asked the chirpy clerk.

'Have you finished your phone call?' asked my daughter. 'Because you said after you'd finished you'd take me to Woolworths.'

'Yes, I've finished,' I said. And we went to Woolworths and bought a packet of felt pens.

So what should we do and who should we vote for? Maybe the most important thing to realise in any state of uncertainty is that you're not alone. This is what people are told when they're anxious about a long-term illness or alcoholism or if their child keeps setting fire to the house. You could have a TV doctor saying on morning television, 'If you feel sick when you hear that a major corporation is funding your local hospital, and when the authorities declare there is simply no other way of providing funds in a modern environment, then don't panic. You're probably one of thousands, or even millions of sufferers of a condition that makes you react to big business by getting irritable and grumpy.' Then they could give you an address to send off for a leaflet or suggest you visit their website.

To me, a socialist explanation of why the inhumanity of the giant corporations takes place, is as pertinent as ever. They're driven by the need to make as much profit as they can, no matter how brutal the human cost, and will act in the interests of that profit, even if it means undermining elected governments, as they've attempted in Venezuela.

At the centre of the debate about 'what should we do?', is to clarify who 'we' is. Most discussions concerning what should be done are really asking 'What should *they* do?' So we debate whether Gordon Brown is better than Tony Blair, whether the Democrats are better than Bush, who should be in charge of the BBC, the FA and the United Nations. Columnists in newspapers say, 'The US government needs to re-engage with Europe' or 'The select committee on benefit reform should reconsider its proposals . . .' And while I might agree with the point they're making, I find myself shifting slightly as I read it.

The reason, I think, is because their solution is to suggest what *they* should do. It's part of the culture of believing only *they* have the power.

Whereas what *we* do determines what they can get away with. The vast march against the war in 2003 defines our times, partly because it showed what is possible, but also because it led many who participated to conclude there's nothing we can do. But there must have been many people who marched behind Martin Luther King who, six months later, said, 'We had our march and they *still* didn't listen – there will *never* be an end to segregation.'

Instead of being disheartened about the ineffectiveness of that march, it should be seen as one important event in an ongoing battle, against a world order that each day spends on arms the amount that could feed the world's starving for a year.

The anti-war campaign may not have stopped the war in Iraq, but there's no telling what it did stop. When the invasion was being planned, the leaders of the Project for the New American Century must have been spinning globes with anticipation, pointing out all the places to go for next, like lottery winners planning a cruise. Iran? Cuba? It all seemed possible. But the global opposition meant that most world leaders who backed the war eventually lost authority with much of their own population. The huge marches, the profile of military families and prominent figures opposed to the war, the films, the songs, as well as the elections dominated by the issue of Iraq, meant they couldn't escape what they'd done. And combined with the fiasco in Iraq itself it meant they couldn't easily do it again.

The scale of the global movement was such that even if Bush and Blair were happy to ignore it, enough politicians, ambassadors and generals became convinced they couldn't get away with it again, and the Project was derailed, and one by one the main players in the war left office in humiliation. The Project clearly didn't go to plan, unless the plan was: 'Now is everyone clear on their role, Rumsfeld, you're going to resign after an election disaster, Wolfowitz is going to resign after a scandal, John Bolton, you're going to resign and then go on television looking increasingly mentally ill – now LET'S GO!' By the time of the next US presidential election, every candidate's campaign message was that they would make the most comprehensive changes from the days of Bush, which by then were almost universally acknowledged as a disaster. None of that change in mood would have happened without the worldwide movement against the war, without the marches, the military families against the war, without the speeches, without Jimmy Hill or the masturbators for peace.

They depend on convincing each of us opposed to the aims of big business that *we* are on our own. Just as the police, if they arrest a group of people, place each of those charged in their own cell and tell all of them separately that all the others have confessed.

The current state of the world amounts to more than a corporate occupation of every corner of life. That may be the aim, but a glance in any direction will find pockets that have defied this shareholders' invasion. In every area there are parks and playgrounds the developers must salivate about but they can't touch because local people don't share their enthusiasm for turning them into profit-driven estates. A hint of a cut in resources for a library or daycare centre almost always leads to meetings, posters in windows and angry letters in the local paper.

Most of the major victories in history for the cause of humanity against greed and bullying have come as a result of millions of tiny actions, carried out by people not in any official governing position. Whether independence for India or votes for women, civil rights in America or the freedom to state the earth goes round the sun, the impetus came from individuals who had been taught they were powerless, until they shook the people taught to hold power.

Who we vote for, seen in this context, takes on a different meaning, as the most effective candidate becomes the one who will give the greatest boost to that movement of the discontented. In many areas there are candidates from outside the mainstream with a following in the community, connected to campaigns, pensioner groups and arms of the socialist and environmental movements, who ought to be able to secure a vote substantial enough to alarm the traditional parties and inspire the opposition.

Maybe the next answer to 'What can we do?' is recognising that opposition is far more effective if it's organised collectively. The sentiment against war and big business is so disjointed. It consists of a vast number of local groups, websites, gigs, individuals producing posters, poems and postcards, and many more quietly seething. It's an opposition that would be so much more effective if these actions were, even loosely, connected. At least people could seethe together.

But we need also to recognise that the very worst course of action in these circumstances would probably be to start up a new far-left socialist group, as if we're just one short of the number of groups we need. Apart from anything else, there are no names left as every permutation of the words socialist, communist, worker, power, party and group has been taken. So a new group would need a random word thrown in and have to call itself something like the 'Socialist Perpendicular Party'.

To play their most effective role, maybe the socialist of today has to accept the predicament they're in, in which millions reject the ethics of our rulers but few are willing to embrace socialist organisation. In that situation surely the socialist has to ensure they're part of that radical sentiment, engaging with its passion and imagination, and trying to inject it with socialist ideas. From this perhaps a new socialist movement can emerge.

It must be possible to bring together in every area a group of people who are appalled by the priorities of those who rule, and agree on a series of values and actions that can dent the agenda of war and profit. It ought to be possible for an opposition movement to unite sufficiently to welcome the beautifully diverse array of modern life and thought that resists the current world order without demanding that everyone agrees with a traditional style or set of ideas.

But the first and most important answer to the question 'What should we do?' is to take the monumental leap to do '*something*', to participate in the continuous rumble against injustice, to donate the pound, respond to the bullying remark, write the letter, harangue the woman with a clipboard who's shut down the tea bar, draw up the petition against the next Tesco Express, boycott the fruit or decide to stop a war.

All my confusions descended on me one night at a rock festival in the Summer of 2007. By now my daughter had recovered from the trial of being the subject of a photography franchise six and a half years earlier and my son was eleven, sitting on my shoulders as we watched Jarvis Cocker in the Suffolk sunset. Jarvis announced his final song, which he dedicated to those who'd started the war, and to the barons of big business. 'I want you to all sing along with the chorus,' he told us, 'which goes: "The cunts are still ruling the world."' And a few moments later I looked up to see my son punching the air and roaring with joy 'The cunts are still ruling the world.' What do you do? What are you supposed to do?

Suddenly someone alerted me to the fact that a few rows ahead of us was Geoff Hoon, defence minister for New Labour, who helped orchestrate Britain's support for the war. And he stood there watching this mighty crowd, even the eleven-year-old boy, yell their verdict across the streams and stiles of the countryside. However confusing it is for us, it must be far far worse for them.

The modest task of opponents of the current order is to bring together the disparate but vast opposition, who agree with the philosophy at the heart of Jarvis Cocker's lyrics, to unite at least part of the army of the angry confused, around the multitude of ideas they agree on, while allowing them the space to express their doubts when they don't agree, without the fear of being belittled, to allow the young to shape the movement with their wit and imagination, and have the humility to acknowledge if it fucked up.

The drive to build a society that rewards humanity rather than greed simmers incessantly, no matter how many setbacks it encounters, just as the drive to fall in love survives the multitude of calamities that love can encounter.

In either case hope shouldn't just be valued because what's hoped for may come true. It's hope that makes life so exhilarating, so it's to be treasured regardless of whether the outcome hoped for ever happens. Hope creates the tingles, the breathless anticipation, the reckless spontaneity. It inspires hope in others, so that if your project fails, the cause it drove can continue, because it fills every aspect of life with purpose and fun.

The Hollywood ending to all this would be to find the solution, to locate the missing figure that makes the equation fit together, and win a Nobel Prize. There's a happier ending than that, however, which is instead of defeating the confusion, to learn to embrace it. The simplest way to avoid further confusion is to withdraw from the world's events and be thankful it isn't you getting clobbered this time round, to abandon the project of love and hope because it only leaves you heartbroken, and to genuinely grow old. But that must be the most frightening outcome of all, to retire from the cycle of manic over-optimism and gruelling disappointment that fuels life. To no longer be livid at the cruelty of dictators, the rumours of ex-lovers and the existence of vacuous celebrities, is truly to be forty. Confusion is a symptom of living, of searching for the answer to how we mobilise the immense generosity too often locked up in humanity and unleash it to build a world upon a set of values the oil companies, the arms dealers and the supermarket chains could never understand, so it was *them* sitting in confusion pondering, 'What's going on?' It is the search itself that makes the world such a thrilling cauldron of potential, of compelling uncertainty, and of hope.

ACKNOWLEDGMENTS

Firstly I would like to thank the cafes of Crystal Palace, without which this book could not have been written. For five or six hours at a time I've sat in them writing the thing, spreading paper over tables and asking other customers questions like 'what's a funnier animal – llama or iguana?', until they must have expected me to start knocking up some shelves and putting in my own switchboard.

I should also thank the cafe in Horwich in Lancashire where I wrote quite a bit of it and in particular the lad with a very distinct accent who works there. Because one day, after he'd brought my soup I went and asked him for some pepper, and he looked around for a while a bit confused, and then said 'What sort do you want – a newspepper or some pepper to write on?'

Thanks to Jonny and Doug at Curtis Brown, for all their splendid work but also for putting up with my rants. Audiences are locked in and have little choice but they've sat and listened to them when they could easily have left the room or put the phone down.

Thanks to Mike Marqusee and Liz Davies for their invaluable comments, and for much else, not least of which is Mike's story about the day he found himself sat opposite a man reading the *Daily Mail*, around the time the Burmese army were firing on protestors. The man looked up and said to Mike, 'Isn't this dreadful what's going on in Burma?' 'Yes, dreadful,' Mike agreed. And the bloke said, 'I mean – you can't have monks running all over the place like that.'

Many thanks to Pete Sinclair, as diligent as ever in pointing out flaws both big and small, from 'The entire beginning is wrong' to 'I'm sure that colon should be a semi-colon.'

Thanks to Anthony Arnove for his entirely accurate comments and for the way that, being American, he said, 'Who is this guy you mention called Des O'Connor?'

Thanks to Bela, the marvellous copy editor who, despite being Portuguese has a command of English vastly superior to mine, but even more impressively was so full of beans. It was going to be a struggle to go through all our tasks in the short time we had, and then she said, 'Now this part interests me – because my husband and I were very involved in the Portuguese Revolution of 1974. Do you have an opinion on that?' And I had to suppress every instinct and say 'Aaaagh Bela – I can't even start or we'll never get past page twelve.' Even better, she didn't want to finish too late as she had to be up at six the next morning. 'You're working too hard,' I said. 'Oh it's not for work,' she said, 'I support Brentford home and away and tomorrow we're playing in Darlington.' They lost two-nil.

Thanks to the billions of people who've discussed the issues in the book with me, often clarifying matters, especially Pat Stack and Mac Mckenna, who both understand beautifully that when something a socialist does goes hopelessly wrong, the disappointment is at least in part balanced by the fact that it makes for a fucking funny story. And thanks to Mark Thomas for similar reasons, and his infectious inspiring anarchistic instincts.

Thanks to the many people on the left who've kept the spirit of resistance alight, including those who will violently disagree with chunks of this book.

Enormous boundless thanks to the memory of the wonderful Linda Smith, for being so bright, so incisive and so resilient but much more than any of that for being so utterly, utterly funny.

Thanks to my ex-partner, for so many brilliant times. After all there's only trauma in parting if there are a stack of wonderful episodes you lament can never be repeated.

Thanks to Natasha for so many things that, if they were listed, the Acknowledgments would have to be ordered as a separate supplement.

And a bottomless cavern-full of thanks to my children, Elliot and Eloise, partly for putting up with so much but also for being such beacons of brightness and hilarity. Obviously every parent is biased, but in the spirit of rational enquiry, having removed all favouritism from my assessment and thought it through scientifically, I can honestly say they are the loveliest wittiest cleverest funniest most delightful kids there have ever, ever been.